The Synergistic Classroom

The Synergistic Classroom

Interdisciplinary Teaching in
the Small College Setting

EDITED BY COREY CAMPION AND AARON ANGELLO

Rutgers University Press

New Brunswick, Camden, and Newark, New Jersey, and London

Library of Congress Cataloging-in-Publication Data

Names: Campion, Corey, editor. | Angello, Aaron, editor.
Title: The synergistic classroom : interdisciplinary teaching in the small college
    setting / edited by Corey Campion and Aaron Angello.
Description: New Brunswick, New Jersey : Rutgers University Press, 2020. |
    Includes bibliographical references and index.
Identifiers: LCCN 2020004932 | ISBN 9781978818415 (paperback) |
    ISBN 9781978818422 (hardcover) | ISBN 9781978818439 (epub) |
    ISBN 9781978818446 (mobi) | ISBN 9781978818453 (pdf)
Subjects: LCSH: Education, Higher—Curricula—United States. | Interdisciplinary
    approach in education—United States. | Small colleges—United States.
Classification: LCC LB2361.5 .S96 2020 | DDC 378.1/990973—dc23
LC record available at https://lccn.loc.gov/2020004932

A British Cataloging-in-Publication record for this book is available from the British Library.

♾ The paper used in this publication meets the requirements of the American National
Standard for Information Sciences—Permanence of Paper for Printed Library Materials,
ANSI Z39.48-1992.

www.rutgersuniversitypress.org

Manufactured in the United States of America

Contents

The Synergistic Classroom

Introduction

• • • • • • • • • • • • •

Building Bridges in
a Land of Colleges

COREY CAMPION

Each fall thousands of recent high school graduates exchange the comforts and constraints of their childhood home for the uncertainty and freedom of a college classroom. The product of years of encouragement from parents, teachers, and coaches, their arrival on campus marks at once the end of one journey and the beginning of another. From the struggle to decide if and when to go to college, students quickly shift their attention to questions about how to succeed in college. Although "Study!" may appear to be the obvious answer, many first-year students will agree that this is easier said than done. With bi- or triweekly meetings, lecture and seminar formats, attention to disciplinary and methodological concerns, and heavy reading and writing loads, college classes bear little resemblance to the world of secondary education with which new students are most familiar. If some of these challenges dissipate with time and experience, one additional burden weighs on students throughout their collegiate tenure: the need to secure a job upon graduation. More than ever, this task, which requires anticipating the demands of future employers, appears challenging, if not impossible, for many students. From globalization to automation, rapid change appears to be the only constant feature of an increasingly ephemeral job market. Echoing the predictions of business leaders across a variety of industries, Dell Technology recently suggested that more than half of the jobs that will be available in 2030 do not yet exist. As today's college graduates enter the workforce, the company advised, they should be prepared for a "lifetime of retraining."[1] Proffered amid soaring tuition costs and constant reporting on the dangers of student debt, such advice offers little solace for students desperate to make their college investment pay dividends.

Of course, students are not the only constituency affected by their uncertain career prospects. Growing expectations for the academy to ensure employment for its graduates challenge faculty and administrators as well. Increasingly, many of the departmental majors and minors that inform today's college curricula and correspond to faculty expertise and interest appear ill-equipped to prepare students for a "lifetime of retraining."[2] Stagnating or declining enrollments in traditional majors like English, political science, and journalism affirm this reality, to which many institutions have responded with the creation of dozens of new professionally focused majors. From nursing, athletic training, and sports management to computer science, applied science, and business, American colleges and universities created over 300 new majors between 2000 and 2010 alone.[3] In addition, faculty and administrators have designed a host of new pathways to enable students to pursue double majors, or an interdisciplinary combination of majors and minors, within the traditional four-year period of study or less. While such innovation has become the norm throughout higher education, the meaning and experience of such innovation at the nation's smaller colleges and universities remain underexplored. The present collection responds to this oversight.

Pursuing innovative pedagogy in a unique setting within the broader American academy, the volume's contributors share their creative responses to a host of recent studies that demonstrate the need for curricular revisions beyond a simple repackaging of current discipline-based offerings. According to one such study, conducted by the Association of American Colleges & Universities in 2009, fewer than half of the employers interviewed felt that the curriculum at two- and four-year institutions was well suited to prepare students for the workplace. Suggesting a shift away from discipline-specific training, the survey revealed a preference for liberal education curricula that provide a breadth of skill sets alongside expertise in a given field. Among those skills most emphasized were knowledge of human cultures and the physical and natural world, effective oral and written communication, collaboration, and an ability to approach an issue from multiple perspectives.[4] More recently, a 2016 study produced by the World Economic Forum, which gathered input from employers both in the United States and abroad, reached similar conclusions. Those surveyed identified a list of skills essential for employment beyond 2025, including cognitive flexibility, effective communication, emotional intelligence, and teamwork.[5] Taken together, these studies suggest that skills, which can be learned in any number of disciplines, are growing more important than training in a particular discipline.

For faculty, this news can prove both threatening and inspiring. On the one hand, disciplinarity provides faculty with an early sense of professional identity along with a pathway toward attaining the PhD, securing a tenure-track position, and earning tenure and promotion. Their disciplines also reflect their interests and house the objects of the intense curiosity that led them to pursue the life academic. From graduate school through retirement, then, most faculty exist, and thrive, within a disciplinary community. They serve in a history, or biology, or English department, and they attend conferences, join associations, and publish papers in those disciplines. Of course, most faculty also teach in their discipline, designing syllabi, delivering content, and assessing student work through the unique perspectives of their chosen field. Although most faculty would rank helping their students succeed among their top priorities, suggestions to weaken or betray their own disciplinary loyalties in order to satisfy the current, and impermanent, demands of employers can prove difficult to digest. Knowledge of the fact that professional advancement has always ranked among the top motivations of college students does little to alleviate the tension that persists between the values of faculty committed to the vocation of learning and students who pursue learning as a means to a vocation.[6]

On the other hand, disciplinary identities can be limiting, restricting an instructor's syllabi, a department's curriculum, and an institution's relationship to the broader student body. Excepting the few who continue to pursue careers in academia, the reality remains that even the most passionate undergraduate students will spend most of their life in a world that bears few of the disciplinary markers of their campus. To the extent, then, that faculty are willing to allow their classrooms to model the world for which they are preparing students, they have an opportunity to serve students in a more enduring fashion. In the meantime, such pedagogical flexibility can pay dividends in scholarship as well. Helping students to approach a topic from multiple viewpoints or to master the skills needed in a variety of fields can free faculty to revise and broaden their own analytical agendas. It can invite collaboration with colleagues normally isolated by the physical geography of the discipline-based campus. Invitations, for example, to a microbiologist to deliver a guest lecture in a historian's class on urbanization can both enrich students' understanding of the meaning of life in nineteenth-century cities and open a line of collegial dialogue that strengthens the historian's forthcoming study of modern Paris or the microbiologist's request for funding to study vaccine administration in inner cities. By helping students, then, to navigate the transitions between fields required by a "lifetime of retraining," faculty can reap their own professional rewards.[7] Addressed, in part, to those faculty open to such endeavors, this volume explores the pedagogical, institutional, and intellectual benefits and challenges that can attend the development of interdisciplinary classrooms.

Tearing Down Silos or Building Bridges?

Among the topics that have most moved the pens of academics and observers of higher education in the last decade, interdisciplinarity has been among the most contentious. From questions about the assessment of interdisciplinary scholarship and its potential value in doctoral programs to calls for a rethinking of traditional curricula and invitations to humanists to engage today's pressing economic and scientific debates, interdisciplinarity is a recurring theme in the news of higher education. The frequency of such coverage, which often features the metaphors of "tearing down disciplinary silos" and "building interdisciplinary bridges," is evidence of the intense, even personal, reflection through which many academics are now reevaluating the character and function of the academy in the twenty-first century.

Adding to such evidence is a steady stream of essays and monographs by faculty and administrators. In addition to calls for the abolition of departments and passionate ripostes detailing the centrality of the disciplines to the mission of higher education, this literature includes a variety of more prescriptive, less polemical contributions.[8] These cover topics ranging from strategies for incentivizing interdisciplinary research to reflections on how to facilitate scholarly exchange across methodological boundaries and inspire administrators and faculty to embrace collaboration as part of their institutional mission.[9] Other authors have located current interdisciplinary initiatives within a broader historical context, exploring how the definitions of successful and failed collaborations have evolved over time. In the process, they offer an important reminder that while our present focus on interdisciplinarity is perhaps more intense, efforts to connect scholarship and learning across the disciplines date at least to the 1920s, when the modern disciplinary landscape was still in its infancy, and were a staple of academic discourse throughout the second half of the twentieth century.[10] Whether one is a proponent of building bridges or maintaining silos, these works offer reassurance by recalling how change rarely, if ever, comes to the academy without careful and lengthy deliberation. Of course, as some of the contributors to this volume demonstrate, the pressure to meet student needs is leading some of the nation's smaller institutions to shift their deliberations from questions of "whether" to pursue interdisciplinarity to discussions of how best to do so.

With this shift in mind, contributions to the last decade of spirited and insightful dialogue have left two issues underexplored. First, most authors neglect the practice of interdisciplinary teaching in favor of discussing interdisciplinary research and institutional organization. While the latter are important, the former merits greater attention in light of the growing demand that colleges and universities provide broader curricula to help students achieve their professional goals. As faculty, departments, and institutions work to meet these demands, the literature would do well to explore the specific experiences of those facilitating interdisciplinary learning in the classroom. From this, a second overlooked issue emerges: the influence of the institutional setting on an instructor's pedagogy. Indeed, many of the authors engaged in conversations about interdisciplinarity work in larger research-driven institutions or focus their work on these. Given the fact that colleges and universities with annual enrollments of more than 10,000 students serve the majority of undergraduates pursuing a four-year degree in an on-campus setting, this focus is not without merit.[11] Still, the landscape of American higher education features hundreds of smaller, teaching-focused institutions with much lower annual enrollments. Operating with fewer resources these schools pursue unique missions in a setting that is often more conducive to teaching across the disciplines than that at larger schools. For these reasons the efforts of small college and university faculty to create innovative, synergistic classrooms are worthy of greater attention in any conversation about interdisciplinarity.

A "Land of Colleges"?

In 2020, America appears to be a land of large public research universities. With medical and law schools that rank among the world's most prestigious institutions, faculty research that leads the world's battles against cancer, poverty and climate change, and athletic teams which now vie with their professional counterparts for popularity and revenue, these schools have come to dominate the higher education marketplace. Thanks to lucrative endowments, a growing online presence, and a branch campus system that creates service webs similar to those of national and global retail chains, this dominance seems to strengthen with each academic year. Combined with images of their expanding campuses, state-of-the-art laboratories, and resort-like dormitories, such realities make it easy to forget the relative youth of large institutions in the longer history of American higher education.

Born in the late nineteenth and early twentieth centuries, large research universities marked a dramatic departure from the traditional smaller liberal arts academies and colleges that had educated the nation's students since the colonial era. As industrialization demanded greater specialization from the American workforce, the professional and pedagogical value of more advanced academic research and training, such as that pioneered by German universities, became obvious to many of the nation's instructors and administrators.[12] Embracing the German model along with its requirement that professors hold a doctorate and demonstrate excellence in their field through scholarship, a number of American colleges, including Harvard and Yale, undertook to transform themselves into research institutions. At the same time, the Morrill Act of 1862 provided public funding for the establishment of a host of state colleges and universities, which soon adopted similar research missions. As the twentieth century began, these new schools continued to grow and, with the dramatic expansion of American higher education that attended the passage of the G.I. Bill in 1944, soon began to assume pride of place in the arena of postsecondary education.

Amid the advent and expansion of larger institutions, however, thousands of American students continued to attend those smaller schools, whose columned brick buildings, grassy courtyards, and cozy campuses offered an alluring alternative to the sprawling universities. Often, these schools catered to students of a particular religious faith or geographic region with a combination of general and specialized education that previewed the liberal arts curricula still in place on many of these campuses today. Unlike their colleagues at larger institutions, whose focus remained on research and whose classroom presence lessened with the advent of graduate assistants, the faculty at these smaller schools functioned as "scholar-teachers," pursuing research when possible yet prioritizing the teaching of young minds.[13] After an inauspicious start, which saw the number of colleges only expand from 9 to 25 by the early nineteenth century, immigration, westward expansion, and economic development inspired a wave of new institutions. Calling for the trend to continue, the Massachusetts pastor Absalom Peters predicted that the United States was destined to be a "land of colleges."[14] Validating his prediction, 250 small colleges had begun to offer instruction by the start of the Civil War. While the struggle to balance small enrollments with rising operating expenses forced some of these to close their doors, 180 institutions survived and became the elders of a small-college community that continued to expand throughout the twentieth century.[15] Today, 1,263 of the nation's degree-granting four-year colleges and universities operate with annual enrollments of fewer than 5,000 students. Of these institutions, 464 enroll fewer than 1,000 students each year. By contrast, large institutions, which enroll at least 10,000 students per year, number fewer than 200.[16] In numeric terms, at least, the nation truly remains a "land of colleges."

Yet, as nineteenth- and early twentieth-century institutions struggling to find their place in the twenty-first century, many of the nation's small colleges and universities now fear for their survival. Shrinking demographics have resulted in smaller incoming classes while rising operating costs have made unpopular tuition increases inevitable. The results have been well chronicled in both the popular and the higher education press. From the trauma of Sweet Briar's near-closing in 2015 to a steady stream of headlines predicting the imminent collapse of many, if not most, of the nation's smaller institutions, it is hard to avoid describing Peters's "land of colleges" as anything but doomed.[17] To be sure, larger institutions also face uncertainty amid the current demographic trends and rising student and parent concerns over the affordability of higher education. Yet there is an important difference between the ways in which small and large institutions can weather this shared storm. As one former small college president observed, the pressures on all institutions are similar, but "the tolerance for institutional error and institutional crisis is exponentially minuscule at the small, the tuition-driven, the experimental, the curricularly focused, and the relatively new."[18]

This "minuscule" room for error notwithstanding, the contributors to the present volume believe that faculty at the nation's smaller colleges and universities have at least three reasons for hope. First, the long history of these institutions speaks to their adaptability and the tremendous value that their students, communities, and alumni have continued to find in them. As recent defenses of the small college experience remind us, these institutions have a cultural currency rooted in both their historic connections to their surrounding communities and the proven value of their more personalized pedagogical approach.[19] Second, smaller budgets can combine with limited institutional resources and shrinking enrollments to create unique incentives, not found at larger schools, to develop the innovative coursework that students most need. Finally, if the current synergy between employer demands and student expectations continues to invite the development of more interdisciplinary curricula, the historic liberal arts traditions of smaller colleges and universities may prove more aligned with the future mission of higher education than headlines now predict.

Written by faculty committed to refuting such headlines, this collection draws needed attention to the practice of interdisciplinary teaching in an underexplored arena of academia. In doing so, it addresses any reader curious about how interdisciplinarity continues to shape pedagogy across the diverse landscape of American higher education. More importantly, however, the volume offers practical reflections written by and for small college and university faculty interested in introducing or enhancing interdisciplinary approaches in their own classrooms.[20] With both audiences in mind, the authors have eschewed theoretical reflections in favor of practical discussions. Together, they offer a broad, though not comprehensive, exploration of the pedagogical, programmatic, experiential, and assessment-related aspects of many common teaching endeavors, including team-taught courses, first-year seminars, honors programs, study abroad initiatives, and campus–community partnerships. With this approach, the volume does not espouse a specific definition of interdisciplinarity but rather invites comparative reflection on the various ways in which faculty across different campuses, or even on the same campus, interpret this contested term.[21] From those instructors who work alone and incorporate multiple disciplinary angles into their lessons to colleagues who have developed new team-taught courses that transcend their respective disciplines, the authors demonstrate how faculty have renegotiated disciplinary boundaries in ways that best serve their unique student bodies.

The essays, which may be read either individually or in sequence, are divided into three sections that focus on interdisciplinary teaching, program development, and experiential learning at the undergraduate level. While the role of interdisciplinarity in the graduate classroom remains an important and welcome subject for future research, the unique institutional and curricular realities that confront graduate programs merit a more comprehensive discussion than the present volume offers. In the first section, "Teaching across the Disciplines," the authors share their experiences in interdisciplinary classrooms and invite readers to consider important questions about the value and practice of team teaching as well as the assessment of student work across disciplines and the negotiation of shared faculty workloads. The section begins with an essay by Aaron Angello, who draws on his own experiences teaching digital humanities to consider the anxiety that interdisciplinarity creates for small college faculty whose institutional setting regularly requires them to teach beyond their discipline-specific training. Paul D. Reich then examines the role of first-year seminars in fostering interdisciplinarity and the ways in which such courses can fail to meet their potential when driven by established disciplinary interests. Addressing an important corollary to first-year programs, Patricia Marchesi explores her experiences using composition courses to expose students to multiple fields. The section then ends with three case studies of innovative approaches to interdisciplinarity within and beyond the humanities. Patrick L. Hamilton and Allan W. Austin review their efforts to combine history and English in a course on graphic narratives in the postwar United States, while Christine Dehne and Jonathan Munson reflect on their work connecting digital media and computer science and the ways in which their collaboration in the classroom has helped to challenge the disciplinary mindset of their institution. Finally, Corey Campion and April M. Boulton discuss their transdisciplinary course Globalization and the Honeybee, which invites students from history, environmental science, and global studies to explore the history and science of apiculture and engage the campus community with a variety of research projects and public education initiatives.

In the second section, "Programming across the Disciplines," attention turns to the design of interdisciplinary programs that serve the unique student populations at small colleges while achieving broader institutional goals. Erika Cornelius Smith and Maryann Conrad explore how their institution leveraged the flexibility of its small size and collaborative culture to create three interdisciplinary programs to enhance the school's business-focused curriculum through the liberal arts. Similarly, Julia F. Klimek discusses how a shift away from discipline-specific programs can help many small colleges meet the needs of their growing populations of low-income, first-generation, and underrepresented students. Christine D. Myers and Audra L. Goach then explore ways to enhance students' professional training through a review of their work developing a multidisciplinary minor in investigative forensics that grapples with limited institutional resources by building on their own existing courses. Hilary Cooperman shifts the discussion to a hallmark of many small liberal arts colleges, the general education program, and considers the challenges and opportunities of building an interdisciplinary curriculum that meets the needs of twenty-first-century students. On a similar note, Winston Ou draws unique attention to the interdisciplinary potential of mathematics and reviews his work designing and teaching math courses for a core curriculum in interdisciplinary humanities. Finally, Lana A. Whited and Sharon E. Stein consider honors programs as a key arena for interdisciplinarity and reflect on both the opportunities and the challenges that such programs present for students and faculty.

In the third and final section, "Exploring across the Disciplines," the volume turns to the development of interdisciplinary experiential learning and community engagement opportunities using the limited resources available at smaller institutions. Recalling the town and gown partnerships that have long informed the mission of many small colleges, Martha Bárcenas-Mooradian reviews her efforts to enhance students' study of medical Spanish through interactions with her school's local Hispanic community. No less innovative, Amanda M. Caleb and Alicia H. Nordstrom share their work teaching a course on mental health that combines the study of English and psychology and empowers students as producers of knowledge through the production of a theatrical performance designed to draw attention to the experience of various mental health conditions. Along similar lines, Tina L. Hanlon and her colleagues discuss their efforts to create meaningful experiential learning opportunities by connecting students at their rural institution to a number of communities in the surrounding Appalachian region. Finally, Paola Prado and Autumn Quezada-Grant examine the ethics and challenges of creating sustainable and socially responsible interdisciplinary study-abroad opportunities.

While readers are encouraged to engage the collection through the lens of their own unique interests and institutional setting, two general observations, which appear throughout the volume, are worth noting at the outset. The first concerns the gap between faculty recognition of the value of interdisciplinarity in the classroom and institutional policies that delay or even discourage collaboration across the disciplines. Indeed, if institutions, large or small, are to meet the needs of an increasingly professional-minded student body destined for a "lifetime of retraining," faculty and administrators must collaborate to develop hiring, promotion, workload, and compensation policies that not only enable but reward interdisciplinarity. Although such efforts demand a thorough, and challenging, review of much of what defines the academy for those employed in it, the essays in this volume demonstrate that progress is not only possible but under way. Fortunately, similar encouragement emerges with respect to a second observation that informs the collection. As many of the authors make clear, faculty understandings of and enthusiasm for interdisciplinarity are not always shared by students. While some students lack a basic appreciation for the disciplinary boundaries and methodologies that make interdisciplinarity possible, others have little interest in deviating from the major in which they enroll. Experienced in addressing both populations, the contributors provide a host of suggestions for instructors struggling to reconcile their own academic purposes with those of their students. Indeed, for the hope that it offers on these two important fronts alone, any reader interested in the future of the American academy will be well rewarded for joining the authors as they reflect on their work in synergistic classrooms throughout the land of colleges.

Notes

1   Institute for the Future for Dell Technologies, "Emerging Technologies' Impact on Society and Work in 2030," accessed August 8, 2018, http://www.iftf.org /future-now/article-detail/realizing-2030-dell-technologies-research-explores-the -next-era-of-human-machine-partnerships/. On the pace of technological change and the unpredictability of the future job market, see also Cathy N. Davidson, *Now You See It: How Technology and Brain Science Will Transform Schools and Business for the 21st Century* (New York: Penguin, 2011); Martin Ford, *Rise of the Robots: Technology and the Threat of a Jobless Future* (New York: Basic Books, 2015).

2   James Axtell, *Wisdom's Workshop: The Rise of the Modern University* (Princeton: Princeton University Press, 2016), 199.

3   Jeffrey J. Selingo, *College (Un)Bound: The Future of Higher Education and What It Means for Students* (Las Vegas: Amazon, 2013), 7. On the broader dilemmas produced by declining and stagnating enrollments, see Gordon Hunter and Feisal G. Mohamed, "Introduction," in *A New Deal for the Humanities: Liberal Arts and the Future of Public Higher Education* (New Brunswick: Rutgers University Press, 2016), 1–17; Corey Campion, "Whither the Humanities?— Reinterpreting the Relevance of an Essential and Embattled Field," *Arts and Humanities in Higher Education*, September 2017, https://doi.org/10.1177 /1474022217730819.

4   Hart Research Associates, "Raising the Bar: Employers' Views on College Learning in the Wake of the Economic Downturn," January 20, 2010, https:// www.aacu.org/leap/public-opinion-research.

5   World Economic Forum, "The Future of Jobs: Employment, Skills and Workforce Strategy for the Fourth Industrial Revolution," January 2016, https://www .weforum.org/reports?page=8.

6   On this tension, see Andrew Delbanco, *College: What Was, Is, and Should Be* (Princeton: Princeton University, 2012), 9–35; Stefan Collini, *What Are Universities For?* (New York: Penguin, 2012), 3–5.

7   For an excellent discussion of the benefits of interdisciplinary collaboration for faculty scholarship, see Elizabeth G. Creamer and Lisa R. Lattuca, eds.

"Advancing Faculty Learning through Interdisciplinary Collaboration," special issue, *New Directions for Teaching and Learning* 102 (Summer 2005).

8 Mark C. Taylor, "End the University as We Know It," *New York Times*, April 27, 2009, https://www.nytimes.com/2009/04/27/opinion/27taylor.html; Jerry A. Jacobs, *In Defense of Disciplines: Interdisciplinarity and Specialization in the Research University* (Chicago: The University of Chicago Press, 2013).

9 Scott Frickel, Mathieu Albert, and Barbara Prainsack, *Investigating Interdisciplinary Collaboration: Theory and Practice across Disciplines* (New Brunswick: Rutgers University Press, 2017); John H. Aldrich, *Interdisciplinarity: Its Role in a Discipline-Based Academy* (Oxford: Oxford University Press, 2014); Myra H. Strober, *Interdisciplinary Conversations: Challenging Habits of Thought* (Stanford: Stanford University Press, 2011); Julie Thompson Klein, *Creating Interdisciplinary Campus Cultures: A Model for Strength and Sustainability* (San Francisco: John Wiley & Sons, 2010).

10 For a study of the growth of interdisciplinary programs from 1975 to 2000, see Steven G. Brint et al., "Expanding the Social Frame of Knowledge: Interdisciplinary, Degree-Granting Fields in American Colleges and Universities, 1975–2000," *Review of Higher Education* 32, no. 2 (2009): 155–183. On the broader history of interdisciplinarity, see Harvey J. Graff, *Undisciplining Knowledge: Interdisciplinarity in the Twentieth Century* (Baltimore: The Johns Hopkins University Press, 2015); Klein, *Creating Interdisciplinary Campus Cultures*, 1–5.

11 Definitions of "small" and "large" institutions vary. In common practice throughout the relevant literature, however, annual enrollments of at least 10,000 students are necessary to describe a four-year, degree-granting institution with a primary focus on face-to-face instruction as large. For the same type of institutions to be classified as small, annual enrollment must not exceed 5,000 or, for some authors, 3,000 students. In this volume, all contributors are from institutions with annual enrollments of fewer than 5,000 students and, in several cases, fewer than 2,500 students. For examples of the varying definitions used to define institutional size, see Center for Postsecondary Research, Indiana School of Education, "The Carnegie Classification of Institutions of Higher Education," accessed August 7, 2018, http://carnegieclassifications.iu.edu/classification_descriptions/size_setting .php; "Data Blog: How Do We Define a 'Small' University?" *Times of Higher Education*, January 2016, https://www.timeshighereducation.com/blog/data-blog -how-do-we-define-small-university.

12 Axtell, *Wisdom's Workshop*, 233.

13 On the history and mission of small colleges, see Samuel Schuman, *Old Main: Small Colleges in Twenty-First Century America* (Baltimore: The Johns Hopkins University Press, 2005), 20–74; Axtell, *Wisdom's Workshop*, 147–220.

14 Absalom Peters, *Discourse before the Society for the Promotion of Collegiate and Theological Education at the West* (New York: John F. Trow, 1851), 13.

15 Frederick Rudolph, *The American College and University: A History*, 2nd ed. (Athens: University of Georgia Press, 1990), 47.; Axtell, *Wisdom's Workshop*, 166.

16 National Center for Education Statistics, Data Collection 2017, accessed August 7, 2018, https://nces.ed.gov/ipeds/datacenter/InstitutionByGroup.aspx.

17 For examples, see Rick Seltzer, "Days of Reckoning," *Inside Higher Ed*, November 13, 2017, https://www.insidehighered.com/news/2017/11/13/spate-recent -college-closures-has-some-seeing-long-predicted-consolidation-taking; Jeffrey J. Selingo, "Small Colleges Fight to Survive, Amid Warnings of Shaky Finances,"

Washington Post, February 9, 2017, https://www.washingtonpost.com/news/grade
-point/wp/2017/02/09/small-colleges-fight-to-survive-amid-warnings-of-shaky
-finances/?utm_term=.90e340d834ae; Laura Krantz, "For Small, Private
Colleges, Fewer Students Means More Worries," *Boston Globe*, March 31, 2018,
https://www.bostonglobe.com/metro/2018/03/31/for-small-private-colleges-fewer
-students-means-more-worries/1jjd8ZFusBt3kGjHOcpIqM/story.html.

18 Will Wooton, former president of Sterling College in Vermont, "The Real Reason
Small Colleges Fail," *Chronicle of Higher Education*, June 8, 2016, https://www
.chronicle.com/article/The-Real-Reason-Small-Colleges/236732.

19 For two of the best recent defenses of small colleges and universities, see Jeffrey R.
Docking and Carman C. Curton, *Crisis in Higher Education: A Plan to Save
Small Liberal Arts Colleges in America* (East Lansing: Michigan State University
Press, 2015); Susan McWilliams and John E. Seery, eds., *The Best Kind of College:
An Insider's Guide to America's Small Liberal Arts Colleges* (Albany: State
University of New York Press, 2015). On the future of liberal arts colleges, see
Rebecca Chopp, Susan Frost, and Daniel H. Weiss, eds. *Remaking College:
Innovation and the Liberal Arts* (Baltimore: The Johns Hopkins University Press,
2014), especially the contributions by Wendy L. Hill on the historic interdisciplin-
ary nature of liberal arts colleges, and David W. Oxtoby, whose essay, though
engaging, stands in contrast to the essays in this volume with the observation that
smaller schools lack "interdisciplinary habits of mind." (78).

20 Few discussions of pedagogy at smaller institutions feature the voices of faculty
from those institutions. A notable, and welcome, exception that addresses
pedagogy amid a host of other institutional topics is McWilliams and Seery, *The
Best Kind of College*.

21 For important discussions of the meaning of interdisciplinarity, see Lisa Lattuca,
*Creating Interdisciplinarity: Interdisciplinary Research and Teaching among College
and University Faculty* (Nashville: Vanderbilt University Press, 2001); Julie
Thompson Klein, *Interdisciplinarity: History, Theory and Practice* (Detroit: Wayne
State University Press, 1991).

Part I

Teaching across
the Disciplines

● ● ● ● ● ● ● ● ● ● ● ● ● ● ● ● ● ● ● ●

1

The Anxiety of Interdisciplinary Teaching
•••••••••••••••••••••

AARON ANGELLO

Imagine yourself in this scenario: it is the first day of class, and you are stand-ing before a group of students. Most of them appear engaged and eager, some look like they'd rather still be in bed, one student in the back of the classroom is obviously struggling to not look at her phone. You feel the familiar nervous-ness that you feel at the beginning of every semester, but this moment is differ-ent. This is the first time you have taught this class. Perhaps this is the first class of its kind to be offered at your institution. Unlike the courses you have taught before, courses that are traditionally discipline specific and in which you con-fidently consider yourself an expert, this course will explore the convergence of multiple topics from different disciplines. After all, faculty at small colleges like yours are increasingly being asked to teach these kinds of courses, either because of institutional pressure to reach enrollment numbers or, perhaps more optimistically, because small colleges offer faculty more opportunities to teach outside their areas of specialization. You consider yourself an authority of sorts in a few of the topics you'll be addressing in the course, but certainly not in all of them. In fact, much of the subject matter is entirely new to you, quite unre-lated to your areas of specialization. You have done your research, but you have a nagging suspicion that some of your students may be more familiar with the information you will be presenting than you yourself are.

This is a daunting prospect for many of us, and an all too familiar one—one that most of us do not have to imagine because we have experienced it. As professors, we are supposed to be the holders and purveyors of knowledge. When we find ourselves in a position in which we may fall short, the very foundations of whom we understand ourselves to be are shaken; our very sense of self-identity is called into question. This chapter examines some approaches to understanding our perceived sense of self, primarily as presented in theories of identity narratives. As we move beyond the anxiety we experience when our identities are challenged, we are enabled to provide a more productive learning environment for students. The chapter presents specific strategies that I, and others, have employed in the classroom both to mitigate our own anxiety and to empower students.

I am a scholar of modern and contemporary poetry. That is, in large part, who I am. While working on my PhD, I developed an academic interest in the meeting of digital media and experimental poetry, and I focused my attention on making myself somewhat of a specialist in it. This specialization is itself interdisciplinary, of course; in addition to knowing poetry and poetics, a specialist in digital poetry must have a grasp of media theory, hardware and software systems, various programming languages, user interface theory, and so on. While I am confident when it comes to my understanding of these things as they directly relate to the composition, distribution, and consumption of poetry, I am by no means a computer scientist. I am a bit of a hack, frankly, when it comes to writing code, and the mathematics often employed in algorithmic structures can at times baffle me.

I am not a programmer or a software engineer, but because of my background, I tend to be the go-to "digital media guy" in my department. I work with an amazing group of colleagues, all brilliant and remarkably capable, some incredibly proficient with technology—but there are six of us. This is a reality of teaching at a small liberal arts college and one of the institutional characteristics that differentiates us from faculty at, say, a research university. When it comes to the courses we teach, we all must extend ourselves beyond our proverbial comfort zone. We have to put ourselves into situations in which we might not feel entirely comfortable and in control more frequently than faculty at larger institutions.

I often find myself teaching media courses with content that extends well beyond the areas of knowledge with which I am comfortable. For example, I recently taught a graduate course titled Introduction to Digital Humanities. This particular course was a part of our Master of Arts in Humanities curriculum, but what I am describing here applies to interdisciplinary courses at all levels. Many students in the course held degrees in English, art, education, and history, and there were several computer science students in the class as well. I have worked on a few digital humanities projects in the past, and I felt entirely comfortable teaching some of the topics covered in the course. I have previously worked, for example, on digital mapping projects; I have done some visual analyses of textual corpora with various software platforms; and I have done a bit of network visualization. I understand these subjects fairly well, and I felt confident introducing them to my students.

However, digital humanities is, by its very nature, interdisciplinary. It is often described as a "big tent" that includes many disciplines, or even a field that exists in the space between disciplines, a meeting place.[1] Teaching it can prove difficult, particularly if a single instructor teaches the course. Instructors teaching courses like this may be inclined to shift the focus to content with which they are more comfortable and neglect areas that might have proven more useful to students. On the other hand, they may choose to venture boldly into unfamiliar territory. In my course, I chose to do the latter. At various times throughout the semester, when the content of the course veered away from areas about which I felt particularly knowledgeable, I was struck with a palpable feeling of anxiety. I felt like a fraud, like I was not who others thought I was. Perhaps more significantly, I was not who I understood myself to be.

Scholars have argued that one way of understanding our subjective experience is through an analysis of biographical narrative.[2] I find this approach particularly useful when exploring the professional/professorial self in the classroom because these narratives are so long-standing and pervasive. We communicate who we are to others with the stories we tell about ourselves, but we also reinforce our own beliefs about who we are by repeating these stories to ourselves: I am a scholar of x, an expert in y; I grew up in a challenging environment, which gives me a unique perspective on my particular field; I come from a long line of academics; I have an aptitude for z because of my social position, gender, class, sexuality, etc.; I worked all throughout my PhD program and still finished my dissertation ahead of schedule; I spent hours in a corner of the library reading everything I could about my field. Story-statements like these are how we understand ourselves and how we communicate to others who we are. These stories will alter and shift depending on audience, environment, and when the story is told. However, as a part of these narratives, we also maintain an image of an essential core that is our constant self. "The story of the self, of the presentation of identity, is . . . fluid but the aim is always to present the story, or part of the story, of an integrated whole being," and we hold tightly to that understanding of ourselves.[3]

These personal narratives are not easy things to isolate or define. Not only are there countless narrative threads that comprise our own stories, all interrelated and overlapping, but also our personal narratives exist within us and in relation to preexisting social narratives. "The individual self and the story are reflected and confirmed by those stories that are the meaning-making currency of the particular culture of the individual."[4] We tell our stories to make sense of our present selves, but those stories are also inextricably tied to the social narratives that establish and perpetuate hierarchies.[5] The stories that we, as academics, often tell about ourselves, along with the stories about how societies are constructed, differentiate us from those who are not academics; they situate us within a position of power and authority that is unique to our position. The professor is the one who knows, the consummate expert, the final word on "proper" knowledge.

Indeed, the narratives that one uses to construct and maintain the self are multiple and fluid.[6] One is a different person at work than at home, different with one's parents than with one's children, different at the pub than at a faculty meeting, but the title "professor" carries with it a set of expectations that can be internalized to such an extent as to become foundational to the professor's very being. A professor might be queer, a person of color, brought up in a particular social stratum, the life of the party, the serious scholar, a nonconformist to a gender binary, very traditional—but the person is always, in the eyes of society and in self-concept, a professor. When their professional identity is challenged, when the authority that in part defines them is undermined, professors can find themselves unmoored from a place of psychological and emotional safety and set adrift on an absolutely unfamiliar sea of insecurity.

Sociologist Keri Lerum began using the term "academic armor"[7] to describe the kinds of protections academics employ, often unconsciously, to maintain their "expert positions or jurisdictions."[8] The term can be useful here. Lerum divides academic armor into three categories: linguistic, physical, and ideological. It is worth taking a moment to explore each of these as they relate to insecurities that arise from interdisciplinary teaching. *Linguistic armor* is the use of jargon or obscure language when simpler, more direct language will suffice. Linguistic armor separates the expert from everyone else, and it creates distance between the professor and the student. Very often, when challenged in the classroom or when encountering information that we feel entirely unprepared to address, we retreat behind linguistic barricades that reinforce our intellectual and educational superiority. *Physical armor* shields the body. It is, quite literally, the costume that the professor wears to signify authority.[9] Finally, there is *ideological armor*. This is the sense that our intelligence or education gives us jurisdiction over those whose knowledge and experience are not institutionally sanctioned. Lerum uses the example of an academic researcher, a sociologist who is working with sex workers in the field, to illustrate the way ideological armor is manifest. When the researcher began to feel challenged by the women she was interviewing, when she felt "sexually intimidated by these women,"[10] her default was to retreat into a position of "intellectual superiority."[11] In other words, there is an established social hierarchy that places the academic's purported knowledge above other kinds of knowledge and provides a place of safety from which challenges to the academic's identity can be successfully parried.

While this sociologist's situation differs markedly from the typical college classroom, Lerum's example does illustrate the ways in which we, when our professional identity is challenged, retreat more deeply into our own self-perception as an academic. When we step into the classroom, that academic armor protects the hierarchical relationship between student and professor. We are supposed to be the ones disseminating information, directing conversation, and guiding the student to the correct answers.

Of course, anyone who is reading this chapter, or this volume, undoubtedly values teaching and is well versed in current ideas concerning pedagogy. We all know that standing in front of a classroom and lecturing is generally considered an ineffectual teaching style. We try to construct "active learning environments" to provide opportunities for student discussion. We work to identify alternate ways students can present the outcomes of their learning. We work to create opportunities for students to contribute their unique perspectives to the classroom environment. In spite of this, however, we continue to understand ourselves through identity narratives, and *we always want to be in control*.

Consider this: you ask your students to read a text before class. Your intention is to discuss the text in class. You read the text (again) yourself, diligently noting the important passages, collecting some outside research about the author and the historical context in which the text was written, noting some of the ways the text relates to other texts you have read for the class. You have some questions prepared that should get the students' discussion started. You are prepared. The class begins, and you write the questions on the whiteboard. The students' desks are arranged in a circle to better facilitate discussion. You are doing everything correctly. The discussion begins, and the students actively engage in a lively conversation (we should always be so lucky).

But then the conversation begins to go off track. A student brings up a bit of "incorrect" information to contextualize the text—a misreading of a passage, say, or some historical event that never happened. What do you do? What is your role in the discussion? Of course, you correct the student. You speak up and redirect the conversation so that it is headed in the right direction because there is a conclusion of sorts at which you want your students to arrive. You are still the professor. You have the knowledge, and you have the power. You are shaping the discussion so that your students arrive at a predetermined conclusion—the right answer. Shifting the classroom to a more active learning environment doesn't necessarily change the way we self-identify. We remain the professor, the expert in our jurisdiction.

When we begin to teach interdisciplinary courses, we are very often confronted with material about which we are not particularly confident; we work in jurisdictions in which we feel insecure. We may recognize the value of interdisciplinary coursework and the importance of bridging the gaps between disciplines as important steps in providing students an opportunity to become well-rounded, critical thinkers. As faculty at small institutions, we realize that it is our duty to push beyond our narrow field of expertise, not only because of institutional pressures to meet our enrollment goals but also because we want to meet the ever-changing needs of our students. However, it can be challenging to step from a place of comfort (within one's disciplinary jurisdiction) into a place of insecurity (outside of it).

So what does one do? The answer is simple in theory: we change our stories. We stop relating to the world as the keepers and purveyors of knowledge. We recognize the systemic, hierarchical narrative structures that reinforce our social role. We reimagine and reconsider the ways students learn, and we stop making ourselves the center of that process. In practice, however, it is nearly impossible to do those things. Indeed, there are professional issues that arise, issues such as administrative expectations, tenure requirements, and pressure from colleagues, but it is the insecurity that accompanies these sometimes monumental shifts in our sense of self—the removal of our academic armor—that triggers the anxiety with which we are all so familiar.

In *The Ignorant Schoolmaster: Five Lessons in Intellectual Emancipation*, Jacques Rancière proposed a remarkably radical pedagogical approach. He tells the story of Joseph Jacotot, lecturer in French literature, who in 1818 finds himself in a position in which he must teach French to a group of students in the Netherlands. Jacotot knew no Flemish, the students' language, and the students spoke no French; the task seemed impossible. Upon this realization, he opted to give the students a bilingual copy of Fénelon's *Télémaque*, and he left them to their own devices. On their own, the students worked through the French text using the Flemish translation. Finally, when asked to write in French about what they read, they "managed this difficult step as well as many French could have done,"[12] and Jacotot was astounded with the result. Until this discovery:

> Like all conscientious professors, he knew that teaching was not in the slightest about cramming students with knowledge and having them repeat it like parrots, but he knew equally well that students had to avoid the chance detours where minds still incapable of distinguishing the essential from the accessory, the principle from the consequence, get lost. . . . In short, the essential act of the master was to *explicate* . . . To teach was to transmit learning and form minds simultaneously, by leading those minds, according to an ordered progression, from the most simple to the most complex.[13]

Still, Jacotot did not explain anything to his students, yet they succeeded in learning French. His revelation was this: the "explicator" needed to become the "ignorant." "To explain something to someone is first of all to show him he cannot understand it himself [*sic*]."[14] There is great pedagogical power in abandoning explication, even if it makes us feel weak, insecure, not ourselves. It is sometimes exactly what our students will most benefit from.

It is important to recognize that Rancière is not making an argument that the teacher is unnecessary.[15] The teacher's role is to facilitate an environment where learning can occur, and often that means setting the stage, then getting out of the way.

I was struck by an article by Chris Friend,[16] an assistant professor of English at Saint Leo University and the director of the online, peer-reviewed journal *Hybrid Pedagogy*. In it, Friend, dissatisfied with the way his classes were running, decided to try something different. As things were, he "wasn't actually letting students try things in [their] conversations. Instead, I expected them to say things, and I waited until they said what I expected. It was a farce, and I should have just told them what was on my mind and waited for them to ingest it, old-school style."[17]

So he decided he was going to *actually* allow his students to dictate the progress of the discussion. He created a Google document on which he would post a couple of questions pertaining to the assigned reading. He projected his laptop on the classroom screen, and he informed his students that he was going to take notes; he was not going to intervene in their conversation. If there was a silence, he would tell his students, "Just talk. You'll figure it out."[18] Occasionally, he would ask a question, but he kept his eyes on the screen to indicate to his students that he was not running the discussion.[19] The resulting discussion was engaged and fruitful, and, importantly, it was driven by the students' own interests and experiences.

When I employed this technique in my digital humanities course, I found that the students embraced the idea of sharing their unique areas of knowledge with their peers. One student, a woman with a background in history, was working on a project in which she wanted to track specific language that news media were using to cover the Dakota Access Pipeline protests. She thought it might be interesting to visualize word frequency across various media sources over time—a fantastic project, and one I enthusiastically encouraged. Other students with backgrounds in different humanities disciplines began to compile a list of words she might target. She was copying and pasting text from various websites, but a computer science student told her that he could show her how to write a bit of code that would allow her to scrape data from some of the websites. Someone suggested she look at social media and compare the occurrences of specific hashtags to the words used in the more traditional news media. Another student searched and found a plug-in for a visualization software we were using that allowed her to compile hashtags from Twitter.

I knew there was a plug-in that allowed our visualization software to access the Twitter API,[20] but I did not have to tell her about it. I would have, eventually, but by keeping quiet, the students were able to figure it out on their own. This is key: when students "figure it out" on their own, they realize the acquisition of knowledge is not something that lies wholly in the hands of the appointed few (i.e., their professors). Rather, it is the result of their own work and inquiry; they have an ownership of the knowledge and a pride in having obtained it that they would not have if they were fed the information.

This is also key: I do not have to know everything. I'm not expected to. The students know that it would be ridiculous to expect me to know everything about history, news media, linguistics, computer science, statistics, network visualization, or whatever else happens to come up in discussion. They respect me as a facilitator of knowledge rather than a disseminator of it. It is difficult to remove that academic armor, to relinquish the power that is so bound up in our academic identity. But it is possible. It is possible to embrace the fluidity of identity and to let go of the stories that we cling to, stories that make us feel as if we are "the professor." It is a matter of letting go and trusting students.

I have used this technique, or embraced this ideology, in a number of discipline-specific and interdisciplinary courses, from traditional literature courses to courses that explore the relationship of film and literature, poetry and digital media, and technology and pop culture. It is particularly useful in interdisciplinary courses about which we cannot possibly know everything. It is remarkably rewarding to trust our students. They are creative, capable, and so very smart.

Notes

1 Patrik Svensson, "Beyond the Big Tent," in *Debates in the Digital Humanities*, ed. Matthew K. Gold (Minneapolis: University of Minnesota Press, 2012), 36–49. http://dhdebates.gc.cuny.edu/debates/text/22.

2 Anthony Giddens, *Modernity and Self-Identity* (Cambridge: Polity, 1991); Dan P. McAdams, "Personality, Modernity, and the Storied Self: A Contemporary Framework for Studying Persons," *Psychological Inquiry* 7, no. 4 (2009): 295–321; Primo Garcia and Cynthia Hardy, "Positioning, Similarity, and Difference: Narratives of Individual and Organizational Identities in an Australian University," *Scandinavian Journal of Management* 23, no. 4 (2007): 363–383; Vera Sheridan, "A Risky Mingling: Academic Identity in Relation to Stories of the Personal and Professional Self," *Reflective Practice* 14, no. 4 (2013): 568–579.

3 Sheridan, 570.

4 Sheridan, 570.

5 David L. Collinson, "Identity and Insecurities: Selves at Work," *Organization* 10, no. 3 (2003): 527–547.

6 Collinson, 529.

7 Kari Lerum, "Subjects of Desire: Academic Armor, Intimate Ethnography, and the Production of Critical Knowledge," *Qualitative Inquiry* 7, no. 4 (2001): 466–483.

8 Lerum, 470.

9 Importantly, Lerum points out that the academics who most readily wear the armor of professional dress to distinguish themselves from those outside of their jurisdiction are those who are already marginalized to a certain extent. It is a privilege of the white, male, able-bodied academic to wear jeans and a T-shirt in the classroom and still signify a position of power.

10 McElroy in Lerum, 471.

11 Lerum, 471.

12 Jacques Rancière, *The Ignorant Schoolmaster: Five Lessons in Intellectual Emancipation*, trans. Kristen Ross (Stanford: Stanford University Press, 1999), 2.

13 Rancière, 3, emphasis in the original.

14 Rancière, 6.

15 The idea that Rancière is not advocating for a teacherless classroom, but is instead arguing for a different approach to teaching, is expertly and fully explored in Gert Biesta, "Don't Be Fooled by Ignorant Schoolmasters: On the Role of the Teacher in Emancipatory Education," *Policy Futures in Education* 15, no. 1 (2017): 52–73.

16 Chris Friend, "Learning to Let Go: Listening to Students in Discussion," *Hybrid Pedagogy*, September 11, 2014, http://hybridpedagogy.org/learning-let-go -listening-students-discussion/.

17 Friend.

18 Friend.

19 This approach has been adopted by a number of educators to great effect. See, for example, Ben Van Overmeire, "Opening the Classroom: Ownership and Engagement," *Hybrid Pedagogy*, March 20, 2018, https://hybridpedagogy.org /opening-the-classroom-ownership-and-engagement/.

20 An API is an application programming interface. It allows a user to interact with an application, in this case, with the website Twitter.

2

Challenging the Discipline

• •

First-Year Seminars and
the Benefits of an
Interdisciplinary Model

PAUL D. REICH

Near the beginning of the third episode of HBO's *Westworld*, Dolores Aber-
nathy opens a dresser drawer and finds a gun wrapped in cloth. This discovery
prompts a flashback to a traumatic scene of sexual assault; when she recovers
from this memory, Dolores opens the same drawer again to find the gun no
longer there. The camera pauses on her face in that moment as she—and the
viewers—attempt to process how, in the space of just a few seconds, this object
could have disappeared.[1] When showing this scene in class, I replay it several
times, asking my students to carefully study the character and objects in the
frame before and after the interrupting flashback. We quickly conclude that
both Dolores and the dresser are unchanged; the only difference is the missing
weapon. I then ask students to attempt to explain this disappearance based on
their knowledge of the series and the previous two episodes they have already
consumed. We know, for example, that Dolores is an amusement park android
programmed to entertain guests; her daily activities in this nineteenth-century
frontier world typically follow a set pattern that includes her returning to this
dresser again and again, to put away clothes. The show has not suggested that

objects in this world can just disappear. How, then, I ask, can we explain the "case of the disappearing gun?"

While this scene occupies barely more than a minute in an hour-long episode of a ten-episode season, I might spend fifteen minutes on this textual analysis. I do so because it offers students an opportunity to think critically about this text and attempt to communicate their ideas in cogent and persuasive ways. For most of my first-year students, this represents the very first time they have thought of television as text, as worthy of considered and thoughtful analysis. It begins their journey to information literacy, to recognizing how most things are *texts*, open to bias and interpretation, waiting to be examined by engaged consumers.

Back to the gun for a moment. Some of my students figure it out; most don't (and I quickly tell them that I didn't when I first watched the series). The post-flashback scene with Dolores, the dresser, and the absent gun is occurring on another timeline, on a different day, from the pre-flashback scene. Since Dolores's days are so similar, it is difficult to distinguish one day, one year, one decade from the next. With this scene, the show's writers are telling us that we must be engaged and active viewers. It is a powerful "ah-ha" moment in class, one that resonates with my students, reinforcing the importance of close textual analysis and critical engagement.

The exercise I just described works particularly well in introductory-level classes—as does *Westworld*, which has enough sex, violence, and mystery to keep a wide range of audiences engaged. I last used it in my first-year seminar course titled "Cyborgs, Androids, and Self," one option of a required course for all incoming first-year students at my institution. Rollins College provides its residential students with this course in their first semester in the hopes of preparing them to succeed both academically and socially on campus. We call these classes Rollins College Conference (RCC) courses, and they are marketed as "a seminar class in which approximately 16 students meet with a faculty member to explore a topic in the professor's area of expertise."[2] As part of their summer registration, incoming students select their top five choices from around thirty-five RCC courses, and while there is a diverse range of disciplinary perspectives represented in these courses, they do not necessarily correlate to the students' more narrow range of interests. More than a quarter of our students, for example, eventually choose one of our business majors—and many had that interest from the beginning—but we do not provide them with an equivalent number of business-themed RCC courses. So, in any given year, I might find most students in my RCC course without a particular interest in my area of expertise, struggling to understand how this class will ultimately relate (or contribute) to their preferred program of study.

Beyond the academic component of the course, RCC courses are also designed to help students integrate themselves into campus life. Our residential college includes around two thousand students, all of whom are required—except for those from the immediate area—to live on campus their first two years. From classrooms to faculty residences in student dormitories, Rollins takes advantage of the opportunities residential campus life creates. My past RCC course, for example, was taught in the same residence where most of my students lived. (One can only imagine the great fun I had in directing my student down the hall to wake up her friend for class.) To help with this transition to college life, every RCC course has two peer mentors assigned to assist the faculty member and serve as counselors and point-persons for the first-years. They are responsible for planning outside activities that introduce students to campus life and help build community. These events range from attending a college soccer game to a movie night, but as one might imagine, even the most benign of activities can prove challenging to cohorts with wide-ranging interests and personalities.

It is quite easy to see how our RCC courses can have varying degrees of effectiveness for the students in them. As discipline-specific courses with social components that may not have expressed connections to the class (or one's course of study as a whole), these seminars confuse many of our most pragmatic students, who fail to see the value or purpose in this particular enterprise. And while, institutionally, we recognize the importance of RCC courses for their preparatory nature and their value for the purposes of student retention, they do not serve our students well when they are taught from the perspective of a single discipline. Based on my experiences, the first-year seminar courses that serve students best have interdisciplinarity as their defining feature.[3] As I have engaged and reengaged with RCC and its goals over the last two years, my courses have evolved from discipline-specific, content-focused classes that served as introductions to my major to outcome-based courses that employ appealing content so students can learn skills applicable to every class on campus. In so doing, my students understand better the purpose of the seminar and are set up for success in whatever discipline captures their attention.

As I prepared to teach my fall 2016 RCC course, Murder Mysteries, however, interdisciplinarity was the furthest thing from my mind. Our workshops for these courses were led by faculty serving in administrative roles who often recruited first-year seminar instructors with the promise of potential majors. They stressed the importance of viewing these classes as "abbreviated introductions to our major" while reminding us that close to a third of the course meetings might be given to college acclimation activities. While none of these activities—which ranged from library tours and lectures on the liberal arts to spring course registration—were superfluous, they did prove challenging and, at times, disruptive to the rhythms and pedagogies of a typical introductory course. Added to this was the class time and discussion we were to put into the first-year common read, Junot Diaz's *The Brief Wondrous Life of Oscar Wao*.

Many of my colleagues in other disciplines found it difficult to integrate this text into their syllabi and expressed concern about their ability to discuss many of the text's problematic themes. As a member of the Department of English who routinely teaches texts that deal with race and gender, I had no particular anxiety about discussing Diaz's work, but I did wonder how such a text would fit into Murder Mysteries. And so, like my colleagues outside the humanities, I, too, was frustrated about "losing" another two or three class periods away from material best suited to my course's theme.

It is instructive to spend a moment on our collective mindset here. We could have—and should have—viewed the common read as an opportunity to capture our students' attention, to engage them, as Diaz does, with issues relevant to them and perspectives they have not encountered. Instead, many of us considered it lost time away from our disciplinary agendas. Only after we saw the overwhelmingly positive response so many students had to Diaz's campus visit after our individually led discussions did we realize what truly had been lost. This, unfortunately, is the by-product of discipline-specific courses.

Introductory courses to the English major in our program have specific learning outcomes that include the articulation of basic literary and language terminology, the focus on active over passive reading, and the ability to perform basic textual analysis (or, as my discipline defines it, close reading). Because our department also staffs all the sections of first-year writing—a required course for every Rollins student—my course would need to satisfy the introductory learning outcomes of the English major along with those of the writing competency program. The latter includes a specific paper sequence that moves students from rhetorical analysis through synthesis analysis toward a research-based argumentative essay. Moreover, as a writing-focused course, additional class periods are expected to be spent on the conventions of writing, drafting, peer review, and individual conferences with the instructor. Finally, as a first-year seminar instructor, I also had to incorporate those college acclimation and social activities required by the first-year program.

Murder Mysteries, then, had three sets of course goals with two sets of learning outcomes that did not always overlap. Because of the time that was going to be devoted to college transition activities, both of the English and writing competency learning outcome sets had to be accomplished in what amounted to twelve weeks of class time. It was not a recipe for success. In previous semesters, I had taught both introductory courses to the major and writing competency classes; my attempt here was to teach a hybrid of the two. In practice, this meant viewing the rhetorical analysis assignment as a close reading essay, the synthesis analysis as a comparative textual analysis, and the argumentative essay as a research paper. While the course texts would still be a combination of fiction, film, and television series, I reduced the number of them in favor of more in-class writing discussions and activities. When coupled with the reduction of class periods for RCC-related activities, I found by the end of the semester that my course had done no one thing particularly well. I do not believe that my students received an adequate introduction to the English major, nor did they become competent close readers; I do not believe they received the type of writing instruction needed for success at Rollins; and I continue to be concerned about how well they have transitioned to college life.

As I began to consider how the course might be improved, I thought first about student engagement. Those enrolled in my RCC course would be interested in a variety of disciplines, and few might initially be interested in the humanities. I spent the first decade of my teaching career teaching first-year composition and felt comfortable engaging non-major populations.[4] At Rollins, I also teach the introductory section to the American Studies major/minor, an interdisciplinary program that draws a diverse group of students. As I taught that course in spring 2017, I was reminded how much more effective a range of disciplinary perspectives was in capturing student interest. My American Studies course was also organized around a central theme—the 1920s—and presented students with an examination of changing gender and class expectations in disciplines ranging from history to literature, sociology, and the visual and performing arts. Students were initially drawn to the class because of the theme—Gastby-esque parties remain a popular pastime at Rollins—and enrolled in the class as a general elective. But despite their wide-ranging majors and perspectives, they could engage with the course material because of the diversity of its approaches to the decade. At a time when I questioned how effective I could be in a class of non-majors, this course and its interdisciplinary approach provided a clear pedagogical path for success.

I also began to feel the influence of two larger initiatives, and both speak to generational shifts in approaches to learning occurring on college campuses. The first emerged within my own department after we recently revamped our curriculum, moving away from content-driven learning toward the increasingly more common skills-based approach. In practice, this meant the elimination of compulsory survey courses in favor of a distribution model that requires both historical and geographical breadth. Our new major also emphasizes clearly defined developmental stages of learning with specific outcomes for lower- and upper-level courses. This transition was not an insignificant one for our department. It involved a lot of hand-wringing, particularly for faculty who could not imagine an English major completing our program without studying William Shakespeare or Emily Dickinson, a distinct possibility with the new model that emphasized skill over content.

Once we moved past that hurdle—some of us more begrudgingly than others—we had invigorating discussions about what exactly we wanted students to learn in our classes. As I described in the learning outcomes for introductory courses to the major, there is now a clear and deliberate focus on our discipline's primary mode of inquiry: close reading. This method of interrogation focuses on textual analysis with an emphasis on critical thinking and written communication. Students continue to improve on this skill as they progress through our program while also demonstrating a proficiency in their use of secondary critical sources and literary theory. Graduates under the new curriculum, we believe, should be able to critically analyze a text (in whatever form it may take) and communicate that analysis in a clear and effective manner.

The second initiative that impacted how I restructured my RCC course proved even more influential because of its close ties to the first-year seminar program. In the spring of 2015, Rollins introduced a new general education curriculum entitled Rollins Foundations in the Liberal Arts (rFLA). Our previous general education courses were typically viewed as introductions to liberal arts disciplines with little explicit connection among the courses. In response to worthwhile questions concerning the value of liberal studies for twenty-first-century students, our faculty wanted to make concrete the importance of these foundational courses for all students' educational experiences regardless of their major. Like our new major, the rFLA program stresses a progressive, developmental approach with specific learning outcomes assigned to each course level. This program, though, relies on the Association of American Colleges and Universities (AAC&U) VALUE rubrics.[5] The required 100-level course focuses on the Information Literacy VALUE Rubric;[6] the three required 200-level courses focus on the Critical Thinking VALUE Rubric;[7] and the required 300-level course focuses on the Information Literacy, Critical Thinking, and Written Communication VALUE Rubrics.[8] While the course goals work students toward proficiency in these specific learning outcomes, 100- and 200-level courses continue to be discipline specific, and students are required to take one rFLA course in each division: Expressive Arts, Humanities, Social Sciences, and Natural Sciences. The 300-level course, however, is meant to be interdisciplinary, a capstone of sorts to students' general education at Rollins with a reinforcement of the learning outcomes in which they should now be proficient.

In addition to the five required rFLA courses, students must also demonstrate competency in five additional areas: health and wellness, ethical reasoning, mathematics, foreign language, and, as previously mentioned, writing. In some ways, these competencies are the last holdovers from our previous general education curriculum, which focused on introducing students to many of the college's discipline-based departments and ensuring that each graduate would have to take a class from philosophy, political science, English, history, and so on. In the new program, no such requirement exists; students could, for example, satisfy their Humanities divisional requirement with an English course and, in fact, never take a philosophy class.

Not surprisingly, the transition to our new general education curriculum has been challenging, and, as with any programmatic shift, certain courses and programs got left behind. RCC has been one of those pedagogical and administrative casualties. While it is identified as a structural part of the rFLA program, we have not spent enough time thinking about its place within the larger general education curriculum. For now, that work has to be done by individual faculty members. And so, as I considered how to improve my first-year seminar in the spring of 2017, I found myself teaching a successful interdisciplinary American Studies course influenced by the new outcome-based curricula of my department and the college's general education program. What, I asked myself, would an RCC course look like if it married interdisciplinary approaches with a focus on learning outcomes over discipline-specific knowledge? And how might that kind of course address many of the problems I faced in my previous first-year seminar? Most importantly, would such a course provide students with the tools they needed to succeed in college and as productive citizens when they graduated?

With those questions in mind, I fashioned a new first-year seminar course for the fall of 2017 entitled Cyborgs, Androids, and Self. Like my RCC course the year prior, it aimed to acclimate students to college life and also fulfill the writing competency. But I decided the class did not need to meet the specific learning outcomes of an introductory English course. Instead, following the models I found in rFLA courses, I focused student attention on the three AAC&U VALUE rubrics most valuable to their broader long-term success on campus: Critical Thinking, Information Literacy, and Written Communication. I sought to deliver an understanding and basic proficiency in those outcomes by focusing on textual analysis through a range of disciplinary approaches. As Harvey Graff in *Undisciplining Knowledge* argues, here, "in the dynamic, simultaneously critical and complementary interplay between disciplines," I can demonstrate how aptitude in critical analysis and written and oral expression are universally prized by a variety of scholars from sociologists to physicists and philosophers.[9] By making the course interdisciplinary and outcome focused, I hoped to address two of my most pressing concerns from the previous year: improving student engagement and establishing clear connections between this class and postcourse success.

My experiences the previous year and the deliberate consideration I put into the course and its goals gave me an advantage going into the fall 2017. So too did the fact that my section ended up being one of those open to honors students. While these students had the same range of academic interests as those in my previous RCC course, their participation in the program promised a higher level of engagement and commitment to the learning process. Drawing on this fact as well as my more extensive preparation, I framed the course as an examination of the differentiating lines between authentic and artificial life, including the debate over how that line challenges our sense of self. This theme, I hoped, would provide ample opportunity for class discussion where students could develop and hone their critical thinking and information literacy skills. I also incorporated a range of writing assignments, including online discussion posts, short and extended textual analyses, and a final analytical essay. This, along with our discussions and conferences outside of class about the writing process, would ensure that my students could meet the expectations for written communication.[10]

First-year students typically arrive on campus five days before classes begin, and Rollins does its best to keep students engaged in acclimation activities during that time. RCC classes meet once during that period, and I used that occasion to provide students with a quick overview of the course, including the three learning outcomes on which we would focus. Whereas in my previous RCC course I would have used this time to introduce discipline-specific concepts, here I stressed how critical thinking, information literacy, and written communication were skills essential to their success in all majors at Rollins and beyond. This initial meeting was followed by short advising sessions with each student—RCC instructors serve as academic advisers for their students' first year—and in these meetings I continued to emphasize connections between our course and their other courses when appropriate.

For our first "official" meeting, students read Isaac Asimov's "Evidence" (1946), a short story that examines the political, philosophical, and sociological ramifications of the integration of artificial life into human society. In Murder Mysteries I used this session to lay the groundwork for the discipline-specific conversations that were to come over the next sixteen weeks: character, point of view, theme and symbolism, and structure. In Cyborgs, Androids, and Self, I instead focused our discussion on the political and sociological questions Asimov's story raises and began the semester-long process of developing their critical thinking skills. The AAC&U Critical Thinking VALUE Rubric defines this skill as "a habit of mind characterized by the comprehensive exploration of issues, ideas, artifacts, and events before accepting or formulating an opinion or conclusion."[11] I developed this habit by doing what all good seminar leaders do: ask probing questions, challenge student assumptions, offer and invite illustrative contexts, and clarify ambiguities. My discussion questions ranged from the sociological to the political. How would artificial life (and the possibility of its potentially limitless life span) impact traditional human institutions like marriage, family, and mortality? Could an artificial life governed by an innate drive to serve and protect humanity be a better public steward? In each case, I asked the class to use the text and our own observations of human behavior to help construct arguments and their counters.

As we moved from Asimov to Philip K. Dick's novel *Do Androids Dream of Electric Sheep?* (1968) to contemporary podcasts dealing with the current state of robotics, the basic format of our discussions remained the same. While I may have had trouble in my previous RCC course with student engagement as we discussed characterization and points of view, this group of students actively participated in discussions that asked them probing interdisciplinary questions. What, for example, are the essential qualities that define human (real) life? Is expressed emotion a necessary part of our social contract? I soon found that students began to take a more active role in determining the course of our conversations, and since the course was not content or discipline focused, these deviations were not only permissible but a testament to the "habit of mind" I wished to instill in these critical thinkers.[12] For example, in our discussion of NPR's *Hidden Brain* podcast "Could You Kill a Robot?" I had planned on discussing the program's main theme: the ways in which we can measure people's empathy using robots.[13] Instead, we had a robust discussion on one of the show's tangential points: the fact that most digital personal assistants like Amazon's Alexa are given female names because the technology is developed by young, white men who do not recognize their own personal biases. We also had one of the most thought-provoking conversations I have ever encountered in a classroom as we discussed the show's assertion that robots designed specifically for sexual activity might serve as an outlet—or safety valve—for behavior that society considers morally repugnant or illegal. As we confronted, challenged, and synthesized our perspectives, I could not have planned a better lesson to actively engage my students in the practice of critical thought. It became all the more meaningful because the students themselves did much of the work to get us to this position of deep intellectual engagement.

I do not mean to suggest in the preceding paragraphs that every moment of our meetings was devoted to these broader, interdisciplinary questions. In every session, I emphasized the importance of textual analysis and grounding one's argument in supporting evidence. At times, this kind of analysis even looked like something I would do in a traditional literature class. During a class period on William Gibson's novel *Neuromancer* (1984), for example, I walked students through a close reading of a single paragraph in that text. We discussed Gibson's use of repetition, punctuation, historical referents, and other stylistic devices. I pressed students, too, on why he employed a definite article in some places and an indefinite article in others, exploring the ramifications of that choice on our understanding of the noun phrase. We closed our discussion by synthesizing these observations into a unified reading of the passage that helped to further our understanding of Gibson's text, connecting the technical parts of his writing with the larger themes in the novel. But because these textual analyses happened in concert with larger, historical or sociological questions, my students this semester found such sessions more relevant to their future courses of study and could more clearly see how our interdisciplinary approach would help them develop skills critical to their success.

As we explored television and film, the move from print to visual texts was relatively seamless, but I used the genre switch to remind students that the methodologies and practices we were developing could be applied to all texts. The exercise I used to open this chapter was, in most ways, no different than the one I employed with *Neuromancer.* As students began to select topics for their larger writing assignments, I reminded them of the variety of texts—films, podcasts, short stories, articles, and novels—upon which they could focus. The first major writing assignment in the course asked students to perform an extended textual analysis by selecting and analyzing a passage or scene from one of our texts. The AAC&U Written Communication VALUE Rubric, which guided this assignment, emphasizes five elements: "context of and purpose for writing," "content development," "genre and disciplinary conventions," "sources and evidence," and "control of syntax and mechanics."[14] As I distributed the first essay assignment, we reviewed the first of these and established a clear understanding as to the purpose of this written exercise. I also used this time to model the kind of interrogation students should have with their assignments across campus; simply put, I taught them how to "read" an essay prompt. After students began working outside of class on this assignment, I used part of our in-class time to discuss common writing conventions like thesis development, topic sentences and transitions, and even some grammar and mechanics. I also dedicated class periods and office hours to individual conferences with students on their essays. As they often do, these sessions proved invaluable for handling specific developmental issues and writing concerns.

The final essay assignment built on the extended analyses students had refined in previous written exercises but asked them to think more broadly about a topic *and* include evidence from sources they had collected on their own. To help point them to local resources for their research, we spent a class period in the campus library, where one of our reference librarians gave a presentation on source acquisition relevant to our class theme. Because we had operated that semester in a larger sociopolitical environment dominated by accusations of "fake news," discussions of information literacy had been frequent in our meetings. But I also used this assignment to discuss how to evaluate sources and use them effectively, both components of the Information Literacy VALUE Rubric.[15] In my evaluation of their final drafts, students in Cyborgs, Androids, and Self routinely exceeded the benchmarks in the Writing Communication VALUE Rubric and consistently outperformed those in my previous class.

As I reflected on the course at end of the semester, I felt confident that my 2017 RCC course had provided students with a stronger foundation for their study at Rollins. By shifting the focus away from the narrow learning outcomes of my discipline, I enabled students of all interests to practice the critical thinking, information literacy, and written communication skills that would serve them well in courses across campus. Students in my class were engaged and enthusiastic, and I found our conversations to be an excellent laboratory for sustained critical discussion. As I look to future first-year seminars, I will continue to employ this interdisciplinary, outcome-based approach and work to integrate our college acclimation activities with our efforts in the classroom. Group attendance at a women's soccer game, for example, can also yield relevant, thoughtful questions. How can we apply similar methods of critical analysis to the crowd size and type? What do our observations suggest about sports and gender, class, and privilege? Once this loop is closed, students will experience a first-year seminar that provides them with a clear path to becoming lifelong learners and engaged and productive citizens regardless of their chosen profession.

Notes

1 *Westworld*, season 1, episode 3, "The Stray," directed by Neil Marshall, performed by Evan Rachel Wood, aired October 16, 2016, on HBO, https://play.hbogo.com.

2 "Residential Life & Explorations: RCC Courses 2018," Rollins College, accessed June 29, 2018, https://www.rollins.edu/residential-life-explorations/explorations/your-first-semester.html.

3 As there are competing definitions of interdisciplinarity, I employ Strober's: "teaching and research that relies on multiple disciplines, regardless of the level at which those disciplines are integrated." Myra H. Strober, *Interdisciplinary Conversations: Challenging Habits of Thought* (Stanford: Stanford University Press, 2011), 27.

4 Like many of my colleagues who did their doctoral work at large state universities, my graduate studies at Purdue University were funded, in part, by teaching assistantships for which I regularly taught first-year composition. Despite being located in the English department, though, I earned my PhD in American studies, where I was well-trained in the practice of interdisciplinarity in both my scholarship and my teaching. And while I had to make several transitions in teaching style as I moved from a large university to a small college, one that I most enjoyed was the ability to engage non-major populations in interdisciplinary work.

5 "VALUE Rubric Development Project," Association of American Colleges and Universities, accessed July 9, 2018, https://www.aacu.org/value/rubrics.

6 "Information Literacy VALUE Rubric," Association of American Colleges and Universities, accessed July 9, 2018, https://www.aacu.org/sites/default/files/files/VALUE/InformationLiteracy.pdf.

7 "Critical Thinking VALUE Rubric," Association of American Colleges and Universities, accessed July 9, 2018, https://www.aacu.org/sites/default/files/files/VALUE/CriticalThinking.pdf.

8 "Written Communication VALUE Rubric," Association of American Colleges and Universities, accessed July 9, 2018, https://www.aacu.org/sites/default/files/files/VALUE/WrittenCommunication.pdf.

9 Harvey Graff, *Undisciplining Knowledge: Interdisciplinarity in the Twentieth Century* (Baltimore: John Hopkins University Press, 2015), 233. In this final

chapter, Graff speaks more about these shared skill sets, including "the ubiquity of 'reading' and 'writing' across multiple media." I share this belief and present my version of interdisciplinarity to students through a range of "texts," all designed to provide multiple disciplinary conversations.

10 It is important to note that I have not included interdisciplinary thinking as a learning outcome. While students in my American Studies courses become proficient in that skill, I provide first-year students with interdisciplinarity so they may develop competency in other critical skills. For those interested in interdisciplinary thinking as a learning outcome, I suggest looking at Woods's "model of Interdisciplinary Communicative Competence" (858–862) in Charlotte Woods, "Researching and Developing Interdisciplinary Teaching: Towards a Conceptual Framework for Classroom Communication," *Higher Education* 19, no. 6 (2007): 853–866, https://www.jstor.org/stable/29735154.

11 "Critical Thinking VALUE Rubric," Association of American Colleges and Universities, accessed July 9, 2018, https://www.aacu.org/sites/default/files/files/VALUE/CriticalThinking.pdf.

12 "Critical Thinking VALUE Rubric.

13 Shankar Vedantam, "Could You Kill a Robot?" July 11, 2017, in *Hidden Brain*, produced by NPR, podcast, 00:33:00, https://itunes.apple.com/us/podcast/could-you-kill-a-robot/id1028908750?i=1000389750420&mt=2.

14 "Written Communication VALUE Rubric," Association of American Colleges and Universities, accessed July 9, 2018, https://www.aacu.org/sites/default/files/files/VALUE/WrittenCommunication.pdf.

15 "Information Literacy VALUE Rubric," Association of American Colleges and Universities, accessed July 9, 2018, https://www.aacu.org/sites/default/files/files/VALUE/InformationLiteracy.pdf.

3

More Than Just Another Core Class

● ●

The Interdisciplinary
Composition Course

PATRICIA MARCHESI

The idea of going to college to prepare for a specific career holds great currency in the minds of students and parents. Year after year, I hear students say they came to college in order to get a job afterward. On some level, I understand: students and parents alike want to know that their time, effort, and money will translate into a bright future with a secure job and a generous income. Few students say they are going to college to become better people, to find meaning, or to broaden their horizons and become more interdisciplinary.[1] More than these intangible outcomes of the college experience, parents and students alike want to *see* results, and they want to see them as soon as possible. Often, this translates into students' reluctance to explore a variety of disciplines or an unwillingness to risk taking courses that could lower their GPA.

Yet according to a 2013 study published in *Liberal Education*, the flagship journal of the Association of American Colleges and Universities, employers affirm that "the world now requires interdisciplinary knowledge and awareness of complex issues that go beyond the skills of a particular profession. Being aware of those, and writing about them, will prepare our students for an ever-changing global marketplace, and will also enable them to be responsible citizens and make informed decisions."[2] The same study also found that most employers believe future employees will need "a broader set of skills (93 percent total agree; 52 percent strongly agree) while facing challenges . . . that are more complex than in the past (91 percent total agree; 50 percent strongly agree)."[3] If success in the future workplace, then, will be determined by one's ability to "excel in more than one discipline or area," colleges and universities should introduce students to interdisciplinarity early in their academic careers.[4] In so doing, long-established core curriculum requirements, such as first- and second-semester writing courses, can find renewed value as important venues in which to help students establish their interdisciplinary critical thinking skills while increasing their awareness of global issues and cultures.[5] I have focused on precisely these outcomes while teaching introductory writing at a small liberal arts college.

Composition with a Focus on Sustainability

LaGrange College, the oldest private college in the state of Georgia, is a liberal arts institution affiliated with the United Methodist Church. The college started out as a women's academy and is now a coeducational college with "an interdisciplinary, broad-based general education curriculum, rigorous study in the major disciplines, innovative learning opportunities and integrative co-curricular programs."[6] With its dedicated faculty and about a thousand students, the college prides itself on its goals to "challenge the minds and inspire the souls of its students."[7] The small class sizes do, indeed, allow students to receive individual attention from faculty, because with fewer students faculty can quickly see what individual students understand or struggle with. This is particularly advantageous when helping students to learn across and beyond their areas of interest. Moreover, smaller class sizes also allow faculty additional time for preparation, exploring the diverse course materials and methodologies required for interdisciplinary pedagogy.

Prior to my arrival at LaGrange College, I taught large undergraduate classes and had little room to explore teaching outside the focus of my professional training in early modern literature and Shakespeare. At LaGrange, however, English faculty, like their colleagues at many smaller institutions, teach courses both on their primary field and on writing. I welcomed the latter and elected to teach one of my composition courses, Rhetoric and Composition I, with a focus on sustainability, a topic I had become interested in while a graduate student in Boulder, Colorado, but one that I had not yet been able to explore in my own classroom. The city, as well as the University of Colorado at Boulder, have many green initiatives, and I learned about their importance for local, state, and global well-being. When I first mentioned my idea of teaching first-semester composition using a sustainability reader, the English department at LaGrange welcomed the idea, especially as it would relate to the then-existing Oikos program, which constituted an interdisciplinary minor sponsored by the departments of biology, political science, religion, and sociology and anthropology. The program aimed to expose students to "the dual aspects of ecological and social responsibility" as well as how they "might contribute to a just, sustainable, and peaceful future."[8] During my time at LaGrange, the program has been revised and renamed the Global Sustainability Minor, a process in which I was fortunate to participate along with the original founding faculty members.

Predictably, Rhetoric and Composition I consists of an "introduction to expository writing, emphasizing the essay form, the writing process, and rhetorical modes of thesis development."[9] The goal of the course is to introduce students to academic writing and lay the foundation for competent analysis and argument development. Typically, students have a variety of writing assignments: low stakes responses, reflections, and three to four essays (the hardest of which is usually the last one, a five- to six-page research paper). There are no assigned themes for Rhetoric and Composition I, and professors usually pick a composition reader or a series of articles including a variety of topics and writing styles. Until recently, I was the only one teaching Rhetoric and Composition I with a theme (now there is one with a journalism focus), and eventually the class became English 1101S instead of just English 1101, so that students who took it could earn credit toward the college's Global Sustainability Minor.

I am able to teach writing with a focus on sustainability, in part, because I teach at a small college that has no environmental studies or environmental sciences degree program. Although I have a degree in English, I also have an international background, which I am able to highlight to my students' benefit because of the lack of specialization that attends a smaller faculty. I am originally from Brazil, and I strive to infuse my classes with a multicultural and global perspective. Because sustainability is a global concern—climate change and other environmental problems no longer affect just one area of the world these days—the topic also fit nicely with the college's emphasis on global engagement, and I was ultimately able to secure funding to complete the Earth Charter's Online Programme on Education for Sustainable Development (January 20–June 17, 2017), a six-month online certificate program with a focus on training educators and community leaders.[10] The certificate program covered a wide range of sustainability issues, as well as pedagogical strategies and resources. I was fortunate to meet participants from all over the world and learn about some of the particular challenges and initiatives that exist in different countries. The international focus of the program was particularly helpful to me, as it made clear to me how many sustainability initiatives exist around the globe. Depending on where students in the United States live and study, however, they may be seriously undereducated on environmental issues, or—worse—have views that are incompatible with the facts and the science that exist. Preparing students for the future means educating them to understand the current trends of their world—which may or may not run counter to those of their home town or home state—as well as teaching them a variety of skills that lead to competence as well as ethical responsibility and citizenship.

In addition to the opportunity to explore a topic beyond my area of academic expertise, the small college setting also afforded me the independence to focus my course on sustainability on the issues, fields, and skills I found most crucial for helping students to "see the big picture, listen, synthesize ideas and connect the dots."[11] Given that sustainability is interdisciplinary by nature, the course readings fell naturally under a broad umbrella covering multiple disciplines. Topics ranged from the importance of biodiversity to the positive impact of bird-friendly coffee and the ecological and political weaknesses of the fast fashion industry. Beyond these, my students may read, discuss, and write about the following topics in a given semester:

Christian perspectives on sustainability
Hunting, conservation, biodiversity, and animal rights
Pollinators (bees, bats, hummingbirds)
The oceans, marine life, and plastics
Overfishing
Industrial recycling
Nature writing
Desertification and regenerative agriculture
Overpopulation and resources
Refrigeration
Local and state sustainability initiatives
Green sports
Food waste
Fast fashion
Fair trade and why
Water conservation
Diet and its effects on the environment
The Earth Charter
The United Nations Sustainable Development Goals
Forests and trees
Fossil fuels and renewable energy
Experimental technologies
Women's education and emancipation around the world

These topics align with the student learning outcomes of the college's Global Engagement Quality Enhancement Plan of 2013, which expects the following:

- Students will demonstrate awareness of global issues by construct-ing solutions to complex problems in a diverse world.
- Students will demonstrate global thinking by their ability to acquire, interpret, synthesize, and evaluate information about global issues.
- Students will demonstrate communication proficiency (oral, written, visual) in efforts to share their global experiences and understanding.[12]

Moreover, the mission of the college emphasizes a "commitment . . . to nurture students' intellectual, social, and personal development. This commitment, in turn, is grounded in the College's responsibility to prepare students to live, serve, and lead in a global community."[13] With its emphasis on reading, ana-lyzing, and writing about complicated global issues, then, English 1101S simul-taneously accomplishes the goal of developing students' writing skills while increasing their understanding of the diversity and complexity of the world as called for by LaGrange's programmatic and institutional learning objectives.

The variety of sustainability topics in English 1101S also allows students with different interests to find reading material they are interested in. Students keen on becoming engineers, for example, gravitate toward subjects related to energy, building, green technologies, and biomimicry. In addition, the readings are suit-able for a general audience and are relatively short. Students are also often given the opportunity to select their own writing topics.[14] For their first essay, for instance, they select a theme from the textbook, summarize the relevant information, and explain how reading about the topic has affected their behav-ior in their community. Such an assignment gives them the opportunity to practice the important skill of summarizing, and it encourages them to reflect on their own actions and make connections to larger contexts and issues. As Walker observes, "Dedicating time to active and purposeful reflection can give us new insights that then plant the seeds for new ways of thinking."[15] I truly believe that new insights and ways of thinking lead to innovation—and "novel and adaptive thinking" is also on the list of the top skills employers often cite as important for the future. As Cathy Davidson points out, "Students need new ways of integrating knowledge, including through reflection on why and what they are learning. . . . This is an engaged form of student-centered pedagogy known as 'active learning.' Students are encouraged to create new knowledge from the information around them and to use it to make a public, professional, or experiential contribution that has impact beyond the classroom."[16]

A reflective assignment, such as the one I described earlier, asks students to reconcile information they have learned with assumptions, behaviors, and pat-terns in their own life. They have to connect the dots, to examine how their actions affect an existing global context. The nature of such a task is interdisciplinary by definition and has the added benefit of contributing to students' self-awareness and personal growth. No less important, students do not feel as nervous about writing their reflections as they do with more formal essays. They generally enjoy such assignments, which is crucial for keeping them engaged in the practice of writing. No less important, the assignment helps me to become better acquainted with all students, especially students who may be quiet in class.

Although there are many interdisciplinary topics that professors could pursue in composition courses, I have found that sustainability is particularly good at getting students to see the so-called big picture and extend their learning across multiple disciplines. As Cullingford and Blewitt describe it, sum up why the topic provides an academic challenge: "Sustainability is complex and complicated, with no single discipline definitively addressing either the problems or the solutions: it incorporates technological, philosophical, economic, social, ecological, political and scientific dimensions. This may be illustrated through an examination of real-world issues or projects that are motivated by concerns over sustainability—for example, Green architecture, eco-design, gender and development; integrated and sustainable transport; global citizenship; and lifelong learning."[17] At the same time, sustainability lends itself well to efforts to refocus students away from passive to "whole person learning," which aims to develop "new ways of thinking through problems with no easy solutions."[18] For example, after watching part of the documentary *The True Cost*, which tracks the environmental impact and poor working conditions behind the fast fashion industry, students often begin to make connections among their buying habits, the degradation of the environment, and the exploitation of people in other parts of the world. These students then start doing research on organic cotton clothing and fair trade. Generally, they are disappointed to discover that such alternatives are more expensive, but this allows us to discuss, and write about, issues such as market demand, business ethics, consumer responsibility, and the laws needed to prevent companies from hiding the "true cost" of some practices. We even examine the debate between minimalism and consumerism and analyze the psychological implications of both. Do we want to *be* more, or *have* more? Is harming others (people, animals, the natural environment) without being aware of it morally excusable? Thinking and writing about such questions is challenging not only because students are practicing the craft of writing, but because these are some of the most challenging questions of our time.

Of course, the interdisciplinary composition classroom is not without challenges. Indeed there are also risks to venturing "beyond the inherited disciplines, departments, and silos" of academic disciplines.[19] Although education today should include "an array of intellectual forums, experiences, programs, and projects that push students to use a variety of methods to discover comprehensive and original answers," professors can encounter student resistance to assignments that require creativity, group work, and originality.[20] Some students have mastered the five-paragraph essay and want to continue doing that for as long as possible. Even students who declare that they are not good at writing (as if "good" happened by an accident of birth rather than practice) may prefer traditional assignments simply because they are familiar. Other students may have different reasons for resisting: some want to know exactly what will give them this or that point, even though a rubric for a creative project may have to be more general to allow for a variety of creative explorations of a topic. In my experience, student resistance fades when professors explain that an assignment is designed to develop a particular set of skills that are important both for personal development and for competitiveness in the job market. In my classes, I often take time to explain such topics like market trends and employer preferences and connect them to a given day's lesson plan.

In addition to student resistance, interdisciplinarity can pose additional challenges for faculty and administrators. Indeed professors who use interdisciplinary approaches can face the disapproval of other faculty who think instructors should stay within their discipline or who believe that incorporating other disciplines makes a course less serious or demanding.[21] Thankfully, this has not been my experience in the small college setting. Still, I have witnessed the difficulty that interdisciplinary majors or minors can have in drawing or retaining students. In general, this appears to be less the fault of a given program than the product of expectations by undergraduates and their parents for field-specific job training. Faced with such expectations, even the most understanding college administration may find it hard to support programs that do not recruit significant numbers of students or are so innovative that they defy connection to a particular occupation. Hopefully, research on marketplace trends and awareness of the growing importance of interdisciplinary experience will secure more support (enrollment and funding) for such interdisciplinary programs.

At LaGrange College, such analysis of market conditions has led not only to the college's global engagement initiative but also to a practice of encouraging students to declare a minor. The college website tells students the following: "Minors can make you more attractive to employers. An additional area of study shows a prospective employer that you're versatile, that you're interested and accomplished in more than one topic, and that you're ambitious."[22] It also reminds students that it may make their graduate school applications more competitive. In order to encourage students to learn more about a minor, there is usually a Minors Fair each semester, with tables and faculty representatives who are there to represent different areas and answer any questions. Any major can be turned into a minor, and the college also offers minors in Entrepreneurship, Gender Studies, Latin American Studies, East Asian Studies, Public History, Social/Behavioral Sciences, Pre-Journalism/Communications,

Poverty Studies, Sports Management, Writing, Marketing Design, French, International Business, Physics, Coaching, and (more relevant to my chapter) Global Sustainability.

To facilitate such wide offerings, smaller institutions, such as LaGrange College, often welcome faculty who are versatile and can fill in missing gaps.[23] In my case, since there is no environmental studies program at my institution, my first-semester composition course ends up being a type of "introduction to sustainability" course, even though the goal of the course itself is to teach the writing process (effective thesis statements, strong topic sentences and paragraphs, textual support, concise writing, ethical documentation, etc.). I am not the only one teaching with an interdisciplinary focus, either. The college's study abroad courses, for example, often feature co-teaching by faculty from different departments. In addition, a variety of departments participate in the interdisciplinary global sustainability minor, the goal of which is for students to acquire an "understanding of sustainability issues in economic, social, and environmental areas," as well as an "awareness of the importance and urgency of such issues in today's world."[24] In addition to required foundation courses, which provide a broad overview of sustainability, students can choose from relevant courses in English, religion, business, biology, modern languages, and political science. The minor also requires a capstone project, but the guidelines of the minor are flexible enough to allow for a wide range of projects: a Servant Scholar, for example, could help create a community garden for low-income areas, an art student could create an installation about famine, and a biology student could examine the effects of pollution on a particular species.[25]

By their nature, smaller institutions like LaGrange invite and facilitate the kind of faculty collaboration required to offer these and other interdisciplinary programs. Because I was interested in sustainability, I was quickly introduced to professors from various departments who shared the same interest, and ultimately we were able to update the curriculum of the minor and brainstorm over courses that could be included. Those of us interested in sustainability also serve on the college's Sustainability Council, whose mission is to promote sustainability on campus. The council organizes events, field trips, and an annual outdoor sustainability fair during Earth Week. Ultimately, a small faculty body means that faculty know each other well. Faculty at LaGrange, for instance, can propose "study away courses," the topics of which often emerge during numerous informal faculty conversations in which colleagues become familiar with connections between their areas of expertise. Indeed the closeness of faculty results in study away trips that are interdisciplinary in nature (for example, a study abroad trip to Iceland with a focus on astronomy and celestial phenomena, but that also includes the Icelandic cosmic worldview through myth and fairy tales), and that provide unforgettable interdisciplinary experiences for students.

Beyond faculty connections, the small college setting also invites campus–community partnerships which also benefit students. Since my arrival at LaGrange College, faculty members have introduced me to local representatives of the Sierra Club, Chattahoochee Riverkeeper, and other organizations. I have learned much about the city and have come to appreciate many of its community initiatives. Because I met local leaders and got involved, I was able to secure a class trip aboard the Miss Sally floating classroom at West Point Lake. My students, in turn, learned about the history of the Chattahoochee River, as well as the importance for wildlife of water monitoring efforts and pollution control. Establishing a network of resources is considerably easier, I think, when a fellow professor knows the local community.

Faculty relationships across and off campus have, in turn, made my writing assignments more meaningful for my students, who have capitalized on our small school setting to interview faculty, staff, and administrators about a given course topic. In my first composition course focused on sustainability, for instance, students had to complete the following assignment: "Choose one aspect of sustainability on your campus. This might include sustainability in campus architecture/buildings, sustainability in the curriculum, landscape design and horticulture, sustainable foods, campus sustainability/environmental committees, energy and water use, and so on. You will conduct research, interviews, and other forms of information gathering, and you will write a 2–3 page report on your findings."[26] Students could go to the library's archives and ask the archivist about past sustainability-related events, or they could go to the cafeteria and speak to the catering manager about sustainability initiatives in food sourcing and within the dining hall itself. One student interviewed our physical plant manager, who told him about all the sustainability practices in the college's daily maintenance and grounds keeping. The student was also able to interview a professor who was one of the earliest advocators of sustainability on our campus and knew the history of sustainability at LaGrange College like no one else. The student's final draft reflected the kind of interdisciplinary experience small colleges can provide: it was full of interesting details about the college and its history. The student had fun completing the assignment, met interesting people, and gained a new appreciation for the sustainability initiatives on campus.[27]

Naturally, the student could have done the same assignment at a larger academic institution, but the point here is that personal contact is *much* easier at a smaller institution—and it makes a big difference. Students at smaller institutions do not feel lost in a sea of people: they can talk to faculty members more easily, get to know faculty members in different areas more easily, and even do research more easily. If the value of an assignment often has to do with the *process* students engage in, a smaller institution can be the perfect setting for students "to become independent and demanding researchers who can use an array of creative, critical, and computational methods to solve problems, wherever they face them."[28] The kind of mentoring and individual attention students receive at LaGrange means that the college can truly pride itself on "transform[ing] the lives of its students."[29]

Notes

1   Emily Esfahani Smith, *The Power of Meaning: Finding Fulfillment in a World Obsessed with Happiness* (New York: Broadway Books, 2017). Smith aptly summarizes such a shift in focus:

> As tuition skyrockets and a college degree is seen as the ticket to economic stability, many people today consider education to be instrumental—a step toward a job rather than an opportunity for moral and intellectual growth. The American Freshman Survey has tracked the values of college students since the mid-1960s. In the late sixties, the top priority of college freshmen was "developing a meaningful life philosophy." Nearly all of them—86%—said this was an "essential" or "very important" life goal. By the 2000s, their top priority became "being very well off financially" while just 40 percent said meaning was their chief goal. Of course, most students still have a strong yearning for meaning. But that search no longer drives their educations. (6)

2   Hart Research Associates, "It Takes More Than a Major: Employer Priorities for College Learning and Student Success," *Liberal Education* 99, no. 2 (Spring 2013), https://www.aacu.org/publications-research/periodicals/it-takes-more-major -employer-priorities-college-learning-and.

3   Hart Research Associates.

4   Terri Williams, "Are Interdisciplinary Degree Majors the Key to Job Security?" GoodCall, June 9, 2017, https://www.goodcall.com/news/interdisciplinary-degree -011140.

5   Although there are many definitions of critical thinking, I adopt D. F. Halpern's view of it: "a habitual willingness or commitment to engage in purposeful deliberation about claims or ideas rather than simply accepting them at face value. It is the foundation of critical thinking behavior and consists of the willingness to (a) engage in and persist at a complex task, (b) use plans and suppress impulsive activity, (c) remain flexible or open minded, (d) abandon nonproductive strategies, and (e) remain aware of social realities (such as the need to seek consensus or compromise) so that thoughts can become actions." D. F. Halpern, *Thought and Knowledge: An Introduction to Critical Thinking*, 4th ed. (Mahwah: Lawrence Erlbaum Associates, Inc. Publishers, 2003), quoted in Michael Sweet and Larry K. Michaelsen, *Team-Based Learning in the Social Sciences and Humanities: Group Work That Works to Generate Critical Thinking and Engagement* (Sterling: Stylus Publishing, 2012), 8. Sweet and Michaelsen provide a useful overview of the concept of critical thinking: "The literature on critical thinking goes all the way back to Socrates, though much contemporary scholarship on critical thinking in education builds on a study by Glaser (1941) in which he identified three aspects of critical thinking: a thoughtful attitude or disposition, a range of reasoning skills, and the ability to apply those skills. Later scholars, such as Paul (1995) and Halpern (2003), added a fourth element: a habit of reflecting upon one's own thinking to continually improve it" (7).

6   "LaGrange College Mission," LaGrange College, http://www.lagrange.edu/about
    /history.html.
7   "LaGrange College Mission."
8   "The Oikos Program," LaGrange College, http://www.lagrange.edu/academics
    /political-science/oikos.html.
9   "English Courses," LaGrange College, http://www.lagrange.edu/academics
    /english/courses.html.
10 According to the LaGrange College website, "The college's Quality Enhancement
    Plan is the Global Engagement Initiative. LaGrange College's QEP is the Global
    Engagement Initiative. The objective of the program is to transform students'
    learning experiences by enlarging their 'local world' perspective to a global
    perspective. The Global Engagement Initiative is in perfect harmony with the
    mission of LaGrange College. Students' search for truth, and their need for an
    ethical framework to foster their lives of integrity and moral courage, will be
    greatly enhanced through this initiative" ("QEP—Global Engagement,"
    LaGrange College, http://www.lagrange.edu/academics/qep/index.html).
11 Reuven Gorscht, "Are You Ready? Here Are the Top 10 Skills for the Future,"
    Forbes, May 12, 2014, https://www.forbes.com/sites/sap/2014/05/12/are-you-ready
    -here-are-the-top-10-skills-for-the-future/#cb5b997c34a5.
12 "Global Engagement Quality Enhancement Plan, Class of 2013," LaGrange
    College, http://www.lagrange.edu/resources/pdf/qep/QEP_Global_Engagement
    .pdf.
13 "Global Engagement Quality Enhancement Plan, Class of 2013.
14 In the past two semesters, our textbook has been Paul Hawken's *Drawdown* (New
    York: Penguin, 2017), but there are a number of sustainability-themed composi-
    tion readers instructors could use instead. I have supplemented the readings in
    Drawdown with newspaper articles, literary texts, documentaries, and YouTube
    videos.
15 Jennie Walker, "Reflection: The First Step in Transformation." *Inside HR*,
    February 6, 2015. https://www.insidehr.com.au/reflection-the-first-step-in
    -transformation/.
16 Cathy Davidson, *The New Education: How to Revolutionize the University to
    Prepare Students for a World in Flux* (New York: Basic Books, 2017), 8.
17 Cedric Cullingford and John Blewitt, *The Sustainability Curriculum: The
    Challenge for Higher Education* (London: Routledge, 2004), 2.
18 Davidson, *The New Education*, 8.
19 Davidson, 13–14.
20 Davidson, 13–14.
21 The attitude is probably due to assumptions inherited from the "new" academic
    institutions of the nineteenth century. Julie Thompson Klein, *Humanities,
    Culture, and Interdisciplinarity: The Changing American Academy* (State Univer-
    sity of New York Press, 2005). Klein examines such institutions' process of faculty
    evaluation: "Professional distinction was reinforced by a new prototype based on
    the German research university. It offered advanced training in research and
    scholarship supported by a comprehensive system of libraries, material resources,
    and specialized programs. Americans studying in Germany brought back the
    model of a research university, although the German academic environment
    differed. The broad, contemplative concept of German *Wissenschaft* connoted a
    connected search for truth and all-encompassing idealism and sense of unity.

Returning Americans interpreted the concept more narrowly, emphasizing 'pure research' over 'pure learning,' scientific aims, and the production of new knowledge"(27).

22 "Minors and Concentrations," LaGrange College, http://www.lagrange.edu/academics/minors.html.

23 In an analysis of the future of liberal arts colleges, Eugene M. Tobin forecasts that such places will necessarily have to "explore intellectual themes that connect departments and disciplines without creating new majors or adding new faculty." See Rebecca S. Chopp, Susan Frost, and Daniel H. Weiss, *Remaking College: Innovation and the Liberal Arts* (Baltimore: Johns Hopkins University Press, 2014), 131. Small colleges therefore offer the perfect opportunity for faculty to create interdisciplinary programs and courses.

24 LaGrange College Global Sustainability Minor brochure, LaGrange College.

25 For more information on LaGrange College's Servant Scholar program, please visit http://www.lagrange.edu/campus-life/servant-scholars.html.

26 The prompt is from the Macmillan Learning's Bedford Spotlight Reader website and can be found in the instructor resources. For more information, please visit https://www.macmillanlearning.com/Catalog/product/sustainability-secondedition-weisser/instructorresources#tab.

27 The student's essay can be read on *The Hilltop News*, LaGrange College's student newspaper, at https://lchilltopnews.org/the-first-word/. The essay is entitled, predictably, "LaGrange College and Sustainability."

28 Davidson, *The New Education*, 14–15.

29 I have deliberately paraphrased the college's vision statement, which is that "LaGrange College will be distinguished as a college that transforms the lives of its students and its communities." More information about the vision of the college can be found at http://www.lagrange.edu/about/index.html.

4

Breaking Boundaries

• •

Reflections on an
Interdisciplinary Course on
Race and Graphic Narrative

PATRICK L. HAMILTON AND
ALLAN W. AUSTIN

Introduction

At first glance, the small college setting seems unconducive to developing innovative teaching practices such as interdisciplinary courses. One might be tempted to ask, after all, how faculty at a small liberal arts university like ours can so innovate given the myriad demands on their time. At Misericordia University, as at most small colleges and universities, faculty take on a heavy teaching load (four classes per semester, in our case), considerable service (to the department, college, institution, and profession), and significant expectations in terms of scholarship (including books, articles, conference papers, and/or grants, among other things). In addition to such explicit expectations, of course, unwritten expectations create numerous additional obligations for faculty at such institutions: being on campus and available beyond class time and required office hours, taking on various and often multiple administrative functions, recruiting students (ever so crucial due to our dependency on tuition), and attending various extracurricular and community events throughout the year.

Faculty members teaching at smaller institutions are, of course, all too familiar with this litany of pressures and barriers working against interdisciplinarity and pedagogical innovation. But we are also increasingly aware of the ways in which the size and nature of these colleges and universities do not only delimit our work; indeed, these very same factors also afford faculty exciting, if unexpected, pedagogical opportunities to break boundaries as they begin to imagine how traditional materials might be delivered in less traditional ways. A quick glance around our institution reveals significant, if nascent, interdisciplinarity. Specifically, the number of team-taught classes—including our own—already on the books suggests that whatever limits exist at small, teaching-centered schools like ours are balanced by the opportunities generated by the very places at which we work.

First offered in spring 2008 and subsequently every other spring semester through 2018, our team-taught class, Race and Graphic Narrative in the Postwar United States, presents a case study in how the small college setting can impede but also facilitate interdisciplinary teaching. Colloquially known by students and faculty alike as "the comic book class," this team-taught course is offered by the Department of English and the Department of History and Government at Misericordia, with students offered the choice of receiving credit for it in one of the two disciplines. Stemming from our mutual scholarly interests in the study of race and ethnicity, as well as comic books and superhero popular culture more broadly defined, the course is the longest-sustained interdisciplinary class at our institution, allowing us a broad experience—the better part of a decade's worth, in fact—upon which to reflect. This experience speaks directly to the factors that can constrain interdisciplinary teaching but also how these limits can be challenged and maybe even broken, in the process providing insight into the potential of such experiences to transform the classroom, its students, and even its instructors.

Developing Interdisciplinary Courses at a Small University: Barriers and Benefits

When it comes to the development of interdisciplinary courses, our experience suggests the ways in which the small college or university environment can function as a double-edged sword. The "origin story"—to draw on a trope of the comic books that our course examines—of Race and Graphic Narrative in the Postwar United States speaks, first, to one of the main features of this environment that facilitated the creation of the class. Ironically, the class grew out of conversations between the two of us that had *nothing* to do with creating one. Instead, the course evolved out of discussions about our shared scholarly interests in examining issues of race and ethnicity in the American experience as well as a shared love of comic books from early childhood. These overlapping interests led to various conversations about the ways in which these subjects intersect, conversations that were (even if unknowingly) paving the way for the creation of the comic book class. For example, we discussed how the Superman newspaper comic strip embarked upon a not-uncontroversial storyline concerning Japanese American exile and incarceration during World War II; for weeks, the strip portrayed Japanese and Japanese Americans alike in the racially scurrilous terms of the time.[1] Talking about Superman's war against Japanese Americans led to another discussion, this time about the late-1980s DC Comics comic book series *New Guardians* and its well-intentioned struggles to promote tolerance in the era of multiculturalism. The series, we agreed, foundered on any number of racial, cultural, and sexual stereotypes that maintained power in that decade.[2] Coming to understand the ways in which these conversations clearly and dramatically demonstrated how Americans have struggled both to understand and to confront racial inequality, as well as the ways in which comics have reflected and contributed to these struggles, we eventually realized that we had the material and approach at hand for an innovative class. In particular, the comic book angle provided a hook that we expected would, first, draw students to sign up and, second, and more importantly, deeply engage primary materials; their interest, in turn, would help to draw them into increasingly complex conversations about race in American life as informed by secondary readings from a variety of disciplinary perspectives.

At the same time, the conversations providing the initial impetus to the development of this course exposed some of interdisciplinarity's challenges. Team teaching requires a willingness to lay bare one's pedagogical methods, and thus an openness that is, in many ways, the cornerstone of interdisciplinarity. This can be uncomfortable, especially as a partnership is developing, and is not always an easy thing to do, even in the best of partnerships. Working so directly with another faculty member raises questions about both professors' methodologies: how they approach texts, in-class discussion, grading, and more. But once a working partnership and trust are established, faculty can have searchingly deep and truthful conversations about what is working and what is not, as well as about—on a deeper level—how most effectively to deliver material. These conversations, it seems to us, happen less often outside of the team-taught environment.

Another significant factor impacting the germination of our course was the environment we enjoy, an environment that is unique to the small university. To start, the very geography of faculty offices at Misericordia (and other small universities like it) provides immense possibility and even encouragement for interdisciplinary work. This is particularly true for those working in the humanities: the third floor of Mercy Hall, on which most of these departments are located, is inherently interdisciplinary in how it mixes humanities faculty members. Our layout for faculty offices does not follow departmental affiliations; rather than faculty being segregated by disciplinary boundaries, they are intermingled. In fact, no members of our history and government, English, philosophy, religious studies, or fine arts departments have their office next to those of only departmental colleagues. Further diversifying the floor is its inclusion of faculty members from outside the humanities. Political scientists, sociologists, and communications faculty are thrown into the mix as well. Resisting strict departmental organization, the third floor cultivates spontaneous (and often lively) interdisciplinary conversations, such as that which led to the development of our course, on a daily basis.

Another facet of the small college environment that allows for greater interdisciplinarity relates to its size. Smaller schools generate and nurture the creativity, the willingness to experiment, and the collegiality that are fundamental to team teaching and interdisciplinary work in general. At the faculty level, this stems from the smaller size of our academic units. Given the relatively small number of humanities faculty at Misericordia, we naturally find individuals working in closer proximity to our own fields of expertise more readily outside our departments than inside them. Our reality is that the "next-closest" expert here is often more likely not in one's own department. But while this may initially seem like it would be a weakness (contributing to a paucity of colleagues and feelings of isolation, among other potential problems), the result at Misericordia has often been the opposite. This engaging and varied environment presents fertile ground from which interdisciplinary classes might emerge, inspired by any number of wide-ranging discussions that are commonplace at Misericordia (and undoubtedly other smaller schools as well). Given, for example, our shared interests, even if from two different disciplinary perspectives, we began discussing how we teach (as well as reading and critiquing each other's scholarship) almost as soon as we met. And the conversations that ultimately led to the development of the comic book class similarly derived from the cross-disciplinary interaction encouraged by the fact that our offices are located next to each other. Both of these factors, in encouraging interdisciplinary work and teaching, are ultimately attributable to the size and environment of our institution.

The size of such small universities at an institutional level is likewise a factor contributing to successful interdisciplinarity, especially, in this case, in regard to pedagogy. A willingness to try new things like team teaching inevitably comes up against a fundamental (and often rightfully dreaded) reality of modern life in the university: bureaucracy. The realities of administration and governance can work either to support or to impede (or, more accurately, both support *and* impede) innovation. At small schools like our own, that bureaucracy is most likely a bit less impersonal and distant than it might be at larger institutions, encouraging the development of personal relationships and allowing for some flexibility that can create openings to try something new.

In our case, a short trip down the hallway to the chairs' and deans' offices to discuss a new idea often suffices to get the ball rolling. We were lucky enough to work as we developed the course with chairs and deans who were quite supportive of team teaching, understanding the kinds of benefits that accrue to students (as well as faculty) in such classes.

Small universities provide faculty a similar proximity to those higher up the chain of command in the bureaucracy, though with varying results. At Misericordia, our chief academic officer is our vice president of academic affairs (VPAA). The extent to which the VPAA has impacted our teaching of the class has varied; we have had four different persons (one serving in an interim capacity) occupy this position since we first offered the class. In particular, the manner in which these courses are loaded for faculty has arisen not infrequently, as our institution actually reduces the compensation for team-taught classes—despite, as explained in the next section, the extra work they involve—in comparison to individually instructed courses. As a result, some of our VPAAs have required us to make up the difference by either taking on additional duties or using other overloads to compensate. Such demands on top of what is already a demanding activity obviously work to the detriment of interdisciplinarity, potentially discouraging faculty from taking it on. Another VPAA supported this innovation but demanded accountability along with it. In this case, the VPAA asked hard questions about what we were doing (in loftier pedagogical terms of our goals and methods rather than more bottom-line issues like loading), honestly listened to our answers, and proved willing to support our endeavor after this very serious and engaged discussion about why such courses matter and make a real difference for students. These hard conversations were ultimately useful in helping to clarify and identify the importance of the course, not only to administrators but to us as well, and thus speak to ways the less distant relationship with administration at small universities can more positively impact interdisciplinarity. But there have been negative impacts as well. With the course coming up on the schedule again in spring 2020, we sought to engage these same administrators in a similar conversation regarding the course and its loading. We were unable, unfortunately, to come to a mutually agreeable solution this time around, and the course was removed from the schedule.

The Practice of Team Teaching at a Small University: Design and Delivery

Just as the small college or university environment plays a key role in both enabling and impinging upon the pursuit of interdisciplinarity, so too the design and delivery of a team-taught class proves equally crucial in its achievement. Scholars have already noted the ways in which interdisciplinary research presents challenges across disciplines (i.e., horizontally) and between a hierarchy of individuals (i.e., vertically).[3] These same challenges manifest when *teaching* interdisciplinarily. A similar horizontal boundary presents itself dually: between instructors, obviously, but also between students coming to the class from different academic backgrounds. That hierarchical/vertical dimension functions uniquely as well, between instructors/experts and students/novices. We have designed and delivered the course to ameliorate these boundaries, creating an intellectual and educational space in which, to borrow our institution's motto, "all are welcome." Doing so is, again, facilitated by the unique freedom we at smaller institutions possess, as it has allowed us to craft a practice of team teaching that thoughtfully pursues these goals.

To start, it is important to make clear that the team-teaching model we practice asks a good deal of faculty; it in fact requires more work on the part of each of us than a traditional three-credit class would. This is perhaps one of the main constraints on team teaching, at least in terms of our approach. Constructing and delivering a team-taught class requires additional effort in a variety of areas, work not required for either traditional teaching or other shared models.[4] The work, from development to delivery, is significant, but we decided to take it on (and to continue taking it on) as it is more than balanced by how team teaching contributes to an enriched, interdisciplinary classroom that produces potentially transformative learning experiences for students (as well as for those teaching the class).

The potential of the team-taught classroom should not, of course, obscure the challenges that come along with it. Students often arrive in the classroom with no or at best fuzzy ideas about just what we actually mean when we use the term "interdisciplinary." In our class, students with a background in history often enter it with trepidation regarding the literature, just as the students majoring in English worry about lacking a background in American history. That our class typically draws majors other than history and English—for example occupational therapy, government, and nursing students, to name some of the more recent examples—can further elevate such concerns. More concretely, students are sometimes less well prepared with background historical knowledge or the ability to analyze primary and secondary sources. Although such problems arise in more traditional formats, of course, they can be compounded by the ambitious nature of team teaching in general. Faculty, as a result, must always be ready to slow down when necessary, and to meet individual students at their own level. No matter how natural interdisciplinary synergy seems to the instructors, it can be—just as a concept in and of itself, let alone a class—quite daunting to students new to the philosophies and methods that underlie such team-taught classes.

In terms of course design, then, one of the most significant challenges we faced at the start was in fact achieving an authentic, yet accessible interdisciplinarity. Our goal for the course was for it to do more than just include different disciplinary perspectives or sources in the manner of a checklist. Simply presenting such sources in this way, we understood, might lead students to "box" them off into separate sessions run by the different "experts" teaching the class. (In a previous team-teaching experience, in fact, we had observed students initially bringing two notebooks to class—one marked "History" and the other "English"—and then shifting from one to another as the subject material changed, demonstrating all too clearly the ways in which students have been trained to think of disciplines as entirely distinct from one another in ways that run counter to real interdisciplinary thinking.) Avoiding such structures required that we work in tandem, carefully consulting each other at each step of the process to ensure the smooth and purposeful interaction of the different materials and disciplinary points of view across the semester.[5]

This hoped-for interaction factored into the design of the course in multiple ways. For one, it ultimately convinced us to teach the class as a once-a-week, three-hour night class. Both the extended class time and extended time between class meetings allowed us to include more materials and provide students with time not just to read but to also to thoughtfully prepare for each class. Second, the reading list was identified in face-to-face meetings, and the syllabus was written with both of us in the same room, debating and discussing the ways in which best to integrate source materials and disciplinary perspectives. Such integration occurs on two levels. Most basically, each class meeting combines materials from the disciplines. But more importantly, the primary materials in the class—the comics as well as, at times, film and television sources—are approached both as primary historical documents and as objects for literary analysis. So, for example, when the class discusses the Superman newspaper strip, the students will discuss the text not only for how it reflects racial attitudes of its time (codified in the secondary materials assigned that week) but also explain how, in the workings of the text—its plot, dialogue, and images— the comics communicate and thus constitute such attitudes. Similarly, the class's discussion of *New Guardians* is framed by historicized treatments of multiculturalism, such as in David Hollinger's *Postethnic America*, as well as theories about cultural appropriation from bell hooks.[6] Again, the point is both for the students to discuss how the comics imbricate themselves within these historical and/or theoretical perspectives, alongside analyzing and explicating the same texts for how they promulgate these attitudes via their various devices.

The same care in course design is reflected in the classroom, as we share the responsibility, consciously and clearly, for first preparing and then actually delivering what will be taught, in this way modeling an interdisciplinary approach to course materials in each and every class. Just as was the case with the course materials, we do not divvy up leadership responsibilities in class based on what discipline the material under discussion seems to stem from;

instead, we consciously work to comment across disciplinary lines in emphasizing the cohesive nature of the assigned materials. Overall, doing so provides students a clear and demonstrable example about the disciplinarily seamless class that we want to present from start to finish.

But perhaps even more important to the achievement of interdisciplinarity in the class is our approach to in-class discussion. We put as much responsibility for leading discussion on the students as we do ourselves. On the first day of class, students participate in what we call the draft of scholars. Students' names are drawn randomly, and they then select what texts they will lead discussion about over the course of the entire term. Each student is required to do so at least twice in the semester. Prior to their first discussion-leading opportunity, students are required to meet with us to discuss the material they must cover; they likewise must send their questions to the rest of the class at least twenty-four hours prior to meeting. This tactic allows each of us—after helping students construct their approach to the material beforehand—to participate, when the class runs effectively, as just another voice in the classroom, not the "expert" who is called upon, depending on our expertise in relation to the topic at hand, to provide instant answers to complex questions or issues. As well, this approach allows the students to participate as scholars with us in the pursuit of an interdisciplinary understanding of these texts. The vast majority of students in the class are third- or fourth-year students and are thus well advanced in their studies within a particular discipline. Here, they are able to use their experience and knowledge as the basis to interact with and explore race in the United States with students—as well as faculty—from other disciplinary backgrounds.

The benefits of delivering team-taught material in these ways are significant, encouraging students to understand not only the material but also a variety of scholarly approaches to it in new and important ways. The team-taught classroom, for instance, ought to introduce students to something that most faculty take for granted: scholars don't all agree with each other. While obvious to us, students often seem to have thought little about this truth. Demonstrating not only disagreement, which students see more than enough of in today's popular culture, but more importantly honest collegial debate, also holds great value for students, helping as it does to introduce them to the *ways* in which scholars work. As we state in our syllabus, "Historians do not just verify facts; they argue with one another over what the facts are and what they mean. Similarly, literary critics do not just reiterate the plot and events of a text; they argue over what these mean." Such a classroom dynamic also demonstrates for students, who again often seem not to have thought much about the work that faculty do (either inside or outside the classroom), the creative process of producing knowledge in different fields of inquiry. The mere *presence* of two professors in the same classroom can teach so much, even without overt instruction.

The fact that we also assign reading materials that we do not always agree with reinforces this point; as students watch both of us constructively engage and critique other scholars (and even on occasion each other), they begin to feel more comfortable doing so themselves, a key development if the class is to support students acting as scholars in their own right.

Finally, both instructors complete the grading of every assignment, experimenting with and demonstrating an additional way in which the interdisciplinary conversations started in the classroom can be continued outside of it. We assess student performance through discussion and written assignments, providing a jointly decided grade for each class meeting. We both likewise provide feedback on the papers, both in text (via Microsoft Word's comment feature) and in conferences. More to the point, we often respond to each other's feedback inside a student's draft, bolstering it at times but also questioning it or making alternative suggestions from one another. When grading works in this way, the feedback to the student becomes a three-way conversation between the individual student and the two professors. Disagreements between the two of us, perhaps ironically, are the best examples of how rich these conversations can ultimately be. They not only demonstrate to the student the dynamics between scholars but also present to them the challenge of navigating these dynamics in order to improve an essay. Such conversations and their inherent challenges are, we hope, instructive to students, helping them to understand that there is no one way to write a sentence, nor one simple model that best assembles evidence in all cases, nor one answer as how to mix historical and literary critiques, nor, ultimately, any one "answer" to the questions we ask about race and ethnicity in the United States since World War II. In this way, even grading—as time consuming as this process can be—reinforces the seamless nature of a team-taught class.

Conclusion

We hope—and have seen, in general—that the seamless interdisciplinarity of the comic book class provides any number of valuable outcomes for students. Perhaps most importantly, we want students to leave the course with a richer understanding of both the scholarly discourse about race and ethnicity over the past eighty years and the creative and dynamic processes of producing knowledge in and between fields of inquiry, as well as an enhanced ability and confidence to take part in debates about the meanings of race in American society (which remain, of course, relevant and important today). Our course encompasses not just English and history but also cultural studies and critical race studies as well as popular culture studies of everything from comics to television to films, and students ideally emerge from the class with a sense not of these as separate and distinct areas of study but overlapping and interactive approaches.

While the benefit to the student has been our focus in this chapter, it is valuable to briefly sketch out various ways in which team teaching can benefit the faculty undertaking such work. Team teaching, for instance, actively encourages faculty to engage with different pedagogical styles, which can lead to evolving approaches to more traditional classes taught on their own. History classes can incorporate literature in new and interesting ways that add another layer of interdisciplinarity. Similarly, historical context (and new ways of thinking about it) can add new levels to an English class. Thought of in this way, team teaching becomes a daily exercise in professional development. In our case, as well, team teaching has shaped the kinds of research topics we have taken on as well as added to our arsenal of ways to examine the materials at hand. In this way, it is worth considering the ways in which team teaching can also help to shape a scholar's research trajectory.

Teaching is, ultimately, a collaborative effort between teachers and students. Growing out of a community that starts between cooperating faculty and then extends to include students, classes like ours suggest exciting and worthwhile work for the future. Importantly, working at a small college or university, it seems clear to us, should not be seen as an impediment to pursuing such ambitions. In point of fact, probably the largest factor in facilitating the creation of our course, and thus the interdisciplinarity it embodies, is the freedom the small college or university setting generally affords faculty looking to innovate. A former faculty member once observed about Misericordia—and by extension, small colleges and universities in general—that the great thing about it (and them) is that faculty can teach and thus be, as scholars, whatever they want. That very freedom allowed our class to develop out of a conversation between two faculty members with relatively few impediments along the way. To be blunt, even though there really was nothing like this course—in terms of content, design, or approach—being regularly offered at Misericordia when we started teaching it in 2008, no one significantly balked at the idea of offering such a course or at the idea that such a course was worthwhile. That freedom allowed the class to continue for nearly a decade, in spite of its various idiosyncrasies and challenges, particularly within the institution and in comparison to more traditional courses. This chapter began by noting the ways in which interdisciplinarity might at first seem relatively incongruous at small colleges and universities; the freedom delineated here might be another seeming incongruity: that, in an institution with a small body of faculty, small departments, and less distance from administration, there is actually some significant opportunity to undertake innovative pedagogical practices such as team teaching and thus to achieve lofty intellectual goals like interdisciplinarity. But if there is such an incongruity, it is actually the unique, peculiar nature resulting from it and inherent within the small college or university that affords us these opportunities to break pedagogical boundaries as we innovate as teachers.

Notes

1 "The Sneer Strikes" in *Superman: The Golden Age Dailies 1942–1944* (San Diego: IDW Publishing, 2016), 154–169. For details on the controversy surrounding the strip's publication—including the U.S. government's ambivalent position on its potential problems—see Gordon Chang, "'Superman Is about to Visit the Relocation Centers' & the Limits of Wartime Liberalism," *Amerasia* 19, no. 1 (1993): 37–59.

2 Steve Englehart and Joe Staton, "The New Guardians," *New Guardians* 1, no. 1 (September 1988).

3 See, for example, Julie Thompson Klein, "Prospects for Transdisciplinarity," *Futures* 36, no. 4 (May 2004): 519; Sharahchandra Lélé and Richard B. Norgaard, "Practicing Interdisciplinarity," *BioScience* 55, no. 11 (2005): 967–975.

4 Here, we in particular draw a distinction between our practice of team teaching—where both faculty members attend and participate in all aspects of a class (attendance, participation, discussion, evaluation, etc.)—and what is known at our institution as turn teaching, in which these responsibilities are divided among the faculty members (i.e., where faculty members trade off lecturing and leading class discussions, split grading responsibilities, etc.).

5 In this, our course would be what Olson and Williams describe as a "dialogue-driven" versus an "expert-driven" course. See Rebecca Olson and Tara Williams, "Reimagining the Literary Survey through Team Teaching," *Pedagogy* 14, no. 2 (2014): 199–223.

6 See David Hollinger, *Postethnic America: Beyond Multiculturalism* (New York: Basic Books, 1995); and bell hooks, *Black Looks: Race and Representation* (Boston: South End Press, 1992).

5

Interdisciplinary Interactivity

•••••••••••••••••••••

Team-Teaching App Design at a Small College

CHRISTINE DEHNE AND

JONATHAN MUNSON

The successes and challenges of Manhattanville College's experiments in interdisciplinary courses can best be understood through a deep dive into our Interactive Media course. Through the lens of this course we describe a set of institutional changes we have initiated to foster the development of interdisciplinary curricula. We also discuss the college's strategic plan for infusing Design Thinking across the campus. This framework for interdisciplinary collaboration is a foundation on which we can build, but we must also address policy and process issues as we create an innovative interdisciplinary curriculum that challenges the existing ethos at the college.

Manhattanville College

Manhattanville College has innovated with integrative pedagogy throughout its history. The most well known example of this was the early adoption of its Portfolio system in the early 1970s as part of a revision of the curriculum supported by a grant from the National Endowment for the Humanities.[1] The Portfolio was a space where students demonstrated that they had met the goals of the college's distribution requirements and was an early example of evidence-based learning, where students would submit artifacts of their work alongside a reflection about the experience. Today, although the Portfolio no longer exists, a general interest in reflection and active learning persists on campus. The current interdisciplinary Atlas program, explained in more detail later, grew out of this pedagogical interest.

With a full-time undergraduate population of 1,700 students, Manhattanville's School of Arts and Sciences offers traditional majors common at a liberal arts college, such as philosophy, sociology, and history, as well as programs that are sometimes considered professional, such as communication studies, music technology, marketing, management, and accounting. In addition, Manhattanville has a School of Education that offers graduate degrees and combined programming for undergraduates in conjunction with the School of Arts and Sciences, and a School of Business, which offers master of science degrees that can also be combined with undergraduate studies.

Interdisciplinary Programming at Manhattanville

At Manhattanville we have three truly interdisciplinary programs, where students from a variety of majors take classes taught by faculty in a variety of disciplines. The first of these programs, in which all students who enter the college as first-time college students participate, is our First Year program. The First Year seminars are taught by faculty from across the School of Arts and Sciences, and occasionally from the School of Education. Years ago Manhattanville moved from a "great books"–style seminar, in which all of the seminar instructors were teaching the same texts, to one that offers flexibility of subject to the instructor. This shift occurred with the hopes of encouraging wider participation in and enthusiasm for teaching the First Year seminar. Despite this change, we continue to struggle to recruit faculty to teach these courses, even though there is widespread understanding that first year seminars are an essential part of a liberal arts education.[2] The main reasons cited by faculty for not teaching the First Year seminars are that they are needed to teach courses within their department and that they do not feel confident teaching the material. In the previous model, confidence was lacking because the materials were not within the faculty member's discipline. In the current model the challenge is to teach discipline-specific materials to a class of non-majors who are struggling with first-time college student issues, such as writing and study skills. The faculty who regularly teach in the First Year program include those from academic areas with fewer student majors, particularly those in the humanities, and very few faculty in STEM (science, technology, engineering, and math), arts, or social sciences. Of course, this struggle to convince faculty from across the curriculum to teach in the seminars is not unique to Manhattanville.[3]

The second interdisciplinary program is the Castle Scholars Honors program. Students qualify to apply for the program by maintaining a 3.6 GPA and may apply upon acceptance into the college or during their sophomore year. Program participation includes taking a number of seminars that may be outside of the student's major discipline but are of general academic interest and high academic rigor. These courses are instructed by faculty from across the School of Arts and Sciences who volunteer to teach the classes as part of their course load. Again, we get the same responses as to why faculty do not participate in these courses, and the participants tend to come from the same small pool of disciplines. This is unfortunate, as studies show that students who complete honors programs have the highest academic performance and graduation rates and the shortest time to degree completion.[4] Echoing such disciplinary biases among the faculty, we have found that our students are more likely to participate in an honors program when some of the courses can count toward their major and are periodically taught by faculty within their discipline.

The final interdisciplinary program is Atlas, which comprises a series of integrative courses based on reflective pedagogy and designed to help students connect what they are learning in their courses and co-curricular activities and form solid goals for their futures. The program originated from an earlier First Year course, known as Passport, which was created as a result of a Foundations of Excellence self-study through the John N. Gardner Institute for Excellence in Undergraduate Education. The course is designed specifically to assist students in their transition to college because this element in First Year seminars is seen as having a great impact on students' success.[5] Faculty have remained resistant to embedding transition elements in the First Year seminars, hence the need to create Atlas Passport.[6] The additional Atlas courses are scaffolded across the student's time and assist with selection of a major, connecting curricular and co-curricular pursuits, networking, and professional self-presentation. Again we encounter faculty resistance to teaching those courses that rest outside their traditional disciplines, and in fact the large majority of sections of the First Year Atlas course are taught by professional staff, such as advisers, Student Affairs staff, and staff from Residential Life.

This resistance to teaching outside of one's defined discipline also has a generational component; many long-term faculty continue to teach in the First Year seminars, whereas we struggle to recruit junior faculty to do so. Part of the issue stems from the pressure that junior faculty feel to publish/produce work within their field, out of both a personal commitment to their research and the realization that publications are necessary to support bids for reappointment, promotion, and tenure. Teaching a new course that is not within one's discipline/ comfort zone entails considerable work that will, presumably, take time away from one's research.

An Interdisciplinary App Design Course

Eager to find ways to overcome these roadblocks and encourage greater inter-disciplinarity at our institution, we launched a new experiment for Manhat-tanville College in spring 2017—a joint course offering from the Department of Communications and Media and the Department of Mathematics and Computer Science. Both departments realized that the development of com-puter applications presented rich opportunities for students to learn user expe-rience design as well as computer system design, and that teams of students collaborating from both disciplines would be the most productive approach. This gave rise to the new course, Interactive Media—User Experience/System Design.

We designed the course to include a few key features. The first was to make use of cross-disciplinary teams. We envisioned students in one discipline learn-ing the concerns of students in the other discipline(s) as they made decisions about the projects. As Bobbitt et al. write, "Student group projects that extend beyond the traditional course boundaries and are integrated with other 'func-tional' areas can provide students with the opportunity to learn how these areas are interrelated."[7] This objective arose from the authors' professional experi-ences of working in multidisciplinary teams and their recognition that, first, this is how more and more companies are working and, second, doing so in a classroom would be professional preparation for the students.[8] Of course we also believe that there is great pleasure in working collaboratively.

A second feature of the course was to use client-driven projects. This was based on the experiences of both authors in working with clients and our con-viction that the rewards would outweigh the logistical problems we would inevi-tably encounter. We report on our experience with this aspect in a later section.

A third feature was to team-teach the course, with both instructors in the classroom at the same time. We felt that it would be valuable for the students to hear the sometimes contrasting perspectives of the two instructors and that we could model for them how to resolve the conflicts that inevitably arise with collaboration. Despite the fact that the college has no policy for team teach-ing, and a history of compensating each co-instructor for only half of a course, we accomplished this objective rather easily. What we refer to as a single course is actually listed in the catalog as two separate courses: Interactive Media—User Experience Design, offered by the Department of Communications and Media, and Interactive Media—System Design, offered by the Department of Math and Computer Science. This arrangement was chosen partly because it allowed us to put off the development of new compensation policies for team teaching, which are still needed, and partly because it allowed each course to bear its department's own prefix and have its own course description and prerequisites, and could therefore be easily listed as an advanced elective within a major. We return later to a deeper aspect of this last reason.

Digital media students register for the digital media course, whereas computer science students register for the computer science course. Some class meetings are held as a larger group, whereas others are held separately. Before the beginning of the semester, the professors line up three or four clients, and on the first day, present the client needs to the students and allow them to rank their top choices of projects. After some balancing, the teams are set, and they remain together for the entire semester. We have found that teams of four to six members (two to three digital media and two to three computer science students) work best.

The students' work is guided by the process known as Design Thinking, and we begin with instruction in that process.[9] The students employ the first step when they interview the clients. After this initial encounter, the students attempt to develop user stories. The next step in the process is design research. The digital media students research the user interfaces of analogous applications, whereas the computer science students research systems requirements, such as user sign-in. The teams next present their findings to the joint class and receive feedback. Because roughly three-quarters of the class is not working on the project being presented, these classmates can serve as ordinary users, providing a ready source of immediate feedback.

Following design research, the teams then proceed to develop prototypes. The computer science students develop prototypes of selected capabilities, such as a "skeleton application" with a database and a simple user-sign-in process. The prototypes of the computer science students are based on a set of Web technologies, as they target a platform called Progressive Web Applications. Developing true prototypes in the Design Thinking sense, the digital media students begin with paper prototypes, which they then digitize to create interactive prototypes using software. These prototypes are then shared with their client and the rest of the class for feedback, which is used to influence design iterations. The focus remains on the client and user throughout, with rapid development of prototype iterations, each presented to the client for feedback.

From this point the teams develop prototypes of increasing fidelity, and the joint meetings are used to update each other on progress and get clarification on various points. Troubleshooting is the main purpose for the separate meetings as the semester progresses; for the computer science class, time is often spent in troubleshooting particular issues a team may be having with their code. The digital media class time is frequently used to troubleshoot specific design concepts and the use of technology to achieve design choices.

Among our earliest discoveries with the course was that the skill levels of the students determine the kind of synergy we can expect. One of our hopes for the course was that when the computer science students would make live prototypes from the digital media students' designs, the digital media students would have the opportunity to improve their designs. However, we found that the computer science students were generally unable to complete their application by the end of the semester; thus the digital media students were unable to see their designs fully functioning, much less to make design changes. We determined that we cannot allow computer science students with only two semesters of programming experience to take the class if the goal is to end the semester with a functional app. We have since made a web application development course, which we already required for computer science majors, a prerequisite for the computer science class.

However, even though the applications were not fully realized, we found the digital media students expressing excitement about seeing their designs come at least partially alive. Likewise, we found the computer science students expressing admiration for the designs they were implementing. And the students clearly enjoyed collaborating with students with different expertise, even if the expertise was not extensive. So although the expertise-trading synergy we had anticipated did not materialize as we had expected, it did materialize to a degree, and we are taking steps to leverage it more effectively.

Working with Clients

One of the primary features of the Interactive Media course is to have the teams work with actual clients on projects that are of value to the clients. The first time the course was taught, teams worked with a physical therapist who desired an app that would encourage his clients to be more accountable for their prescribed exercises, a psychotherapist who desired a way to provide suggestions to her clients for cognitive-behavioral therapies at moments of crisis, and a theater for the very young that wanted a way to prepare children for the sights and sounds they would experience during performances. Our primary motive for working with clients was that it would be a more authentic and rewarding experience for the students than designing for a classroom assignment. We found this to be true: only real-world clients had the depth of experience necessary to provide the teams the guidance they needed. The physical therapist was able to tell his team that a certain feature wouldn't be used based on his knowledge of his clients; the psychotherapist was able to make her team understand the relationship between the therapist and the client and how the app might affect that; and the director of the children's theater was able to tell her team that the app would often be used by a parent and child sitting together, which informed the design of the app. This is quite a different experience from working on assignments created for an instructor, and that real-life experience is part of what makes this course more valuable than a typical upper-level design course.[10]

We also realized several other benefits. When a client was involved, we found it easier to get students to iterate on their designs, because what seemed "good enough" to the students did not always seem that way to their client. The students realized the value of doing more iterations on paper and other low-fidelity media, because they could do more versions and get more feedback from their client. In addition, working with clients required discussing and implementing intellectual property and nondisclosure agreements, making these real-life issues concrete, rather than an abstract lesson learned from a lecture. We hear repeatedly from surveys and alumni feedback that "what employers want, and what students need, is a broad set of tools and the ability to practice applying these tools to real-world problems."[11] Finally, having the teams work with clients afforded us the opportunity to teach communication skills. These are among the skill sets most prized by employers, and they are best attained by hands-on, cross-disciplinary projects. As described by McCale, "The core concepts that client based projects can teach and reinforce certain skill sets is a cross-disciplinary premise: liberal arts students as well as business students could certainly benefit from the hands on approach a client based project can provide."[12]

Challenges with an Interdisciplinary Approach

Some of our specific takeaways from the initial iterations of the Interactive Media course involved communication within the multidisciplinary teams. We found that we needed to find and deliberately incorporate appropriate tools to foster communication and collaboration, especially for tracking task assignments and fulfillment, and communications with clients. And we recognized the need to teach team communication skills to equip students to collaborate more effectively.

With team teaching, finding the right mix of shared meeting times to allow for same-time/shared-space meeting is necessary, and our iterations informed our recommendations for Manhattanville's Design Thinking Center, which opened in fall 2019. Space is certainly a consideration for this method of interdisciplinary teaching, and having space in which the teams can both collaborate and work individually is essential for the success of the projects. The difficulty we have had in nailing this down—how often to meet jointly— illustrates what we believe is a fundamental tension between the benefits of a synergistic classroom and the imperative to teach discipline-specific skills and knowledge. Time spent in having the teams jointly reflect on design choices meant time not spent with the computer science students in instruction on the HTTP session model, or with the digital media students on color theory and design choices in user interfaces.

With all of our interdisciplinary offerings, from the First Year seminars to the Interactive Media course, we have encountered the same basic tension, which is that the interdisciplinary courses compete with discipline-specific courses for faculty and students. A strong underpinning of education at Manhattanville, and at most other colleges, is that students must graduate with an expertise and body of knowledge in a recognized discipline. We place responsibility for explaining what that expertise looks like on a department of scholars whose research is within a given field and whose expertise is best suited to develop the requirements for a major in that field. Students cannot graduate unless they meet the requirements for some specific majors. Within the School of Arts and Sciences the number of credits required to complete a single major varies from 30 to 70 credits for a bachelor of arts degree. The full-time faculty teach a 21-credit load per academic year, and most programs also utilize part-time faculty in order to offer all of the courses required for program completion. A department may set a large number of required credits for its major, which has the dual effects of (1) making it difficult for students in that major to participate in interdisciplinary programs and (2) making it difficult for faculty teaching in these departments to participate in teaching interdisciplinary programs. In response, we echo what Association of American Colleges & Universities (AAC&U) president Lynn Pasquerella stated in the spring 2018 volume of *Liberal Education*:

> AAC&U's 1,401 members understand that a liberal education for the twenty-first century mandates the acceleration of integrative learning opportunities that engage students in solving real-world problems. They also know that a graduate's ability to think critically, communicate clearly, and work in diverse teams is more important than one's undergraduate major, and they have demonstrated that such cross-cutting skills can be developed in a wide variety of chosen disciplines, across all types of institutions. Most importantly, they recognize that opportunity results in equity only when focused on quality. Therefore, each student's participation in high-impact practices and his or her achievement of essential learning outcomes must be considered core components of student-success initiatives at every college and university.[13]

Although Manhattanville is one of the member institutions of the AAC&U, this understanding that the "ability to think critically, communicate clearly, and work in diverse teams *is more important than* one's undergraduate major" is not embraced across our institution. Our students' graduation requirements are strongly determined by discipline-based academic departments. According to Larry Shinn, most discipline-based "academic departments, even at select liberal-arts colleges, are better organized to prepare their majors for advanced study in their discipline than to provide courses that provide a strong liberal education for all students."[14] This organization impacts the sorts of curriculum these faculty are likely to create, and where its focus will be. When curricula are built in this manner, with faculty who favor depth over breadth, the deliberate opportunities for integration of knowledge and experience across disciplines are frequently lost, even though that integration is exactly what will assist students to prepare for the complexities of the professional world.

Moreover, in our evolving workplace, students who graduate now will in their professional lifetimes be working jobs that do not currently exist. This should point liberal arts colleges "to embrace the fact that one's choice of major matters less now than it has in the past."[15] However, the specialists in narrowly defined fields charged with the development of major curricula may or may not choose to adapt the curricula to workplace evolution.

This tension between discipline-specific education and integrative learning opportunities emerged in one of our earliest interdisciplinary courses, Game Development Scrum, where we loosely coupled a Music for Games course from the music department with a Game Development programming course from the computer science department. We began the course with a unit that focused on the fundamentals of games, completely independent of game format. We found this to be highly valuable for uncovering problems that came up in the study of the technology for implementing games, and to provide a conceptual framework for game development, but it did not specifically include computer science content. Since we were devoting a significant amount of time to a non-computer-science topic, we debated whether we could justify considering the course an advanced computer science elective.

How shall we resolve this tension? In their 2007 report "College Learning for the New Global Century," the AAC&U argues for moving away from the predominant model where liberal-learning-based outcomes apply only to general education, toward a model where these outcomes apply across every field of college study.[16] The faculty at Manhattanville have taken the initial step toward this model by defining a wide variety of general learning objectives essential to a liberal education and infusing general education across the curriculum. Instead of meeting general education requirements by taking isolated, introductory courses in the first two years, students meet general education requirements by taking courses—in their major or not, and of different levels— that fulfil one or more of the general education learning objectives. These outcomes are rather broad and naturally apply across many fields of study. The approach we are arguing for here involves adding new learning objectives, objectives that are met by students applying knowledge and skills gained from previous coursework as well as their lives in interdisciplinary contexts. If we shift our focus from the "body of knowledge" requirement that currently exists in some of our majors to a set of liberal-learning-based outcomes defined by full college faculty rather than departments, this provides an opening for these interdisciplinary experiences. In adopting this model, we would ask the faculty to expand their notions of "mastery of advanced material" so that the focus is on application and processing of knowledge rather than pure knowledge acquisition. In this model, less pure content in a particular discipline would be covered within a major, yet more methods of approaching and troubleshooting that information can be practiced.

Under such a model, the part of the Game Development Scrum course that was not solidly computer science could satisfy a college-wide "Applied Liberal Learning" learning objective. We have this requirement at Manhattanville, but currently each student is only required to complete one credit toward it. Our argument in this chapter supports significantly increasing the number of credits for this requirement. In addition to this possible approach, we are moving toward resolving this tension between depth and breadth of requirements by adopting Design Thinking, which is naturally interdisciplinary, integrative, and collaborative, across our curriculum.

Design Thinking Curriculum

Manhattanville is exploring how to adopt Design Thinking into its curriculum and campus culture, and to this end, over the summer of 2018, a team of faculty and staff participated in a series of workshops led by IDEO. The participants learned what Design Thinking is by applying it to various institutional questions. Design Thinking is not itself a subject, but rather a system of problem solving, and when applying it to the curriculum, the goal is generally to provide an intentional integrative opportunity for students to apply their own knowledge, gathered from across their academic and personal lives, and work collaboratively to solve a complex problem. Emerging from these workshops are several ideas for discrete courses within academic disciplines like global studies and literature, which would provide problem-based learning opportunities for the students within those majors. A more broadly planned interdisciplinary initiative comprises a pilot of six sections of a first-year seminar that ran in the fall 2018 semester. A blend between shared content and unique content, these pilot courses were taught by a group of faculty from across several disciplines. The pilot sections were deliberately scheduled to overlap, so that there was opportunity to build shared experiences into the course and connect co-curricular experiences to the curriculum. One of the main ideas is to embed the seeds of design thinking into this earliest of college courses with the belief that this skill will help lay the groundwork for students to continue this integrative approach throughout their studies and into the types of complex problems they will meet outside of college. In addition to a foundational development of those skills in the first-year seminar, the opportunity to further refine our upper-level experiential courses to be more interdisciplinary, like the Interactive Media course that we continue to refine, is an outcome of the workshops.

Conclusion

We see Design Thinking, which is naturally interdisciplinary and collaborative, and to which the college is making a major commitment in curriculum, administration, and facilities, as a vehicle through which we can evolve our college toward the inclusion of more integrative learning outcomes. As a result of our experiences while teaching and through participation in the IDEO workshops, existing institutional structure and expected norms of how curricula are created and supported are under review, and the participants in the workshops have been encouraged to propose new approaches. To encourage curricular innovation and scholarship about pedagogy, the provost and dean of the School of Arts and Sciences are discussing how work outside of one's strict discipline may indeed be considered toward the reappointment, tenure, and promotion processes with the Status Committee. The provost will soon be announcing an upper cap on the number of credits a major can require, which will prompt some curricular revision for several departments. A process through which to apply for support for implementing Design Thinking initiatives, whether it be financial, release time, or other, has been put into place. We are working on complex questions (e.g., how faculty involved in co-teaching can be appropriately compensated while also making sure the courses required by the curriculum are all being taught), where the solution is likely a mixture of revision of course requirements within majors and a compensation structure that recognizes co-teaching as not equal to teaching half a course. One innovation already adopted is that each of the instructors of the pilot First Year seminar will be receiving a one-credit release from teaching in order to participate in a community of practice, with the goal of providing faculty with both time and a cohort for support. Curricular innovation is more likely if obstacles to explore it are minimized.[17] Knowing this, the School of Arts and Sciences is revising the course and program submission process for transparency and ease of use. For now, we must continue to navigate the politics of persuading faculty that the depth of their students' knowledge will not realize its potential unless supplemented with an opportunity for an integrative interdisciplinary experience, wherein students can uncover what they really know and put it to use.

Notes

1   Manhattanville College, *The Manhattanville Plan: A Report to the National Endowment for the Humanities* (New York: ERIC, 1973), 19, Education Resources Information Center (ERIC) Archive, June 3, 2015, https://archive.org/details /ERIC_ED084997.

2 Ryan D. Padgett, Jennifer R. Keup, and Ernest T. Pascarella, "The Impact of First-Year Seminars on College Students' Life-Long Learning Orientations," *Journal of Student Affairs Research and Practice* 50, no. 2 (2013): 133–151.

3 Kelly Field, "A Third of Your Freshmen Disappear. How Can You Keep Them?" *The Chronicle of Higher Education*, June 3, 2018, https://www-chronicle-com .librda.mville.edu/article/A-Third-of-Your-Freshmen/243560.

4 John Cosgrove, "The Impact of Honors Programs on Undergraduate Academic Performance, Retention, and Graduation," *Journal of the National Collegiate Honors Council* 5, no. 2 (Fall/Winter 2004): 45–53.

5 Joseph Cuseo, "The Empirical Case for the First-Year Seminar: Course Impact on Student Retention and Academic Achievement," *eSource for College Transitions* 6, no. 6 (2009): 4–5.

6 Alison S. Carson, Gillian Greenhill Hannum, and Christine Dehne, "Manhattanville College's Atlas Program: Designing a Road Map to Success in College and Beyond," *International Journal of ePortfolio* 8, no. 1 (2018): 73–86.

7 L. Michelle Bobbitt, Scott A. Inks, Katie J. Kemp, and Donna T. Mayo, "Integrating Marketing Courses to Enhance Team-Based Experiential Learning," *Journal of Marketing Education* 22, no. 1 (2000): 15–24.

8 Hart Research Associates, "Falling Short? College Learning and Career Success," accessed March 29, 2020, https://www.aacu.org/leap/public-opinion-research /2015-survey-results.

9 Tim Brown, "Design Thinking," *Harvard Business Review*, 86 (June 2008): 84–92, 141.

10 Matthew T. Hora, "Beyond the Skills Gap: How the Vocationalist Framing of Higher Education Undermines Student, Employer, and Societal Interests," Association of American Colleges & Universities, June 21, 2018, https://www.aacu .org/liberaleducation/2018/spring/hora.

11 Jose Antonio Bowen, "Nudges, the Learning Economy, and a New Three Rs: Relationships, Resilience, and Reflection," *Liberal Education* 104, no. 2 (Spring 2018): 30, https://www.aacu.org/liberaleducation/2018/spring/bowen.

12 Christina McCale, "It's Hard Work Learning Soft Skills: Can Client Based Projects Teach the Soft Skills Students Need and Employers Want?" *Journal of Effective Teaching* 8, no. 2 (2008): 50–60.

13 Lynn Pasquerella, "In Pursuit of Quality and Deliberative Democracy," Association of American Colleges & Universities, June 21, 2018, https://www.aacu.org /liberaleducation/2018/spring/president.

14 Larry D. Shinn, "Liberal Education vs. Professional Education: The False Choice," *Trusteeship* 22, no. 1 (January/February 2014): 6–10.

15 Bowen, "Nudges," 28.

16 Association of American Colleges & Universities and the National Leadership Council, *College Learning for the New Global Century: A Report from the National Leadership Council for Liberal Education & America's Promise* (Washington, D.C.: Association of American Colleges & Universities, 2007).

17 Carsten Tams, "Small Is Beautiful: Using Gentle Nudges to Change Organizations," Forbes.com, February 22, 2018, https://www.forbes.com/sites /carstentams/2018/02/22/small-is-beautiful-using-gentle-nudges-to-change -organizations/#12d1f1465a8d.

6

Honeybees and the Transdisciplinary Classroom

• •

Bridging the Gaps between History, Environmental Science, and Global Studies

COREY CAMPION AND

APRIL M. BOULTON

As other contributors to this volume can attest, regular opportunities for dialogue with colleagues in other disciplines are among the many benefits that attend faculty life at a small liberal arts college. Operating with fewer faculty, these institutions often require simultaneous service on multiple committees in order to meet a host of institutional objectives. Though challenging, this service often creates a more consistent forum for interdepartmental exchange than that enjoyed at larger institutions where lighter service loads and larger faculty can do more to reinforce than alter the academy's siloed landscape.[1] As members of the faculty at Hood College, a small liberal arts institution in Maryland, our experience has been no exception. Among the college's 120 full-time faculty members, our work serving the undergraduate-graduate population of approximately 2,100 students involves service on numerous committees with colleagues from all disciplines. It was, in fact, through such service that our collaboration in the classroom began.

We first interacted as members of the Graduate Council. An assistant professor of history and global studies and an expert on modern European and transatlantic history, Corey Campion also directs Hood's interdisciplinary master of arts in humanities program. An associate professor of biology and an expert in ecology and entomology, April Boulton began her work on the council as director of the master of science in environmental biology program before serving as assistant dean and, now, dean of the Graduate School. Over the years, our conversations after bimonthly council meetings and summer workshops often extended beyond the council's agenda to include discussions of our teaching and research interests as well as our shared love of beekeeping. Moreover, our work on the council focused our attention on enrollment matters and inspired many brainstorming sessions in search of pedagogical innovations that could grow and better serve our student body. This naturally led to a series of conversations about increasing employer demands for graduates with the interdisciplinary training and "cognitive flexibility" needed for success in a global economy.[2] Our dialogue continued when, in 2016, we began serving on the faculty advisory board of the undergraduate global studies program. It was, in fact, at the end of an advisory board meeting in spring 2017 that years of discussing pedagogy, interdisciplinarity, and, yes, beekeeping, in a variety of service-related settings, resulted in the decision to offer a team-taught course on the history and science of apiculture.

Concerned about the growing disconnect between our discipline-focused classrooms and graduates' increasingly interdisciplinary workplaces, we found in bees a perfect course topic. For more than a decade, stories of the demise of honeybees (*Apis mellifera*) have produced regular headlines both in the United States and around the world.[3] From pesticides and parasitic mites to insufficient pollination and the collapse of global food markets, newspapers and social media sites regularly recount both the causes and the consequences of the bees' decline. Approaching the issue largely as a matter of science and economics, however, the coverage has left unanswered important questions about the broader origins of and potential solutions to the crisis. From the veneration of the honeybee by many ancient societies to the mechanization of the hive during the Industrial Revolution, the current challenges facing honeybees are, in part, the product of a broader evolution in the way in which humans view nature in general.[4] Understanding this history is essential for any effort to solve the current crisis. Moreover, an awareness of global institutions, laws, and politics is no less important if local and national efforts to help global pollinators are to succeed. In short, the decline of global honeybee populations presents precisely the kind of multifaceted problem that employers increasingly want graduates to be prepared to engage.

In addition to extending students' learning beyond their chosen majors, however, we were particularly interested in the opportunity to facilitate collaboration between the humanities and the natural and social sciences. Our own past experiences teaching courses in European history, insect ecology, food, and human health had long convinced us of the ways in which the perspectives gained from one of our fields could enhance student learning in the other. Just as work in the humanities could help young scientists learn to empathize and communicate with the constituencies whom their research aimed to help, work in the sciences could help humanists contextualize their study of humanity in the broader natural world and substantiate their arguments through statistical and data analysis. Aware of the pitfalls that have long attended efforts to bridge the gap between what C. P. Snow described as "the two cultures," we were encouraged by the growing efforts of many institutions to connect our fields and reimagine a more integrated liberal arts curriculum for the twenty-first century.[5]

Planning a Transdisciplinary Course

Eager to help initiate a similar effort at Hood, we anticipated a variety of challenges as we planned our course. Although college service had offered the forum needed to inspire our collaboration, we knew that the enrollment concerns and departmental competitions for majors typical of small liberal arts colleges like ours could hinder the realization of our ideas.

Among the earliest challenges that we confronted was the practical question of how to list the course on the college schedule. Ideally, we hoped to list one course and make it open to students in three programs: history, environmental science, and global studies. After consulting with our departments and the registrar, however, we learned that this would not be possible. A combination of institutional policies regarding teaching loads and departmental concerns over enrollment required us to list the course with a history prefix for history majors and an environmental science prefix for environmental science majors. Moreover, the best we could do for global studies majors was to advertise the course, with either its history or environmental prefix, as an acceptable substitute for one of the required global studies seminars. The result was a confusing dual listing that to students, and us, appeared void of the very collaboration that we sought to model. The listing also did little to simplify the course advertisements or the advising process. Excited to have created our course, we noted the future need to advocate for registration policies that facilitated the institution's strategic commitment to interdisciplinarity as an essential tool for attracting and serving a twenty-first-century student body.[6]

With our course approved, we turned to designing the syllabus and found ourselves grappling with familiar issues. Reflecting on our colleagues' concerns during the proposal process and the discipline-specific nomenclature at which we had arrived, we confronted difficult questions about the nature and purpose of the course. What about the course would allow it to substitute for a required global studies course that normally focused on a range of issues from politics and economics to culture and religion and served only global studies majors? How would it serve environmental scientists without the lab components that their courses traditionally included? Would a course that dedicated at least one-third of the instruction time to reviews of honeybee biology, evolutionary taxonomy, and bee-related scientific papers really enhance the training of young historians?

The products of both our own disciplinary training and our institution's policies, these challenging, if not discouraging, questions led us to view the course in a different light. Rather than interdisciplinarity, which we understood to entail collaboration between two fields with a sustained focus on the methodological conventions of each, we came to see our collaboration as an example of transdisciplinarity, which encouraged students to approach the material from a variety of disciplinary angles and was less concerned with training them to practice the skills of any one field.[7] In short, our course was *not* a substitute for a traditional history, environmental science, or global studies course that aimed to develop skills inherent to work in those specific fields. Instead, our course complemented these, offering students both a chance to apply skills learned in their majors and the opportunity to enhance their work through exposure to alternative perspectives and methodologies. With this realization, we began to focus less on what made our fields unique and more on the questions, ideas, and practices that connected them: namely, the pursuit of evidence-based research and the communication of our findings to a wide range of experts and laypersons.

Having identified a common foundation on which to build our course, one additional concern informed our planning: enrollment. Like many small colleges, Hood's smaller student body and higher teaching load (21 annual credits) can create pressure on departments and individual faculty as they work to secure sufficient enrollment for their courses. Adding to this pressure are the rigorous demands of a number of majors that leave students with little room for electives and the inability of our smaller faculty to offer multiple sections of individual courses. We knew that our course would count toward any of the history, environmental science, or global studies majors, but we were not certain that enough students from each would be interested in and available for the course. With posters and emails to students and advisers, we marketed the course as an exciting opportunity to acquire precisely the kind of cross-disciplinary, collaborative experience in which employers are interested. Yet, as registration began, we remained nervous. While employers are interested in transdisciplinarity, and students seek the jobs that employers offer, students often remain most comfortable in the disciplinary silos to which we introduce them at orientation and from which we promote them at graduation.

Fortunately, our marketing efforts were effective. We enrolled seventeen students with roughly equal representation from the history, environmental science, and global studies departments. Having attracted a transdisciplinary audience, we felt ready to design lesson plans and assignments that would realize the course description and student learning outcomes (SLOs) on which we had settled:

> This course explores the science, history, politics, economics, and culture of honeybees (*Apis mellifera*) and beekeeping. Given the long-standing relationship between bees and human society and the centrality of bees to modern global food production, the course explores themes relevant to students across a variety of majors. At the same time, the course offers students an opportunity to experience the kind of transdisciplinary collaboration that many employers now require. While exploring a common topic from a variety of disciplinary angles, students will have the opportunity to apply the skills learned in their discipline as they collaborate with students in other fields on a common project.

> Student Learning Outcomes:

> 1 Describe the historical and contemporary meaning of bees in human society.
> 2 Analyze global and local causes and solutions to major socioeconomic and environmental problems affecting bees today.
> 3 Assess the relative effectiveness of various environmental laws, policies, and proposals on honeybee populations.
> 4 Demonstrate an understanding of bee biology and principles of beekeeping.
> 5 Assess the opportunities and challenges that attend transdisciplinary work.

Teaching a Transdisciplinary Course

Amid the rush of finals in early December 2017, we met to finalize our syllabus and draft the assignments on which our students would begin working the next month. Though we had hoped to begin this work earlier, the demands of teaching and serving at a small college with a small faculty offer few opportunities for advanced course planning. Still, we found the chance to engage our shared interest in beekeeping a welcome respite from our end-of-semester work, and we were excited to see the course take its final shape. Having outlined our

SLOs, we now had to decide what exactly we wanted students to do to achieve them. Our fascination with all things bee-related aside, we agreed that our most important task was to engage students in transdisciplinary collaboration. From this it followed that SLOs 1 through 4 would equip students to tackle the kind of project we envisioned for SLO 5. Put another way, we wanted to provide all students with a basic knowledge of the history, biology, and global politics and economics of apiculture, which they could then apply in pursuit of a broader bee-related transdisciplinary group research project.

Essential to providing students with this basic information were daily reading assignments, which were not easy to select. Many of the relevant texts with which we were familiar in our respective fields were geared toward specialists. We therefore agreed that web blogs, media reports, and popular documentaries about honeybees and apiculture would constitute an important, and more widely accessible, literature from which to draw. At the same time, however, we wanted students to experience readings written from a variety of disciplinary perspectives. To a collection of generalist texts, then, we added some more specialized titles. Convinced that students needed a solid reference with which to build their foundational knowledge of honeybee biology and hive structure, we reviewed several biology-based textbooks. Striving to challenge all students in spite of their diverse areas of expertise, we settled on Caron and Connor's *Honeybee Biology and Beekeeping*, which delivered a wealth of biological information in a manner geared more toward beekeepers than biology majors.[8] In addition, we selected Maurice Maeterlinck's classic apicultural treatise, *The Life of the Bee*. A standard work for apicultural historians, Maeterlinck's text remains accessible to all readers and encourages transdisciplinary reflections through its personified treatment of the honeybee colony, which likens basic hive functions, such as queen rearing, to dramatic human interactions rife with melodramatic turmoil.[9] Of similar transdisciplinary value was our final selection: *Vanishing Bees: Science, Politics, and Honeybee Health* by Sainath Suryanarayanan and Daniel Kleinman. Addressing questions of global politics and trade familiar to our global studies majors, the authors also model transdisciplinarity by exploring the current honeybee crisis through the unique "knowledge cultures" of scientists, beekeepers, and policy makers. Echoing our aim for the course, they question the value of disciplinarity and argue instead for "a more complexity-oriented approach to understanding and resolving honeybee declines."[10]

Beyond our interest in transdisciplinarity, our final reading selections emerged in response to our design of daily lesson plans. The first session (Transdisciplinarity—or Why Are We Studying the History and Science of Beekeeping?) included a brief overview of the historical development of discipline-specific majors and a review of employers' recent demands for cross-disciplinary collaboration. We also asked students to share in small groups the defining skills and questions of their respective majors. We thought this would provide a useful introduction to the concept of transdisciplinarity, with which many students were not yet familiar. From this initial discussion, we moved to our course topic and began a three-week section called Bee Basics—the Science of Honeybees. We followed this with another three-week section titled Bee History—the History of Honeybees. Each comprised a series of lectures and discussions and concluded with a brief "quiz" to encourage students to complete the reading assignments and ensure mastery of the basic information presented.

Excited to introduce students to the study of honeybees in our respective fields, we worried that these opening sessions could appear disjointed. To avoid this, we both elected to attend all classes and contributed comments to each other's lectures in an attempt to model the kind of collaboration we expected from students. We also created a transdisciplinary seating chart, which strategically positioned students to interact with colleagues from different majors. The seating chart became a key component of the in-class exercises that followed. This was the case with what was perhaps our most entertaining attempt to maintain a transdisciplinary focus among these more discipline-oriented introductory sessions. Pairing students with their neighbors on the seating chart, we distributed a collection of children's books on honeybees and invited the groups to dissect and critique the stories based on their biological accuracy. The environmental scientists in each group often led the discussion, but the historians and global studies majors applied their newly acquired biological knowledge to advance the critiques as well. The exercise also engaged the groups in interesting conversations about the broader processes of anthropomorphism and representation that inform our collective understanding of many global and environmental issues today. A similar experience followed during the section on the history of apiculture when we reviewed a brief documentary on the recent work of scientists at Harvard University to create robotic bees.[11] Having just explored the implications of the Industrial Revolution for both agriculture and the natural world, the video inspired history majors to reflect on humanity's relationship to the natural world since the nineteenth century and led the environmental scientists to reflect on the broader ecological consequences of robotic pollination. Moreover, the story invited discussion of the political and economic implications of robots that could replace bees and, thus, discourage efforts to alter those human behaviors now responsible for the decline of honeybee populations.

In hindsight, the opening two sections of the course accomplished much of what we had wanted. Students gained a basic background in honeybee biology and apicultural history while engaging in dialogue with colleagues from other disciplines and learning the value of approaching topics from multiple perspectives. Still, we noted one important change to make as the first half of the semester ended: we should have reversed the order of the opening sessions. Given the more technical nature of the biology unit, it would have been better to welcome students into the enchanting world of honeybees *before* covering the rather sterile science that produces the very epiphenomena humans have found so captivating throughout their history. In other words, we took the mystery out of the honeybee with our scientific lectures and later asked the students to appreciate such "mystery" with the historical and literary content that followed.

Setting such reflections aside for future reference, we entered the final eight-week section of the course (Globalization and the Honeybee—Global Problems, Local Solutions) ready to engage the students further in transdisciplinary collaboration. In addition to the dynamics of global agriculture, pollination, and honey-production practices, which were most familiar to the global studies students, we tackled a variety of questions whose relevance defied disciplinary boundaries. Questions about the source and security of our food and the consequences of ecological and environmental change are relevant to all of us, regardless of our profession. Furthermore, they require answers that draw on the collective expertise of the fields represented in our class.

With this in mind, we invited students to explore issues in global politics, agriculture, and ecology through the shared lens of apiculture. We asked them to begin by writing a film review of two apicultural-themed documentaries, drawing on the foundational knowledge gained in the first half of the course to critique the films' content and identifying the broader global political, economic, and ecological questions that they address. Following the film review, we asked students to critique the transdisciplinary text *Vanishing Bees* and enjoyed a vibrant classroom discussion about the unique ways in which experts in diverse fields could engage the crisis now confronting honeybees. With each paper we encouraged flexible, critical thinking by requiring students to include at least three different disciplinary perspectives in their discussions. Students could opt to support their analyses with readings written by entomologists, political scientists, historians, philosophers, and economists, and they had to reflect on how the fields, collectively, contributed to a more comprehensive understanding of the issues at hand.

Each of these assignments offered preparation for a final semester-long group project in which students explored the local and/or national implications of global bee-related problems and discovered how to apply their unique discipline-specific skill sets to communicate their groups' findings to broader audiences. The resulting project titles demonstrated the seriousness with which they approached the transdisciplinary requirements of the assignment. These included The Symbolic Interpretation of Honeybees through the Ages, which offered a modern scientific critique of historical symbolism from around the world, and The Medicinal Uses of Honeybee Products throughout History, which connected regional historical uses of hive products to the current global markets for beeswax and honey. Each group presented its work in a final display board, which was peer reviewed in class before being presented to the campus community. The peer review sessions were informative and featured comments such as those of historians encouraging environmental scientists to limit their use of technical terms or global studies majors asking historians to be prepared to discuss the contemporary political and economic relevance of their findings. After revising their work, the students delivered their final presentations during a poster session that we strategically located in our bustling student center during the lunch hour. For roughly seventy-five minutes, each group shared its ideas with passersby and fielded questions from faculty, students, and staff. The experience required the students to practice addressing both specialist and nonspecialist audiences and encouraged them to lean on their collective expertise as they sought to communicate the relevance of their academic work to a broader public. Feedback from our colleagues and the college administrators was excellent and affirmed our belief in the importance of empowering students as producers, rather than just consumers, of knowledge.

While transdisciplinarity remained our focus throughout the semester, we made little effort to hide our passion for honeybees and felt it important to expose students to the world of apiculture through several experiential learning opportunities. To that end, we led a demonstration of the honey harvesting and extraction process, which included a sampling of honeys from local and international apiaries. The students were excited to see how honey actually moves from the hive to the jar and were shocked to discover the variety of honey flavors that the homogenized offerings of most grocery stores conceal. The pinnacle experience, however, was a field trip to the USDA Bee Research Laboratory, which is located only an hour from the college. Our geographic luck aside, the trip owed as much to the generosity of our provost who, in spite of the institution's limited budget for field trips, saw the value in the trip and the course and agreed to provide the necessary funding. In addition to visiting with several scientists in their labs and discussing their research on the current honeybee crisis, we enjoyed a tour of one of the USDA apiaries. The staff provided full bee suits for the students and enabled them to encounter the subjects of our course in person. As the students looked for eggs and tried to find the queen bee, we realized that the lab visit had provided an unexpected opportunity to clarify for students both some of the historical readings on the mystery of bees and the more abstract scientific studies covered earlier in the term. There is simply no substitute for experiencing an actual honeybee hive in person. More importantly, though, the visit expanded students' horizons, offering precisely the kind of experience that, we believe, all students at a small liberal arts college should have.

Evaluating and Revising a Transdisciplinary Course

As the semester ended, we met several times to discuss the course, review our student evaluations and identify those issues that need attention prior to our next offering. Before dwelling on the latter, we took time to note which of our efforts had worked well. In general, we were pleased with the extent of transdisciplinary collaboration. If our seating chart prevented the initial formation of disciplinary clusters, students needed little additional encouragement to engage with colleagues in other fields as the semester progressed. At the same time, both their individual written assignments and their group projects affirmed their interest in tackling issues from multiple perspectives. Pointing to this interest, one student observed the following: "This is a subject the whole country should be educated on, and the interdisciplinary factor of the course was smart to do because it made the topic open to any major on campus. . . . This was an amazing opportunity and a great idea for a class." Echoing this sentiment, another student commented, "While I was not expressly concerned about the scientific aspect, I learned a lot and I think I am better for it."

Like that of our students, we counted our own collaboration among the successes of the semester as well. Our work together on various college committees had proven that we could collaborate well, yet the prospect of doing so in the classroom had inspired no little anxiety. How could a historian team teach with a scientist during a three-week section on honeybee biology and evolutionary taxonomy? How could an environmental scientist contribute to a three-week section on historical continuities and discontinuities in humanity's relationship to honeybees and the environment? As the semester began, we realized that the answers to such questions were twofold. First, our interest and experience in beekeeping afforded us a unique pedagogical authority, unconnected to our academic training, with which to engage all sections of the course. Second, our pedagogical approach focused on the pursuit of evidence-based research and written communication, which lie at the heart of both of our fields and had informed the development of our transdisciplinary learning outcomes. This latter point may also help explain why our shared approach to grading worked so well. After reviewing each assessment independently, we met to exchange comments and agree on a final grade. Although we may have focused on different aspects of the assessment, our final grade assignments were remarkably similar. In fact, it often proved less difficult to agree on a grade than to navigate our contrasting preferences for electronic and paper submissions and feedback.

Of course, both our own collaboration and that among our students owed much to the course topic as well. The current honeybee crisis lends itself well to analysis from a variety of angles. Still, we can envision humanists and scientists creating similar courses around topics such as food, disease, or climate change, and we would encourage it. As we experienced it, the boundary between the sciences and the humanities is less severe than our course catalogs, institutional structures, and faculty hiring practices might indicate.

Our successes notwithstanding, no new course runs without issues. Ours was no exception. Among the areas most in need of attention are the content and rigor of the sections on honeybee biology and global agriculture. With respect to the former, we dwelled too much on the deep evolutionary relationships of honeybees with other insects and likely offered too much detail on honeybee anatomy and physiology. We would have done better to focus more on the role that honeybees play in the environment that interfaces with humanity. Confirming this conclusion were comments on several student evaluations, such as this one: "The topics were too science focused for what one would consider an interdisciplinary class. A whole day was spent on animal classifications, which was confusing." As for the section on global agriculture, we needed to provide more concrete information about the specific actors, institutions, and dynamics that inform the global food market. We would also have done well to outline the basic functioning of institutions, such as the United Nations and the World Bank, that can effect change in the global agricultural arena. Though perhaps familiar to our global studies majors, such information could have benefited all students and enhanced the global focus of the group projects. A casualty of the calendar and the all-too-familiar inability of faculty to cover topics to their liking, this material will be at the top of the list to include in our revised lesson plan.

In addition to such content adjustments, we identified a need for more instruction about the methodologies of our respective fields. History students would benefit from a brief introduction to reading scientific papers and flow charts. Likewise, environmental scientists would benefit from discussions about the various kinds of evidence and arguments that inform the work of historians and global studies majors. While ensuring that all students have the skills to understand the wealth of material presented in the class, comparative discussions of methodologies would also help students to reinforce their own disciplinary training. Meant to complement, rather than rival, courses within students' majors, our course both invites collaboration across the disciplines and encourages reflections about the unique skill sets that define them. Put another way, specialists can learn much about their own field when working in the presence of colleagues from other fields. To facilitate such learning, we need to help students articulate better their fields' defining methodologies and, thus, the specific toolboxes that they will bring to future transdisciplinary endeavors in or beyond the academy.

Conclusion

As faculty at a small liberal arts college, we enjoy many incentives and opportunities to work and teach across disciplinary boundaries. Eager to recruit students in an increasingly competitive environment, our administrators have
listened to the demands of employers for transdisciplinary training and have
included a shift away from academic silos among the institution's strategic goals.
Yet, as our own course reminded us, practice often lags behind vision. Our
struggle to list a course across three departments revealed how concerns over
enrollment, teaching load, and major requirements inherent to smaller institutions can impede those same institutions' stated commitment to interdisciplinarity. As we push to overcome these institutional hurdles, we have much
to do to continue bridging the gaps between disciplines in our classroom as well.
Essential to both the recruitment and the education of a twenty-first-century
student body, transdisciplinarity demands of faculty a delicate balancing act
between drawing on, while not retreating to, our disciplinary backgrounds. As
we see it, however, this challenge is also one of the greatest privileges of teaching at a small college today.

Notes

1 On the broader challenges of service at small colleges, see Afshan Jafar, et al.,
"Hang Together or Hang Separately: The Importance of Participating in Governance on Small Campuses," *Academe* 103, no. 3 (2017), https://www.aaup.org
/article/hang-together-or-hang-separately#.WzqKJNJKg2w.

2 World Economic Forum, "The Future of Jobs: Employment, Skills and Workforce
Strategy for the Fourth Industrial Revolution," World Economic Forum,
January 2016, http://www3.weforum.org/docs/WEF_Future_of_Jobs.pdf.

3 On the crisis, see Sainath Suryanarayanan and Daniel Lee Kleinman, *Vanishing
Bees: Science, Politics, and Honeybee Health* (New Brunswick: Rutgers University
Press, 2017); Hannah Nordhaus, *The Beekeeper's Lament* (New York: Harper,
2010).

4 Eva Crane, *The World History of Beekeeping and Honey Hunting* (New York:
Routledge, 1999).

5 C. P. Snow, *The Two Cultures and the Scientific Revolution* (1959; repr., Mansfield
Centre, CT: Martino, 2013). Among the most recent discussions of the interde-
pendency of the humanities and the sciences, see Jennifer Summit and Blakey
Vermeule, *Action versus Contemplation: Why an Ancient Debate Still Matters*
(Chicago: University of Chicago Press, 2018), 68–69. For examples of recent
efforts to update the liberal arts and connect the humanities and the sciences, see
Wendy Hill, "Interdisciplinary Perspectives and the Liberal Arts," in *Remaking
College: Innovation and the Liberal Arts*, ed. Rebecca Chop et al. (Baltimore:
Johns Hopkins University Press, 2014), 85–95; Greg Toppo, "New Liberal Arts or
Not-So-Liberal Arts?" Inside Higher Ed, May 2, 2018, https://www.insidehighered
.com/news/2018/05/02/ohios-hiram-college-puts-new-liberal-arts-test; Colleen
Flaherty, "Reviving the Curriculum," Inside Higher Ed, March 28, 2018,

https://www.insidehighered.com/news/2018/03/28/cornell-college-arts-and -sciences-considers-new-general-education-program.

6   "Hood College Strategic Plan," accessed July 25, 2018, http://www.hood.edu /About-Hood/Strategic-Plan.html#Decade.

7   On the meaning of inter- and transdisciplinarity, see Patricia Levy, *Essentials of Transdisciplinary Research: Using Problem-Centered Methodologies* (Walnut Creek, CA: Left Coast Press, 2011), 21–23; Diana Rhoten et al., "Interdisciplinary Education at Liberal Arts Institutions" (white paper, Teagle Foundation, 2006); Julie Thompson Klein and William H. Newell, "Advancing Interdisciplinary Studies," in *Handbook of the Undergraduate Curriculum: A Comprehensive Guide to Purposes, Structures, Practices, and Change,* ed. Jerry G. Gaff and James L. Ratcliff (San Francisco: Jossey-Bass, 1997), 393–415.

8   Dewey M. Caron and Lawrence J. Connor, *Honeybee Biology and Beekeeping,* rev. ed. (Kalamazoo, MI: Wicwas Press, 2013).

9   Maurice Maeterlinck and Alfred Sutro. *The Life of the Bee* (Middletown, DE: ReadaClassic.com, 2010).

10 Sainath Suryanarayanan and Daniel Lee Kleinman, *Vanishing Bees: Science, Politics, and Honeybee Health* (New Brunswick: Rutgers University Press, 2017), 14.

11 "Autonomous Flying Microbots (Robobees)," Harvard University, accessed July 25, 2018, https://wyss.harvard.edu/technology/autonomous-flying -microrobots-robobees/.

Part II

Programming across
the Disciplines

• •

7

Learning, Leading, and Succeeding

• •

Collaborative Culture and Experiential Interdisciplinary Studies at Nichols College

ERIKA CORNELIUS SMITH AND
MARYANN CONRAD

Introduction

In 1890, Charles William Eliot, president of Harvard, commented that a good education for businesspeople requires the development of "accuracy in observation, quickness and certainty in seizing upon the main points of a new subject, and discrimination in separating the trivial from the important in great masses of facts." Along with the ability to communicate, he added, those in business require a "sense of right, duty and honor," which, he believed, directly emanate from a liberal education.[1] Agreeing with Eliot, the community of faculty, students, and administrative divisions at Nichols College have developed four distinct interdisciplinary programs designed to equip our business-minded student body with precisely these skills: the Learning to Lead program (LEAD) and the Emerging Leaders Program (ELP), the Civic Leadership and Politics program (CLP), and the gender and diversity studies minor (GDSM). This chapter discusses how these innovative programs and corresponding experiential learning opportunities inspired interdisciplinary departments and degrees and will examine the challenges and benefits of facilitating meaningful interdisciplinary learning. As a smaller school with limited resources and a focus on professional preparation and business education, we believe that interdisciplinary programming is an essential tool to enable the institution to serve and reach more of its target audience in a highly competitive sector of higher education.

Nichols College

Nichols College is a four-year private, not-for-profit coeducational institution offering associate's, bachelor's, and master's degrees. We have an approximate undergraduate enrollment of 1200 and 52 full-time faculty members, with a faculty to student ratio of 16:1. Our mission is to provide a dynamic, career-focused business and professional education that can prepare "students for careers in business, public service, and the professions, by means of improving their skills and competencies, and to actively engage within our community and the global society."[2] The majority of our students are business majors with specializations in a variety of business concentrations, but we do offer a number of liberal arts majors as well.

At Nichols we believe that business and liberal arts disciplines are not incompatible and, in fact, profit from integration. This is reflected in the structure of our general education curriculum, which aims to foster the growth of the "whole" individual, whose intellect and emotions are capable of processing and integrating technical and cultural inputs and looking at issues in a creative mode from multiple perspectives. Indeed we recognize that an integrated liberal arts and business education produces thoughtful and well-informed civic leaders and cultivates individual freedom through reflection and self-awareness. More specifically, this integrative approach creates an understanding of the larger context of business issues and the role of business in society, politics, culture, and ideology.

Faculty in most programs at the college teach four or five courses per semester, excluding summer and winter intersessions, and, to serve students across the various academic programs, often teach at least three or four different course preparations each semester. This has created a culture where faculty continually develop and offer new course topics to capture the interests of a broad range of students and ensure that our offerings are consistent with the rapidly changing fields in which our students seek employment. Many faculty members are hired for their versatility, with joint appointments in business and liberal arts or multiple business fields. Once they are appointed, they then teach courses in multiple academic disciplines as part of their regular course load, and they often pursue scholarship collaboratively across disciplines. Many faculty also team-teach single courses and collaborate with their colleagues on research. At Nichols, we consciously work to intersect our pedagogy and scholarship. This integrated approach gives our faculty consistent exposure and development in multiple disciplines, which fosters both inter- and multidisciplinarity.[3] Combining a collegial culture and institutional support for innovative programming with the small size of Nichols College reveals an ideal environment for fostering interdisciplinary, collaborative work.

Interdisciplinarity(-ies)

In our view, interdisciplinarity provides students with the opportunity to work with knowledge and frameworks from multiple disciplines. It can be distinguished from cross-disciplinarity, multidisciplinarity, and transdisciplinarity, which are equally valuable and important.[4] As William H. Newell describes them, interdisciplinary curricula "critically draw upon two or more disciplines and lead to an integration of disciplinary insights.[5] Building on this, Lisa Lattuca has categorized four types of interdisciplinary curricula. *Informed disciplinarity* occurs when instructors concentrate on a single discipline but bring in other disciplinary ideas to enhance course content.[6] *Synthetic interdisciplinarity* combines theories, concepts, and methods of research while leaving disciplinary boundaries intact. *Transdisciplinarity* extends across fields to provide students with a variety of disciplinary tools through which to engage and solve real-world issues. *Conceptual interdisciplinarity* has no disciplinary focus and may include themes such as poststructuralism or postmodernism, which do not belong in a single discipline. Lattuca and other scholars have illustrated that the balance between specialization and interdisciplinary activity varies across the contemporary college landscape.

However, the balance has been shifting in favor of interdisciplinarity. This shift owes to a recognition by scholars and practitioners that in the twenty-first century the ability to solve complex problems often requires more than one area of expertise, such as sustainability, poverty, ethics in global trade and governance, and so on. Allen Repko identifies four cognitive abilities that interdisciplinary learning fosters, and each ability aligns with Nichols College's learning outcomes for the student body:

1 *Perspective-taking techniques:* The capacity to understand multiple viewpoints on a given topic, including an appreciation of the differences between disciplines and especially their perspectives on how to approach a problem and their rules of evidence.[7]
2 *Development of structural knowledge:* This is composed of two elements, declarative knowledge (factual information) and procedural

knowledge (process-based information), which are needed to solve complex problems.

3 *Integration* of conflicting insights from alternative disciplines.

4 *Interdisciplinary understanding*: This entails seeing an issue from an array of perspectives and recognizing how each of the alternative approaches influences one another.[8]

Depending on the learning goals and structure of the programs, these four cognitive abilities can be developed to varying degrees in interdisciplinary courses and programs. At Nichols College, our interdisciplinary programs operate with three central objectives: (1) they encourage collaboration, coursework, and unique study opportunities that promote student awareness and abilities relevant to the global economy, including cultural awareness, social responsibility, and diversity; (2) they promote pedagogies that are relevant, experiential, and supportive of student outcomes; and (3) they inspire and engage faculty and students, fostering greater integration and collaboration across the curriculum.

Although our small size and versatility encourage our pursuit of these learning outcomes, they also present us with a variety of challenges. Among the most pressing of these is a lack of financial resources. As Holley notes, many interdisciplinary programs struggle with revenue generation, depending on their organizational structure and their place within the institutional hierarchy.[9] Funding mechanisms vary widely across institutions, with some programs resulting from an initial investment by the central administration and others relying on student tuition or faculty grants. Most interdisciplinary programs do not generate significant revenue on their own, and an increasing number of institutions are assessing program viability in terms of the productivity of the degree or program.[10] Interdisciplinary programs that do not offer a degree are disadvantaged by this form of measurement.

At Nichols, these challenges are all too familiar. The two academic minors we discuss (CLP and GDS) do not generate significant revenue as stand-alone programs and rely on resources (faculty) devoted from other programs and departments to meet scheduling needs. However, courses offered in these minors do fulfill general education requirements, special topic electives in academic majors, and free elective choices for students across the college. In this way, the minors do not divert faculty resources away from serving their "home" programs; rather, they reallocate them to the locus at which two or three programs intersect. Further, like the LEAD program and ELP, the CLP and GDSM support the institutional mission and strategic vision to transform "today's students into tomorrow's leaders through a dynamic, career-focused business and professional education."[11]

Beyond finances, there are many long-term challenges to the organization and administration of interdisciplinary curricula, and small colleges adapt differently to these challenges than do larger universities. First, instructors face challenges in developing courses to support the various programs. This includes first becoming sufficiently knowledgeable to teach a multi- or inter-disciplinary course. At the same time, it can be difficult to identify the appropriate level of complexity for a course and to promote the synthesis of ideas when students are being exposed to multiple disciplines (theories, methods, concepts) for the first time in a single course.[12] In addressing these issues faculty sometimes have difficulty avoiding polarity or territoriality, as it is often easier to revert back to one's home discipline as the primary framework. This can be particularly problematic at smaller colleges, where lower student enrollment and finite resources can create competition among discipline-based departments. Indeed some faculty may perceive growth in one academic major or minor as a threat to their own program's sustainability. In our experience at Nichols, however, many faculty choose to collaborate and pool their resources rather than construct silos around their individual programs. Instead of forcing students to choose between competing academic programs, we integrate our programs and allow students to work across more than one academic field by adopting dual majors or majors with accompanying minors. We believe this more integrative approach supports the creative, innovative, and entrepreneurial problem-solving abilities we hope to foster in our students.

Second, many interdisciplinary programs can struggle to appeal to students, as they do not align with a specific industry and are not widely considered by an increasingly employment-focused student body. The "discipline-focused" structure of higher education creates a strong connection between student education and industry. As an example, accounting programs align accounting curriculum with the accounting profession for students majoring in accounting.[13] The absence of overt industry alignment means that proponents of interdisciplinarity must first convey to students (and parents) the relevance of interdisciplinary knowledge and skill-sets for future employment.

Finally, interdisciplinary programs like ours also face challenges related to course scaffolding and require the development of unique learning paths that build student knowledge and cognitive abilities aligned with program student learning outcomes. With smaller student populations and few students majoring or minoring in any one specific program, our students may not always be able to take courses sequentially to complete degree requirements. At the same time, it is difficult to know with certainty which skills and knowledge bases students will bring into an interdisciplinary course in their second, third, or fourth year of study. This can lead to difficulties in assessing interdisciplinary student learning at both the course and program level.[14] With the foregoing challenges in mind, the following sections of this chapter will discuss the development, delivery, and assessment of three specific interdisciplinary programs at Nichols.

Learning to Lead and Emerging Leaders Program

Though leadership has been a topic of intrigue for centuries, leadership studies only emerged in the twentieth century with the development of the social sciences. As Rost explains in *Leadership for the Twenty-First Century*, the field is rooted in numerous disciplines, including "anthropology, business administration, educational administration, history, military science, nursing administration, organizational behavior, philosophy, political science, public administration, psychology, sociology, and theology."[15] In addition to these fields, leadership learning has since been connected to the broader educational goals of personal competence and caring, emotional intelligence, and knowing oneself.[16] Today, the field has never been more relevant, as leadership skills are often cited as one of the seven keys to professional success in the twenty-first century.[17]

Coinciding with a broader shift toward interdisciplinary curricula, in general, there has been an emerging consensus that leadership studies benefit from interdisciplinary approaches that develop "a shared understanding of differences and commonalities in leadership principles and practices across professions and cultures."[18] In *Assessing Outcomes and Improving Achievement: Tips and Tools for Using Rubrics*, Rhodes maintains that the world needs leaders able to synthesize knowledge and draw conclusions by combining examples, facts, and theories from seemingly unrelated fields of study. This echoes popular arguments that complex problem solving requires diverse proficiencies and perspectives.[19]

While many large colleges and universities approach interdisciplinary leadership study through minors structured from a variety of academic departments, small colleges may not have the capability or student population to support such minors. Integrative approaches that encourage multiperspectives include linked courses, team teaching, civic engagement, service learning, first-year experiences, capstone portfolios, and peer mentoring.[20] Although potentially viewed as challenging, structures and practices such as combining a foundation course with a final capstone course, co-curricular programs, or study abroad engender truly effective connections with students' experiences, rather than viewing them as disconnected events.[21]

With the belief that leadership study is relevant and important to student learning and that exploring concepts of leadership across diverse disciplines and perspectives is both valued and essential, we developed two leadership-focused programs at Nichols College: Learning to LEAD and ELP. The LEAD program grew out of a campus-wide collaborative initiative to create a unique first-year experience aligning with the College's transition to a "leadership" brand and corresponding campus-wide leadership initiatives. As an outgrowth of the LEAD initiative, ELP was launched the following year to offer students deeper leadership growth beyond their required first-year LEAD course experience. Both interdisciplinary programs were conceived under the premise that leadership can (and should) be learned and practiced, aligning with the college's mission of transforming "today's students into tomorrow's leaders."

LEAD 101: Learning to LEAD, is the foundation course in the LEAD program. The program is not an independent concentration in the college's curriculum but resides under the Leadership and Professional Development umbrella of the Nichols general education core curriculum, in addition to the other general education subsection requirements of communication, social/behavior science, global values, humanities, and math/applied sciences. Intended to capture the interest of a broad range of both liberal and business studies students, Learning to Lead replaced a first-year business course, with the objective of immersing students in the study of leadership and exploring their personal leadership style. Other LEAD-designated courses, Leading and Working in Teams and Psychology of Leadership, are elective courses that either fulfill a general education requirement or can be taken as electives within a student's discipline. Leading and Working in Teams, for example, is cross-listed as an option in the general education subsection Leadership and Professional Development or as an elective within the communications discipline. A fourth-year LEAD course, Leading Strategic Initiatives, also serves as the capstone course in the business core.

In programs such as this, small colleges often confront a lack of faculty availability, particularly when engaging those in departments with only a few, or even just one, full-time faculty member. Alleviating this constraint, while broadening the perspective of the LEAD team educators, several key members of the Nichols community, including coaches and the assistant director of Student Affairs, are also LEAD educators. This has proven to be a valuable strategy, as these community members work with students outside of the classroom in other capacities, creating positive campus-wide synergy. On occasion, even the president of the college is part of the LEAD educator team, highlighting the college's commitment to leadership learning and small college versatility.

As the theme of leadership does not reside within one single discipline, and questions of leadership require students to understand, evaluate, and critique knowledge from multiple disciplines, the LEAD program assumes a "conceptual interdisciplinary" approach.[22] Since its inception, LEAD courses have been taught by faculty from different disciplines supporting cross-curricular course design and content. An example of this can be seen in the foundation course with case studies that explore leadership scenarios written by the LEAD educators from the lens of their respective disciplines. At the end of each semester, systematic debriefs among the LEAD team members serve to further develop cross-discipline knowledge and perspectives and foster a learning environment to help students integrate their LEAD experience in meaningful ways.

Whereas the LEAD program is part of Nichols College curricula, ELP is a non-credit-bearing program that offers a leadership designation upon graduation for students who wish to distinguish themselves in leadership development. Over the course of the program, students develop and cultivate their leadership style through workshops, field trips, community service, networking, and speaker events, and they take on leadership roles within and outside the campus community. Like the LEAD program, ELP assumes a "conceptual interdisciplinary" approach but features components that also suggest a "transdisciplinary" typology, as students highly engage with various "real-world" practices.[23]

Both LEAD and ELP partner and pool resources with supportive departments in the college including Athletics, Student Affairs, the Office of Institutional Advancement, and the Institute for Women's Leadership, and take part in shared networking and career initiatives. Additionally, opportunities for LEAD and ELP student leadership and collaboration are promoted through the Fischer Institute, the college's cultural and enrichment center, which has programs that focus on cross-discipline partnerships.

According to Morgan McCall, experience is the primary source for learning to lead.[24] An example of linked experiential learning at Nichols can be seen between ELP and the Hospitality Management program; students jointly travel to Walt Disney World to participate in three days of leadership field study using the Disney Parks as the "classroom." Outside business partnerships for case study competitions, service learning, internships, and a Leadership Summit in Washington, D.C., further enhance students' learning opportunities. These experiential programs offer valuable learning tools for students, support programmatic learning outcomes and initiatives, and leverage the flexibility and collaborative culture of Nichols College.

As with other interdisciplinary programs, approaches to leadership education can be a victim of the challenges of structuring and maintaining a scalable, coherent, and connectible curriculum. Educators may grapple with facilitating leadership theories and training outside of their own program and disciplines, relying instead on familiar frameworks of their disciplines.[25] Scaffolding of courses may also face barriers in a small college as students may not be able to take classes in a sequential path due to a less frequent rotation of offerings aimed at ensuring adequate enrollment. At Nichols, the first-year LEAD course is developed through institutional scaffolding of business core courses, a senior business capstone LEAD course, and cross-listed elective LEAD courses. This design has served to alleviate faculty resource constraints by extending the educator team to Nichols community members, ensuring adequate course enrollment for elective courses, and continuing to foster collaboration between LEAD and other departments.

Nichols has benefited from its size by allowing it to be nimble and capitalize on its shared values and collaborative philosophy. Reflecting and embracing their culture and small college structure, the LEAD program and ELP were designed and developed by a myriad of faculty, staff, and campus leaders. While the programs continue to evolve, their multidisciplinary and integrative objectives remain a core focus and strength.

Civic Leadership and Politics Minor

For students interested in studying business, civic leadership is becoming critically important. The worlds of business and politics are becoming increasingly entangled in the contemporary era, with businesses and government having to adapt together to changing global regulatory and financial pressures. Research shows that leaders who understand the design and function of local, national, and global political systems can afford their organizations a greater degree of political engagement and influence. Rather than treating processes of governance and business separately, then, the CLP program reinforces the linkages between them.

In preparation for the 2016 election and as part of a larger civic engagement program coordinated with Student Services, a series of cross-listed courses and linked projects were developed between political science and other academic disciplines. An Introduction to Political Science course teamed up with a statistics course in the math program to conduct a poll of the college campus. The political science and management departments partnered to offer All Politics Is Local, a public management course themed on the famous Tip O'Neill quote, while faculty in political science and psychology partnered to offer a Washington, D.C., immersion experience during the two weeks prior to the inauguration. The success of these team-taught and linked courses generated further interest in collaborating across disciplines over the following year, with a total of six courses offered in a three-year period.

A number of students progressed through these courses together as they fulfilled various requirements in the general education curriculum, and this gave the students a sense of community built around a shared interest in civic engagement. In fact, conversations with these students and the faculty members engaged in teaching the courses generated discussion of a political science minor. Many soon realized, however, that a political science minor, in its traditional form, would not necessarily capture the essence of what students learned and enjoyed in these interdisciplinary course experiences. They liked the integration of various frameworks, methods, and theories around questions that transcended a single-discipline approach, particularly when they involved synthesizing work from the business disciplines. An illustrative example is the Federal Budget Simulation in the 300-level political science course Business, Government, and Regulation (BGOV). A required course for all business students, BGOV includes a simulation wherein students debate suggested changes to programs impacting mandatory and discretionary spending in the federal budget. In addition to integrating theories of policy making into their preparations, they bring together their learning in courses on finance, accounting, business law, communication, international business, and management to formulate their position statements. They can apply what they are learning beyond their academic fields to questions of governance, democracy, and civic life, and likewise appreciate the relevance of government and policy in shaping their future profession. At a business-specialty school like Nichols College, the students and faculty saw this alternative approach to studying civic life as an important part of their future roles as entrepreneurs or whatever career path they might pursue.

The resulting program proposal reflected elements of "transdisciplinarity" and "conceptual interdisciplinarity," with nearly all courses cross-listed across political science and business fields. In addition to offering courses that serve students in need of social science credits, the program offers a new cross-listed special topic each fall and spring semester. This includes courses connected with business programs in criminal justice, marketing, finance, international business, and hospitality. The college has only one full-time faculty member appointed to political science, like other concentrations and disciplines, so the single faculty member typically teaches a 5–5 course overload with a minimum of four different courses each semester. In some cases, this full-time faculty member, like other faculty members at the college, will teach courses for programs and concentrations outside the primary appointment, and these scheduling needs have to be balanced against offering courses for students in the CLP minor. This leads faculty members to develop course offerings that serve multiple requirements and programs. An example might be a cross-listed political science and criminal justice management course, International Security Studies, that students can select as a social science credit, an elective in the CLP minor, or an elective in the criminal justice management concentration. A single faculty member is serving two programs, and a single course supports the needs of three different scheduling divisions (general education, CLP, and CJM). This benefits both the academic programs and the college, as courses with this level of versatility are likely to see higher enrollment.

By design, the CLP program complements nearly all business concentrations, and because most courses are cross-listed, students can sample the approach and decide later if they want to continue pursuing the minor. If they choose not to pursue the CLP minor, the cross-listed courses often fulfill an elective choice (demonstrated by examples already provided) in their central academic concentration or requirement in general education.

Gender and Diversity Studies Minor

In the second half of the twentieth century, new interdisciplinary fields arose, such as area, gender, and race/ethnic studies. While these programs are common at many colleges and universities, they assume many different forms. Some are housed within a single academic department, whereas others are freestanding, independent schools. In 2013, Nichols College created the Institute for Women's Leadership, which focuses, through campus initiatives, industry partnerships, research analysis, and thought leadership, on the issues and challenges impacting women in business. Between 2014 and 2015, faculty in English and political science conceived of the GDSM as an extension of this mission. In social conversations and at college functions, faculty members recognized common themes across their independently taught courses and academic research. The combination of a new strategic mission for the college, specifically to increase awareness of issues related to women and leadership on campus, and a collaborative culture, led to the creation of this "conceptual interdisciplinary" curriculum and a new academic program. From the faculty perspective, the GDSM was constructed as a conceptual interdisciplinary program for pedagogical reasons—gender and diversity awareness have become integral to disciplinary fields as diverse as history, literature, science, sociology, and economics, in addition to emerging as independent fields of study.

The GDSM comprises an interdisciplinary field of study that addresses the ways in which gender is conceptualized and investigated by diverse disciplines: humanities (literature, history, and cultural studies), behavioral and social sciences (psychology, political science, sociology), biological sciences, and core fields within business education (human resources, marketing, management). The program was not conceived as a self-standing department but as an umbrella program for a series of interdisciplinary and cross-disciplinary courses that address conceptual and practical themes related to gender and race. Developing students' critical skills in a variety of fields, the GDSM explores gender-based inequity, injustice, and oppression; studies gender's impact on career and workplace environments; and focuses on diversity in cultural and social arrangements. It provides academic reinforcement for the programming of the Institute for Women's Leadership and the broader strategic vision of the college to provide professional preparation for our students.

Unlike the two aforementioned interdisciplinary programs, the GDSM struggles from underenrollment and a lack of popularity among students who do not clearly see value in its offerings. In retrospect, the creation of the program was driven by institutional (administrative and faculty) demand, rather than student interest. Currently only a single student is enrolled in the minor, and the program faces challenges in sustaining itself beyond the institutional commitment to diversity. Yet, with our flexible approach to course structure and scheduling, faculty can continue to offer GDSM courses that meet the requirements of other programs and departments, while experimenting with new interdisciplinary course offerings that may attract to students to the minor.

Conclusion

At Nichols College, we believe that as a smaller school with correspondingly limited resources and a focus on professional preparation and business education, interdisciplinary programming is an essential tool to enable the institution to serve and reach more of its target audience in a highly competitive sector of higher education. There is consensus among those researching the forms of interdisciplinarity noted earlier in this chapter, and elsewhere in this volume, that the most successful efforts to create new programs and curricula arise from collaborative efforts of faculty from different disciplines with the support of administrative systems. While there may be challenges related to personnel sufficiency and funding inherent in small colleges, our college's small size and collegial culture encourage and foster collaboration in teaching, research, and academic initiatives, while providing opportunities for students to integrate their learning in meaningful ways.

Notes

1 Charles William Eliot, "Speech to the New York City Chamber of Commerce 1890," in *Modern Eloquence*, ed. Thomas B. Reed (New York: Stationers' Hall, London, 1923), 4:94–98.

2 See "Nichols College Educational Goals and Outcomes," accessed March 19, 2020, https://www.nichols.edu/academics/educational-goals-and-outcomes.

3 Lisa R. Lattuca, *Creating Interdisciplinarity: Interdisciplinary Research and Teaching among College and University Faculty* (Nashville: Vanderbilt University Press, 2001), 55–77.

4 Karri Holley, "Interdisciplinary Curriculum and Learning in Higher Education," in *Oxford Research Encyclopedia of Education* (New York: Oxford University Press, 2017), http://education.oxfordre.com/view/10.1093/acrefore /9780190264093.001.0001/acrefore-9780190264093-e-138.

5 William H. Newell, "Interdisciplinary Curriculum Development," *Issues in Integrative Studies* 8, no. 1 (1990): 89.

6 Lattuca, *Creating Interdisciplinarity*, 55–77.

7 Lynda Baloche, John Hynes, and Helen Berger, "Moving toward the Integration of Professional and General Education," *Action in Teacher Education* 18, no. 1 (1996): 1–9.

8 Allen F. Repko, "Assessing Interdisciplinary Learning Outcomes" (working paper, School of Urban and Public Affairs, University of Texas at Arlington, 2009), https://oakland.edu/Assets/upload/docs/AIS/Assessing_Interdisiplinary _Learning_Outcomes_(Allen_F._Repko).pdf.

9 Karri Holley, "Interdisciplinary Strategies as Transformative Change in Higher Education," *Innovative Higher Education* 34, no. 5 (December 2009): 331–344.

10 For more on assessing program viability and measuring institutional productivity in higher education, see Teresa A. Sullivan et al., *Improving Measurement of Productivity in Higher Education* (Washington, D.C.: The National Academies Press, 2012).

11 "Nichols College—Mission," accessed March 19, 2020, https://www.nichols.edu /about/nichols-at-a-glance.

12 Synthesis reflects a higher-order cognitive ability in Bloom's taxonomy. See Benjamin S. Bloom, *Taxonomy of Educational Objectives* (Boston: Allyn and Bacon, 1956).

13 Tony Becher and Paul R. Trowler, *Academic Tribes and Territories: Intellectual Enquiry and the Culture of the Discipline*, 2nd ed. (Buckingham: Open University Press, 2001): 41–57.

14 The Association of American Colleges & Universities (AAC&U) recognized two common means of assessing student ability to analyze in an interdisciplinary manner: the pre- and postsurvey method, and the grading rubric approach. Student surveys can be designed and used to capture perceptions (subjective information) and the capacity to think in an interdisciplinary manner (objective information). Grading rubrics provide objective feedback on the status of both multi- and interdisciplinary thinking. Course sequencing or scaffolding and student learning goals at the various levels will ultimately determine the approach, but it is worth noting that this is particularly challenging in interdisciplinary programs, and more research on "best practices" should be pursued on the topic.

15 J. C. Rost, *Leadership for the Twenty-First Century* (Westport, CT: Praeger, 1991), 45.

16 Julie E. Owen, ed., *Innovative Learning for Leadership Development*, New Directions for Student Leadership, 145 (San Francisco, CA: Jossey-Bass: 2015), 49–57.

17 Anna Rosefsky Saavedra and V. Darleen Opfer, *Teaching and Learning 21st Century Skills: Lessons from the Learning Sciences* (Washington, D.C.: RAND Corporation, 2012), http://asiasociety.org/files/rand-1012report.pdf.

18 Susan R. Komives, Nance Lucas, and Timothy R. McMahon, *Exploring Leadership: For College Students Who Want to Make a Difference*, 3rd ed. (San Francisco: Jossey-Bass, 2013), 6.

19 Terrel L. Rhodes, ed., *Assessing Outcomes and Improving Achievement: Tips and Tools for Using Rubrics* (Washington, D.C.: Association of American Colleges and Universities, 2010).

20 Owen, 52.

21 Mary Taylor Huber, Pat Hutchings, and Richard Gale, "Integrative Learning for Liberal Education," *peerReview* 7, no. 4 (Summer/Fall 2005): 4–7, https://www .aacu.org/publications-research/periodicals/integrative-learning-liberal-education.

22 Huber, Hutchings, and Gale, 55–77.

23 Huber, Hutchings, and Gale, 55–77.

24 Morgan W. McCall, "Leadership Development through Experience," *Academy of Management* 18, no. 3 (2004): 127.

25 McCall, 51.

8

Why Can't It Be Both?

● ●

Supporting Students across
the Spectrum of Abilities
and Ambitions

JULIA F. KLIMEK

Meeting Students Where They Are

Coker College is a small college with a liberal arts core—in fact, it is so small
that it does not even make the cut as a small college by some definitions. We
enroll about a thousand traditional day students, most of them housed on
campus but some of them living with their families in town or commuting
from communities nearby. Many of our students are from South Carolina,
Georgia, and Florida, but our athletics programs attract students from the
northeastern United States, Europe, and South America. About 40 percent
are first-generation college students, and just over 50 percent are Pell Grant
recipients—two data points that put many of our students at risk for not completing their studies. Indeed, financial hardship and family pressures are two
hurdles that many of our students struggle to clear. No less challenging can be
the pressure that they face to pursue a degree that promises a stable career—even
if that career is in a field in which the student has struggled or has little or no
interest. The student who excels at dance, for example, will likely face family
pressure to at least add a minor in business, yet the extra semester or more

required for this can pose significant financial and academic roadblocks toward graduation.[1]

To better serve these students, I helped develop an interdisciplinary studies program to offer an alternative to the traditional major to students struggling with academic, financial, or professional pressures. Having completed my undergraduate work at Evergreen State College, which promotes interdisciplinarity, and my graduate work in comparative literature at the University of California, Davis, another interdisciplinary environment, the position of director of interdisciplinary studies (IS) at Coker posed the interesting challenge of creating an unconventional program within a more conventionally structured college.

Established in 2016, the program built on an obscure and ill-defined existing "individualized major" option found in the college catalog. The new interdisciplinary program requires students to complete both a 3-credit introductory course (IS200) and a 3-credit capstone course (IS400) while ensuring their fulfillment of the 30 credit hours of junior/senior standing coursework required to complete any major at Coker. The content for these upper-division courses often comes from two or three disciplines determined through advising consultations between the student, the program director, and the relevant disciplinary faculty. To offer such personalized curricula while keeping staffing costs low for the college, the program relies overwhelmingly on courses that are already taught for traditional majors in the disciplines. This avoids placing an additional burden on faculty already stretched thin by a teaching load of four courses per semester and allows IS students to work alongside their peers in traditional majors in almost all their classes.[2] Beyond these offerings, two optional 300-level courses (one for research projects, the other for internship credits) are available to IS students to create individualized opportunities for skill development. Speaking to the value of such consultations, Dr. Lynn Griffin, vice president of athletics and athletics facilities at Coker, notes how "carefully listening to a student's desires and then selecting courses and faculty members who are experts in those fields are crucial to the success of the student. . . . Students no longer are pigeon holed into a particular degree."[3]

With this structure, the IS program lends itself to bridging the liberal arts intentions and the preprofessional realities of a small college, both for student learning (finding relationships between required liberal arts courses and professional interests) and faculty partnerships (uniting instructors across disciplines as we share responsibility for a student's success). Moreover, the program has benefited the institution, as its founding coincided with a new strategic plan that called for the creation of a Student Success Center aimed at retention. With this broader goal in mind, the program offered an important, and inexpensive, way to attract and retain students by offering a flexible, alternative approach to the traditional majors (biology, English, communications, etc.) while still preparing them for an increasingly competitive and fluctuating career market.

At a small college such as ours, it is imperative that we adapt to meet the needs of our student population, for whom education is crucial and yet fraught with challenges (the pressure of student loans, time constraints, family obligations—and, often, limited academic preparation preceding college). At the same time, the program also serves those students for whom the identification of a career path was more challenging than anticipated. As a faculty member who has worked with its students explains, the program accommodates "students whose interest and scholarly passions have evolved throughout their college experience."[4] The first three students attracted by the new program had all reached a point in their studies where they were discouraged and on the verge of dropping out of college. Their original majors (math, computer science, and education) had produced road blocks that frustrated them (coursework that was unmanageable or unappealing, a timed certification exam that could not be passed at the right time), and at the beginning of what was supposed to be their final year, graduation was slipping from sight. The program sequence as I had conceived it could fit into a single year, although this stopgap version proved to be less than ideal. In individual advising conversations, we identified interests that could be added to existing knowledge to shape a coherent new direction for each student: to education we added business courses to prepare a student to open up her own daycare, to computer science we added math and communications courses for a student who wanted to develop and market his own apps, and we added communications and art courses for another who wanted to design web pages. In each case, we were able to build on existing coursework in one field (e.g., education) and add skills in a second field (e.g., business), and thereby create a path across the finish line and provide solid preparation for employment; all three graduated after two semesters in the program, completing capstone projects (a business plan, an app with a marketing campaign, a website) co-directed by faculty mentors whose support the students had enlisted.[5] These final projects served the dual purpose of giving the student a chance to apply skills learned in the disciplines and to produce evidence of the professional value of a degree in IS. In fact, even before graduating, one of the students had already secured a job offer by presenting the website she had designed (about interdisciplinary learning, no less) during an interview.

Designing the Program

When designing this program, my aim was avoid sacrificing academic standards while bringing graduation into reach for students who had become discouraged or were running out of time to complete their degree. To achieve this, I elected to maintain the 30-credit requirement for junior/senior-level coursework but offered students the opportunity to select those courses that they and their mentors saw as relevant to their career interests. In the same way, the senior capstone course required for a discipline-specific major was not eliminated but rather replaced with an individualized project that had to be inter- or multidisciplinary in focus. I was looking for efficiency for the student (maximum use of existing coursework and credit hours as we adjusted direction) as much as for the college (minimal additional course- or workload for faculty, small price tag for the college), and the program delivered both.[6]

Operating with the belief that all students profit from having access to an education that is relevant to them and their goals, I elected to design interlocking and mutually reinforcing pieces that allow students to master the basic skills of interdisciplinarity (perspective taking, problem solving, research, bias awareness, etc.) while pursuing their unique interests and ambitions. Research and internship opportunities can be adjusted to any student's ability, and the interactions between stronger and weaker students in small groups, as well as the presentations followed by questions and feedback, engage every student in a positive way. More importantly, I have found that the generally encouraging atmosphere of the IS classrooms fosters exactly the skills (listening, patience, willingness to acknowledge and support differences) that any interdisciplinary work environment will require.

This has certainly been my experience teaching one of the program's core courses, IS200. To guide the course, I use a text book, *Introduction to Interdisciplinary Studies* by Repko, Szostak, and Buchberger, which is, admittedly, a bit overwhelming for my students. Still, they have commented on its value for introducing them to the concept and benefits of interdisciplinarity.[7] For each textbook reading, students complete individually (and encouragingly) graded weekly homework assignments on Blackboard, which help me gauge comprehension and prompt me to follow up both through written feedback and through discussions and applied exercises. The first few chapters require quite a bit of adjustment from the disciplinary approach—rather than presenting subject content, they explain more abstract ideas about knowledge, the organization of knowledge, the formation of disciplines—topics that my students have not ever given much thought to. I have found that students who join the program late in their college career and feel on comparatively solid ground reading material in their original disciplinary major can become frustrated with the new challenge of having to explain learning *processes* rather than simply *learning* a single subject. To foster this much-needed metacognition, I employ partner and small-group work; students are asked to explain to each other, under acknowledgment of their disciplinary background and using specific examples, definitions and aspects of disciplinarity, multidisciplinarity, traits and skills needed to think interdisciplinarily, and so on. We slowly work our way into the field, exploring together ideas and challenges presented in the textbook, and right around chapter 5, it seems to "click." Throughout this process, the student interaction across fields and experience levels is overwhelmingly positive, and students enjoy their increasing awareness of, and control over, the subject, as the following student comments demonstrate:

> At first I was intimidated when I realized how many Seniors were in the [IS200] class, but when we started group work, it ended up being really fun and easy. I didn't even know about some of the disciplines [represented], and in the group projects, we could make sure that the projects worked for the different disciplines. The whole dynamic and diversity was really cool. (Bailey, sophomore)

> I think [the diversity] was obvious every time we went around the class and talked about what we were working on. It was really interesting to hear about the different fields and perspectives, especially the sciences and education fields. . . . For the [interdisciplinary] study itself, you have to look at that as something positive, because the degree is about making connections. Sometimes group work could be frustrating because [another student] had a more scientific way of approaching a problem, more rigid, just on a different wavelength—but it was part of the experience. (Scott, senior/transfer)[8]

Like the textbook, class meetings deal exclusively with interdisciplinarity as a subject; when examples draw on field-specific information, students rely on their previous classwork or I prepare some quick background or definitions. Questions checking comprehension and asking for application of ideas are included in the textbook; students post their answers on Blackboard a day in advance. There is no particular lecture; Tuesday work begins with the homework questions and adds depth where needed. At least one of the homework questions assigned intentionally draws on students' individual experiences with a specific idea presented in a chapter (bias awareness, decision-making process, etc.) without adding the pressure of "getting it right." Thursday work is very different: we follow up with interactive workshop exercises, prompting cross-major small group collaboration and high-energy activity as poster paper, markers, sticky notes, and whiteboards are put to use for brainstorming, communication, and presenting.[9] I rely on a series of interactive activities, such as deciding on a "complex problem" and developing a flowchart of disciplines involved in addressing it; or a design competition for a new multipurpose building in downtown Hartsville—with assigned pretend-characters collaborating (and exploring their opposing perspectives and ambitions); or assembling a spaceship crew to conduct interdisciplinary research on a distant planet. All these activities promote a range of skills (creativity, communication, problem solving), and students anticipate and enjoy the mayhem—but we start and finish each activity lesson with a conversation about how it relates to the information presented in Tuesday's chapter.

Beyond classwork, all students must complete a forty-five-hour internship, which they identify and apply for with the help of the college's admittedly understaffed (i.e. one-person) career-planning center.[10] An internship presentation to the group and a written internship reflection (focused on work situations that demand the application of interdisciplinary skills) further bridge the theoretical with the practical. The internship experiences vary widely: while second-year students use them to simply learn more about the career fields they are considering (finding out, for example, that graphic design is not the same as game design) and learn basic skills (how to choose and edit images in Photoshop), students in their final year actively start networking and seek out responsibilities that serve as résumé builders. As the following comments show, students are both aware of the benefits of internships, but also see them as filling different needs at different points in their academic careers:

[The internship placement] wasn't exactly what I wanted to do, but learning how to draw things on the computer helped me understand how to do graphics. It was really interesting. I still go into the office to further my skills in Adobe. . . . I felt I could learn more. It wasn't really about the course grade anymore. (Gabrielle, junior)

I appreciated the fact that I was kind of forced to do an internship like that. On my own I would not have done that, but it turned out to be really helpful. . . . I will be working with children—that is now 100 percent, because of my experience with children in that therapy setting. (Bailey, sophomore)

The internship gave me a direction. I worked for thirteen years in an industry that did not interest me, and coming back to college was a search for a passion. Working in sports information gave me a vision. I did not know it was out there, but it was exactly what I was looking for. It really opened my eyes to a new career. (Scott, senior/transfer)

Because the internships are, except for the number of required hours, highly individualized experiences, each student's work and progress are evaluated based on his or her own report (aside from the completion of basic expectations), allowing for scaled grades for this course component. In the internship reflection, which I modeled on similar assignments in education courses, I ask for an overview of tasks, a description of several challenges encountered and mastered, and an assessment of the internship as an interdisciplinary experience. Students who are farther along in their studies discuss more complex situations, linking coworkers to "disciplines" with specific biases or assumptions. Here their answers often highlight the more nuanced aspects of our class conversations about interdisciplinary work. By contrast, students who are just setting out on their path, and who are using the internship to simply gain an overview of their field, usually offer more simplistic observations. Both can earn a high grade for completion and earnest engagement of the questions, as well as for the inclusion of details and examples. A basic expectation (without which no passing grade for this aspect of the course can be earned) is the completion of minimum hours.[11] My assumption, from the get-go, was that the internship would simply "move the needle"—that gains would be made appropriate to each student's starting point, that encouragement would lead to each student taking full advantage of the opportunity, and that the emphasis lies, once again, on reflection.[12]

A final reflective exercise is the research process paper, which focuses on individual interests. Students are immensely relieved when they find out that they are not producing an actual *research* paper, but rather further encouraging metacognition by writing about the *process* of conducting interdisciplinary research. While students usually choose a topic that is directly related to their study and career interest, the project must contain interdisciplinary elements. Each student formulates a research inquiry (the steps are outlined in their textbooks, over the course of three chapters/three weeks), spending in-class time to refine and explain the questions in partner work. They follow up with librarian-supported research in multidisciplinary databases, either applying research skills already gained in previous courses or just developing those skills. Here, too, the quality of work is assessed based on the starting point of each student individually, and I emphasize that the resulting essay need not satisfy any particular vision I, the instructor, may have, but should reflect honestly the learning process the student has completed. This focuses the effort and the accomplishment on the students, shoring up their investment in and responsibility for learning. In a conversation about this project, students showed their growing awareness of disciplines and their relationships:

> I had worked in my ENG102 class on an assignment about philanthropy and looked at organizations that work with adolescents in addiction recovery. At the time, I started on this topic from a psychology perspective, and I wanted to look at it from a biological and sociology perspective. We learned about deviance and group behaviors in sociology classes, and I wanted to develop that more, so that's what I used this research project for. (Bailey, sophomore)

> I was working on my research paper [on business and weight loss], and when I talked to [another student], she helped me out a lot, because she knows a lot about biology. And food intake and how your body processes that, that's really about biology, and I did not know that much about that. So that was helpful. (Charity, senior)

Seeing the Results

After completing IS200 and their remaining disciplinary coursework, one final graduation requirement remains: the capstone course (IS400). This is conducted as an independent study, allowing for a great range of options as long as the course outcome meets two criteria: it must be interdisciplinary, and it must be useful to the student. A student whose next step is to find an entry-level position in information technology (IT) will benefit from a hands-on internship with the college's IT team, using her capstone course learning how to operate a ticket system, how to research different tools and solutions, and how to work as a member of a focused team. A student who will be applying to pharmacy school, however, probably needs to complete an extensive research project under the guidance of faculty in biology and chemistry. Both options are available, and individual advising determines what is most helpful and appropriate for each student.

It is perhaps at this final point that faculty in traditional disciplines are anxious to see work of a caliber that truly reflects the standards of college graduation and attests that comprehensive understanding of a field has been attained. Conversations with faculty in all disciplines at the college are ongoing, and faculty who have worked as mentors or advisers with IS students are usually impressed with the work these students complete.[13]

Students whose frustration is replaced with newfound interest and hope, and who suddenly see themselves in charge of their education, experience a second wind. My colleagues report noticing a pronounced change in their attitude toward learning, class attendance, and work. The students who have been struggling to earn Cs and Ds suddenly earn Bs and As as they apply themselves with new enthusiasm. Mentoring IS students, Dr. Peter Gloviczki (communications) explains, "I have the opportunity to remember the experience of discovery that is central to the liberal arts tradition. . . . It's an exciting thing to witness and affirm so much of why we do what we do."[14] The change is pronounced and rewarding. Students come to the program from a range of situations, some more intentional about it than others, but in interviews conducted after completing the introductory course, all of them speak with enthusiasm about their new direction.

> I did not know anything about interdisciplinary studies until I knew I was not going to finish my PE major in time to graduate. My adviser told me about combining PE with something else to graduate on time, and I researched what I wanted to do, and I decided to add business. So that's the approach I took. . . . I want to one day own my own facility, so I knew I needed to learn about management. Even my internship was about managing a sports facility. (Charity, senior)

I wanted to do premed, but it would have added two years at the college. So my adviser pointed me toward IS. I researched the prerequisites for occupational therapy graduate school at the Medical University of South Carolina. Interdisciplinary studies wasn't anything I had ever thought about before, but I am able to combine two disciplines I really love and pursue something I really wanted to do. (Bailey, sophomore)

For me [coming to Interdisciplinary Studies] was a two part thing: as a returning student, I had all these credit hours in different disciplines and they needed to combine into a degree. At the same time, Coker did not offer a journalism degree.... So I cobbled together credits from English, communications, and PE to create something like a sports journalism track. (Scott, senior/transfer)

To the traditional majors and programs at Coker College, the IS program offers great enrichment and enables faculty and the institution to serve better those students who struggle for a variety of reasons to complete their studies. While maintaining the institution's high academic standards, it empowers these students to create a personalized sequence of courses and learning opportunities that leads them toward meaningful studies and, most importantly, graduation. All constituents benefit from the outcome: the student, who graduates with a degree, knowledge, and skills; the family members, who take pride in their son or daughter as the first college graduate and hopefully, gain trust in the process of education; and the institution, which can count the student among its success stories. Moreover, because it also reaches across departmental boundaries by bringing together a team of professors from different disciplines to support an individual student, it allows faculty to gain a better understanding of each other's fields and expectations. In this way the program builds a learning community.

As I see it, education seeks to "move the needle." The Interdisciplinary Studies program at Coker College does this by meeting students where they are and provides them with the space to move forward in a direction that is productive. Putting the student back in the center of the educational experience, and providing a balance of structure and flexibility, can reinvigorate a student's curiosity and engagement, thereby providing a path to academic, professional, and personal success that benefits all stakeholders.

Notes

1 The college also sustains a program for nontraditional students as well as several (mostly online) graduate programs, and maintains bridge programs with local two-year colleges to facilitate transfers. A pilot program to offer bridge and other

nontraditional students an interdisciplinary studies degree is under discussion; currently the introductory course is offered as part of the general education requirement path for nontraditional students.

2 The often continued enrollment of IS students in some courses of their original major helps the relationship between IS and traditional majors: faculty, who often feel protective of students, see improved grades and attitudes as students move toward graduation, and while the students may not "count" as their major anymore, they continue to fill the seats of sometimes small upper-level courses. During its first year, the possibility of the IS program "poaching" majors was of some concern among some colleagues; a reemphasis on student success over specific department numbers and the ongoing actively solicited involvement of interested faculty members in the teaching and advising of these students has helped foster a positive environment.

3 Email correspondence with Dr. Griffin on June 7, 2018. Dr. Griffin supervised the capstone internship of an IS graduate and commented on the student's experience: "One of the best things [the student] did was having to sit down with [a representative of the downtown business organization] and discuss the rental needs" of the facility for which she was writing a plan. "By combining the areas of PE, communications, and business, she had the opportunity to learn about event management, how to communicate, how to organize, and how to look at a business. No one major will allow this."

4 Dr. Peter Gloviczki, email correspondence, May 25, 2018.

5 Upon choosing the IS major, each student is charged with developing a strong mentoring relationship with a faculty member in each of the disciplines to be combined. Coker is a small, student-focused college, and instructors, some of whom are excited about a new perspective for their students, make time to go over schedules and create lists of relevant courses. These faculty mentors take on a more official role during the capstone course, when they serve on a committee to ensure appropriate breadth and depth in the final project.

6 Originally, a reorganization of the English major freed me to develop and teach the courses for this new major; the position of Director for Interdisciplinary Studies then became a 50 percent position in which I taught a single in-seat IS200 introductory course a year and supervised about six to ten capstone projects, with around fifteen to twenty students enrolled in the first years. With the growth of the program and the expansion into online/bridge offerings, the position is now 75 percent to allow for additional course teaching, development, and advising; the program has grown to about thirty students, with fifteen graduating seniors in May 2020. The main challenge in terms of my workload is the advising—students have very individual needs, and I am charged with assembling a course track that makes sense for them and helps them fulfill graduation requirements; at the same time I am working with prerequisites and course sequences that can present challenges in scheduling. Once a student leaves the carefully designed course rotations in a specific major, finding and accessing upper-level courses can be frustrating. I rely a great deal on the support of colleagues in each department, who are often flexible about taking alternative prerequisites into consideration or overriding other program-specific requirements that do not have a direct effect on student success.

7 I am currently using Allen F. Repko, Rick Szostak, and Michelle Phillips Buchberger, *Introduction to Interdisciplinary Studies*, 3rd ed. (Thousand Oaks, CA: SAGE, 2019). The textbook provides overviews of disciplines and disciplinary

studies, and one of my students commented on its helpfulness: "Going over some of those tables of disciplines in the textbook provided a really interesting bird's-eye view of education. I think most students just choose one lane and then stick with that, so we never are aware of the big picture" (Scott, senior/transfer).

8 All student quotes were collected via open-ended questions in phone conversations between May 20 and June 10, 2018; students quoted have reviewed all content and agreed these quotes are accurate and they are comfortable with the publication.

9 Students commented positively on the weekly shift from lecture/textbook work to the playful and spirited interaction of hour-long group challenges and small projects. The college has recently moved to employ iPad technology throughout classes for a variety of excellent reasons. For the time being, I am continuing with the old-school approaches, as I find that students enjoy moving around the room, spreading materials out on the floor, and they generally benefit from the kinetic energy. Individual presentations make use of PowerPoint or Google Slides, however.

10 The challenges this process presents have been revealing; in response to difficulties encountered by the first couple of cohorts, I am now providing detailed instructions and a homework assignment post to draft an inquiry to an offer, include several scaffolded timely deadlines for researching and applying for an internship, and require individual meetings with our internship coordinator. Members of my last cohort, except for two students, were able to secure and complete internships much more smoothly, regardless of their years at college.

11 The college sends out a brief survey to each internship provider/supervisor, and if I do receive an assessment of the student's work in response, I can take it into consideration in my grade—realistically, although the survey is electronic and only requires a few clicks from the respondent, I do not see a lot of responses returned, which leaves me with the student's report. We do use signed time sheets to assure that the time requirement (forty-five hours) has been completed, and informal conversations with the students allow me to get a sense of what kind of work is being done.

12 My undergraduate experience at Evergreen State College, which did not employ grades but widely trusted students to evaluate their own work, prompts me to carefully consider the purpose of grades for specific assignments.

13 The schedule for the capstone course calls for initial, mid-semester, and final presentation meetings that bring faculty mentors, the program director, the student, and any internship supervisors (if applicable) around a table; the student is charged with scheduling, preparing, and directing these meetings. These conversations help keep a project on track and facilitate productive and positive feedback at multiple points.

14 Email correspondence, May 25, 2018. Dr. Gloviczki also reports that "students speak with excitement and a good deal of well-earned pride" about their work in the Interdisciplinary Studies program and "take ownership" of what they have learned and what still lies ahead, actively making connections across course work, years of study, and disciplines.

9

From Chemistry to History to Psychology

• •

Creating a Multidisciplinary
Minor in Investigative
Forensics

CHRISTINE D. MYERS
AND AUDRA L. GOACH

Establishing the Minor

In 1918 a "committee was appointed to inquire what provision is now being made in our colleges . . . for instruction in the various subjects that contribute directly or indirectly to the understanding and solution of the problems that are presented by the criminals and delinquents in our communities."[1] The academic interest in the causes of crime and methods of deterring or solving crimes was established in the nineteenth century and has continued to evolve as new technologies become available to aid in its study. The 1918 committee concluded that proper education in these subjects was only possible in "the larger universities" and "is done very hastily and superficially by necessity in the smaller colleges in which the teaching force is limited."[2] At Monmouth College, in western Illinois, where we have a student body of fewer than a thousand students, we humbly disagree with the conclusions written so long ago and feel, instead, that a small liberal arts college is an ideal place to have a program in investigative forensics.

Beginning in the fall of 2018, students at Monmouth College will be able to minor in what we decided to call investigative forensics. In our proposal, we contended that the courses included would enable students to consider a career in fields related or attached to the civil and criminal court systems, or simply to deepen their understanding of how evidence is studied and applied in a variety of academic disciplines. Unlike programs at larger schools that train students for specific positions, such as crime scene technician or criminalist, the minor at Monmouth takes a multidisciplinary, liberal arts approach to investigating incidents that may or may not be crimes. In this way, we encourage students to think about the field of forensics in relation to a variety of majors.[3] Interest in forensic investigation can be seen on a daily basis in the news and popular culture. The fact that many of the courses included in this minor have typically high enrollments shows a particular interest in this area among college-aged students. As our admissions office reminds us, many students enter college as undecided or "exploratory" with respect to a possible major. The creation of the investigative forensics minor gives those students a number of fields to explore so they can find one that is a good fit for them. Recent data from students taking the PSAT indicates a steadily increasing interest in multi-/interdisciplinary programs and a sharp increase in those wishing to study what they categorize as security and protective services (with subsets that include forensic science and criminal justice).[4] Furthermore, the number of students who have taken one of the courses listed and gone on to take another, even without doing so as part of a minor, shows that a multidisciplinary interest already exists on our campus; this minor will help provide guidance to those students.

One of the educational goals from our college's mission statement is "fostering the discovery of connections among disciplines and of larger patterns of meaning."[5] Working to understand the reasons behind actions or methods to deter crime and violence requires the use of many disciplines in order to find a larger pattern of meaning. No single piece of an investigation will reveal the complete picture, so students who are able to take multiple approaches will be more successful in investigative work. Students in this minor will also enhance their ability to "understand the methods of inquiry and expression in the arts, humanities, sciences, and social sciences."[6] At times, despite the best efforts of faculty, students see their major as their identity and are closed off to the possibility that another discipline's approach might be useful in solving a problem. This minor can serve as a catalyst to those students by encouraging them to look at the same topic in a variety of ways, one of the key attributes of a liberal arts education.

The idea for this minor began at a Curriculum Committee meeting on, perhaps fittingly, Halloween in 2017. It was prompted by the submission of a course proposal from a new colleague, Tara McCoy, in forensic psychology. The catalog description states that the "course will provide an in-depth review of how psychology and the law interact. A review of theories from a variety of areas of psychology, which have been influential forces in the creation and implementation of laws, will be explored. Topics include: police psychology, eye-witness testimony, false confessions, violent and non-violent crimes."[7] As Professor McCoy explained further in her proposal, the course will look at common misperceptions of forensic psychology and individuals connected to the legal system, such as jury members, who play important roles and are often less studied because of the traditional focus on the criminals themselves. Knowing that this approach to the study of crimes overlapped with numerous disciplines, and having a new colleague who could be added to a collective endeavor, made the timing appear right to create a minor that would enhance many existing majors and appeal to the incoming students we hope to recruit. After securing sufficient buy-in from faculty across campus, the minor was approved by a full faculty vote in December 2017.

Structuring of the Minor

All of the courses in the minor—in art, biology, chemistry, communication studies, English, environmental studies and sustainability, history, political science, psychology, and sociology—are ones already established in our curriculum, so it was possible to create a new area of study without incurring additional expenses. If the minor proves successful, then there is the possibility of requesting a new tenure line; in the meantime we knew we would encounter less resistance from colleagues, who are all grappling with the limited resources available at our small institution, if we did not ask for additional staffing. The only required course in the minor is CHEM 102: Forensic Science, which provides students with an overview of both the history and the current state of criminalistics and investigative methods. The minor requires a minimum of five course credits coming from at least three different disciplines. To ensure sufficient academic rigor, no more than two 100-level course credits can be taken. And to push students into unfamiliar academic territory, no more than two course credits can come from the same discipline. We had to make the wording of the requirements precise, as there are some departments at Monmouth that house more than one discipline, and not all courses are taught as a full credit.[8]

We have a wide range of electives for students to choose from, and all the faculty have committed to teaching them regularly in the coming years to provide students with a great deal of choice as they move through the minor. Electives in the arts and humanities include an art course, Photography—Digital; two communication studies courses, Argumentation and Fake News;

two English courses, Nineteenth-Century Mystery and Sherlock Holmes; and two history courses, Archival Science and Violence in Victorian Britain. Social science options include courses in political science, Civil Liberties and Politics of Criminal Justice, the new course Forensic Psychology, and a sociology course, Criminology. And finally, the science electives included in the minor are Field Botany, Human Anatomy and Physiology, and Introduction to Cartography and GIS (geographic information systems).[9] Having such a variety in electives limits the impact on any single department and will make scheduling the minor easier to facilitate.

Most interdisciplinary minors at Monmouth College have some sort of capstone experience. In many cases these are courses designed to facilitate assessment of the minor. Though we could see the benefit to that approach, we did not see a sensible way of organizing such a course that could incorporate the array of course combinations possible in investigative forensics. We decided on a different approach, taken by a few minors at the college, to allow students to choose an upper-level capstone experience in consultation with us, as the co-coordinators, and their other faculty. These capstone courses might be internship opportunities at a law office or courthouse, a research paper/project done via independent study, or a course with a topic that draws together several interdisciplinary threads from the minor. As a complement to their major, we ask students to connect material from different disciplines within each of the courses in the minor, as well as across those same courses.

We chose not to have a prescribed set of courses for this minor beyond the required course in forensic science and expect students to tailor the minor to their academic interests, culminating in the capstone experience that is appropriate to their major(s). Keeping the minor low impact in as many respects as possible enabled it to go through the Curriculum Committee remarkably quickly. Including courses from so many departments inadvertently resulted in support from many faculty members, who all share the enrollment concerns of a small college, resulting in a positive faculty vote. Moreover, students are able to enter the minor from any of the courses included, and we hope that a student interested in a single discipline might become intrigued by the methods used in other departments and choose to pursue those in tandem, as a result of the minor. Similarly, we feel that having students grounded in other disciplines taking courses outside their field will make those courses more engaging to teach because of the additional perspectives brought to discussions—a hallmark of liberal arts education.

Learning Objectives and Assessment

Assessment in each course will be at the discretion of the faculty member teaching it, with assignments, papers, projects, and tests that require students to consider multiple disciplines, as already happens in each of the courses included in the minor. We pulled from the related course learning objectives to develop a list of goals for students taking the minor. Investigative forensics students will achieve seven goals:

1 Develop skills of analysis, critical thinking, and problem solving.
2 Consider ways to approach evidence in an unbiased fashion.
3 Learn to use precision in laboratory experiments and how to document findings/results systematically.
4 Expand their understanding of society's responses to crime in relation to the time and place in which crimes occur.
5 Develop oral and written communication abilities in an effort to convey material concisely and effectively.
6 Appreciate the value of collaboration across disciplines to aid in investigations.
7 Gain knowledge about careers, graduate programs, internships, and other opportunities to pursue in fields related to forensic investigation.[10]

We plan to ask questions on course evaluations about the effectiveness of the minor, anticipating that students taking their fifth course in investigative forensics will produce more insightful answers than they did in their first course. In the future, we plan to survey graduates of the program to ascertain not only if they chose a career in a related field but also the ways in which the skills or concepts they learned as an investigative forensics minor are used in their lives.

Once students have determined which course will serve as their capstone experience, we will provide them with a rubric of four assessment criteria for the minor that at least three faculty members will evaluate in their final paper and/or public presentation:

1 Explain the methods used in the study of crime/violence in at least three disciplines.
2 Identify bias in sources and determine the relevance of the evidence to the problem at hand.
3 Analyze the application of concepts learned in courses to real-world examples.
4 Present material effectively in oral or written format to a multidisciplinary audience.[11]

It is assumed that, as co-coordinators of the minor, we will be two of the three faculty assessing the capstones, with the third being a faculty member in the student's major. This makeup will guarantee consistency across disciplines and will enable us to identify any needed adjustments to the minor. To help illustrate the cross-disciplinary advantages of the investigative forensics minor, we will now each describe the pedagogical approaches used in the course we teach within it and how the overlap between them led to the organic development of the minor.

CHEM 102: Forensic Science Taught by Audra Goach

CHEM 102 has been offered as a non-majors science course since fall 2010. The chemistry department at Monmouth College at the time offered a non-majors course in environmental science, and the department thought it would be more relevant to students' interests to offer forensics instead. The course I currently teach was developed after I attended a National Science Foundation Chemical Workshop at Williams College in 2008.[12]

The overall goal of this course is to instill an appreciation for chemistry as a discipline that is related to one's own life. The class has four goals for students to achieve:

1 Understand the science and legality involved in analyzing crime scenes.
2 Master the concepts of chemistry, mostly analytical, organic, and biochemical.
3 Gain quantitative skills.
4 Appreciate the science involved in famous case studies.

With the onset of the investigative forensics minor, I will be adapting these goals to reflect and enhance the interdisciplinary nature of the current assignments in the course.

The course begins with a discussion and lab on the early identification of the area of criminalistics, that of body measurements, or anthropometry.[13] This allows us to do quantitative exercises as well as to discuss historical and literary examples in the field. The students are asked to pair off and then measure the forearm, hand, and torso of their partner and then put their data on the board. We then analyze the data to see if body measurements differ between men and women or within a gender. After this lab, we move into fingerprints as a more accurate way to identify and discriminate between people.[14]

A central premise of this course is that it is not a chemistry course disguised as forensic science. I try to integrate the concepts of chemistry into the discussion of forensic science, but there are a few weeks where it may seem to the students that we are only doing "pure" chemistry. To help with this, I have the students write papers throughout the semester in which they research different aspects of forensic science and their relation to various course topics. I also periodically assign articles from newspapers and magazines such as *Discover* and *ChemMatters*, which address topics we are discussing in class.[15] I truly believe in the concept of communication across the curriculum and that writing and speaking are important in all classes.

In the spring of 2018, I utilized the *Innocence Project* web page to discuss with the students real-life forensic science cases in which innocent people were sent to jail.[16] We have also on occasion had a Skype session with a Monmouth College alumnus and Texas State Crime Lab scientist. When Forensic Science and Violence in Victorian Britain were taught in the same semester, we made this a joint Skype session of both groups of students. Labs are also a large portion of the course grade. It is in the lab that students learn about "fake news." They learn that data do not come as easily as shown in crime shows and that it is not easy to lift fingerprints. It is also in the lab that they learn collaboration, a skill that is important in all academic fields.

One of the assignments that the students do in CHEM 102 that I believe ties the entire semester together is the group case study presentation. The students are put in groups of five and asked to research a famous case with the ultimate goal being a final presentation involving their critical analysis of the forensic methods used. Halfway through the semester, each group creates a PowerPoint presentation that includes the history of their case, along with their own investigation of the evidence. The students present what was discovered by authorities and what analysis they would do differently today if the case were reopened. In particular, we ask what new instrumental techniques could be used to analyze evidence that was not available previously. This project offers the students a chance to reflect on what they learned throughout the course and how chemistry and the law apply to forensic science. In order to understand the science involved in the crime scenes and case studies and the instrumental analysis used, the students need to master concepts of chemistry.

At the end of the semester, students analyze a crime scene and then present their findings as a class. The professor, lab teaching assistants, and lab manager, Steve Distin, fashion a crime scene in Monmouth's Center for Science and Business and act out a scenario of the crime. The students then process it by sketching, photographing, packing evidence, lifting fingerprints, analyzing evidence, interviewing suspects and witnesses, and taking suspects' fingerprints. They work as a class to analyze the crime scene and then present their findings on a specific aspect of the case. If a student chose the photography course in the art department to count toward the investigative forensics minor then that student can apply those skills to photographing the crime scene. Or, conversely, after photographing the crime scene, the students may appreciate the need to take digital photography to improve their skills.

Students feel challenged by this course but also recognize that they learn a great deal in terms of the field of forensic science and criminalistics in general.

Three students from the twenty-seven-student class in the spring 2018 semester have already decided to become investigative forensics minors. The students' majors include biochemistry, business, accounting, and computer science, illustrating the appeal of the subject across disciplinary lines.

HIST 230: Violence in Victorian Britain
Taught by Christine Myers

My course on the Victorian era is crucial to include as part of the investigative forensics minor because it is the period when forensics began to find a place in legal proceedings. Public interest in crime was also enhanced by an increased availability of publications, making the 1800s a time of rich and debatable course material for young adults. The moral questions raised can be easily related to twenty-first-century situations, and the textbook I have chosen is perfectly in line with this pedagogical aim. *Criminal Conversations: Victorian Crimes, Social Panic, and Moral Outrage*, edited by Judith Rowbotham and Kim Stevenson, features chapters from economic, legal, police, religious, and social historians, as well as those who specialize in crime history itself.[17]

In the expanded, full-credit version of the course in the fall of 2017 I added a second textbook, *The Dynamiters: Irish Nationalism and Political Violence in the Wider World, 1867–1900* by Niall Whelehan.[18] This book provided greater depth of analysis on a single form of violence than the chapters in *Criminal Conversations* or journal articles can, plus it showed the interconnectedness of crimes in the United Kingdom with political movements on the European continent and in the United States. As a special, interdisciplinary activity I invited chemistry professor Bradley Sturgeon and lab manager Steve Distin to visit the class to teach the students more about the development of explosives and demonstrate some of the basic science that would have been available to Irish nationalists in the nineteenth century.

The third iteration of the course will shift the focus, and interdisciplinary possibilities, by replacing *The Dynamiters* with *Violent Victorians: Popular Entertainment in Nineteenth-Century London* by Rosalind Crone.[19] The choice of violent entertainment as a new concentration is also due to the fact that Monmouth's theater department will be producing *Oliver!* as their spring musical. A flexible syllabus means that collaboration with theater faculty, made even easier in the small college setting, can draw in an additional element to the investigative forensics minor that might not normally be possible.

As the course has always been interdisciplinary, I anticipate no need to change it to fit the new minor. Each day I provide students with handouts to keep their notes organized. This method is especially helpful when I have students from a number of majors who do not always ask the same questions of reading that we do in history: Who is the author and what is their background? What is the chapter's thesis? What types of evidence are used to prove the thesis? These are followed by key vocabulary and a concluding question: What would you say is the most important conclusion from this chapter you should keep in mind moving forward? On different days I focus more on different aspects of the handout. Sometimes I might spend ten to fifteen minutes on a single term, if I think it warrants extended description ("eugenicist" and "phrenology" have been two such terms).

The highlight for several students in the 2016 and 2017 version of the course was the Skype session we had with Professor Ann McClellan, then chair of the English department at Plymouth State University in New Hampshire. We discussed the book she was writing on Sherlock Holmes fandom, having done research on fans from Conan Doyle's time to the present.[20] In 2017 we were also able to Skype with Professor Anne-Marie Kilday, a historian of crime at Oxford Brookes University in England, about her ongoing research on women and crime, the collections she has edited, and her own course, Jack the Ripper and the Victorian Underworld.[21] Because Violence in Victorian Britain also counts toward Monmouth's women's studies minor, having the chance to speak with other female scholars provides students with perspectives about the importance of gendered analysis and how that impacts society's views of crime and criminals.

Student feedback on Violence in Victorian Britain reinforced why I chose to teach the course initially and why it is a valuable element in the investigative forensics minor. When asked if I "effectively challenged [the students] to think and learn" one student said, "Prof. Myers always asked us to relate the history to current events today, something that is useful and thought provoking." And in talking about what they found most memorable about the course, another student commented, "[I] learned a lot from relating the Victorian attitude toward violence and criminals with the attitude we have toward violence and criminals today." These connections are what will truly impact the students as they proceed through life, even if they forget facts or definitions of vocabulary terms, so I consider these comments evidence of an effective course.

Future Plans for Expansion and Collaboration

Unfortunately, the society we live in is one that will continually need forensic investigation, making the minor viable for the foreseeable future. Alumni from Monmouth College have gone on to careers in related fields as forensic engineers, forensic scientists, police officers, and public defenders. One even owns a forensic accounting firm. In the future, we plan to tap these alumni connections to help us promote the possibilities of the minor. Just as we believe more students will consider pursuing such career paths if exposed to them during their time as undergraduates, we are hopeful that these alumni will be excited by the minor and support it, whether through offering internship opportunities or with financial contributions, in the years to come. To encourage connections with our alumni, we have a wish list of future courses that we would like added to the minor when faculty have time to teach them. These include computer forensics, handwriting analysis, the history of art forgeries, and nuclear forensics, to name a few.

While we wait for the resources needed to add new staff and courses, we will continue to function within our existing structure and expand the collaboration between disciplines that will raise the profile of the minor—a modus operandi with which many small college and university faculty will be familiar. In the fall of 2018 students taking Nineteenth-Century Mystery and Violence in Victorian Britain will have the chance to speak with Professor McClellan in person when she visits campus in October to speak about her new research on race and Sherlock Holmes. Her campus-wide talk will be the first event sponsored by the investigative forensics minor, along with the departments of English and history. Such collaborations will help recruit more students to all of the courses in investigative forensics.

Another new endeavor is a course we are creating for travel to England and Scotland in May 2019 to study Chemistry, Codes, and Crimes in Britain. The faculty are Audra Goach and Laura Moore from the chemistry department, Christine Myers from the history department, along with an emeritus faculty member of computer science, Professor Marta Tucker. Centerpieces of the trip include a tour of Jack the Ripper sites in London and an excursion to Bletchley Park where the British centered their code-breaking efforts during World War II. The chance to see numerous museum collections will also reinforce and expand students' understanding of the techniques of investigative forensics about which they have learned in their courses on campus. And, since the travel course will not be limited to students who have declared the minor, we anticipate that the others who join us will be inspired to take more courses in the minor upon their return to Monmouth. If this first trip goes well, we feel travel could become a valuable and exciting component of the minor that will keep it in the forefront of people's minds in a way that traditional on-campus courses may not.

Conclusion

The investigative forensics minor at Monmouth College was brought to our Curriculum Committee a month after we started putting it together, then approved by the faculty in December 2017, and was in place for the first time for the 2018–2019 academic year. Subsequently, true assessment of the minor is not practical at this point, but we can draw some conclusions about how it is structured based on the courses already being taught and the skills developed in these courses. Because the minor was not created as the response to a specific need, or as an attachment to a specific department or major, it was able to evolve quickly and will remain flexible in the future.

For the time being, we want to leave the course order fluid to allow students to add the minor at any point in their college career and to have an organically derived, diverse group of students in the required course (CHEM 102) at any time, thereby allowing for rich discussion of topics. The beauty of this minor at a liberal arts institution is that it shows students (no matter the order of the courses) that various disciplines connect on newsworthy, often controversial, topics in our world.

Notes

1   Robert H. Gault, "On the Teaching of Criminology in Colleges and Universities (Report of the Committee of the Institute)," *Journal of the American Institute of Criminal Law and Criminology* 9, no. 3 (November 1918): 354.

2   Gault, 355, 356.

3   University of Wisconsin–Platteville, Academic Catalogs 2017–18, Forensic Investigation Minor, accessed August 19, 2018, http://catalog.uwplatt.edu/undergraduate /liberal-arts-education/criminal-justice/forensic-investigation-minor/.

4   Data provided by the College Board and supplied to us by our vice president for Enrollment Management and Communications on November 7, 2017.

5   Monmouth College, "Mission Statement," accessed July 8, 2018, https://ou .monmouthcollege.edu/about/mission-statement.aspx.

6   Monmouth College, "Mission Statement."

7   Monmouth College, *Monmouth College Academic Catalog 2018–2019*, 180, accessed July 8, 2018, https://ou.monmouthcollege.edu/_resources/pdf/academics /advising/catalog-2018-2019.pdf.

8   Monmouth College, 113.

9   Monmouth College, 114.

10 Monmouth College, 113.

11 Christine Myers and Audra Sostarecz, New Minor Proposal Form: Investigative Forensics, November 28, 2017.

12 "NSF Grant Establishes Workshops in Novel Topics and Innovative Ways to Teach Chemistry," Williams, Office of Communications, News Release, June 7, 2001, https://communications.williams.edu/news-releases/nsf-grant-establishes -workshops-in-novel-topics-and-innovative-ways-to-teach-chemistry/.

13 James E. Girard, *Criminalistics: Forensic Science, Crime, and Terrorism* (Burlington, MA: Jones & Bartlett Learning, 2018), 115.

14 Girard, 116–124.

15 *Discover*, http://discovermagazine.com/; *ChemMatters: Demystifying Everyday Chemistry* accessed July 23, 2018, https://www.acs.org/content/acs/en/education /resources/highschool/chemmatters.html.

16 Innocence Project, "The Cases & Exoneree Profiles," accessed July 23, 2018, https://www.innocenceproject.org/cases/.

17 Judith Rowbotham and Kim Stevenson, eds., *Criminal Conversations: Victorian Crimes, Social Panic, and Moral Outrage* (Columbus: Ohio State University Press, 2005). See also HIST 230: Violence in Victorian Britain, accessed July 8, 2018, http://cdmyers.info/VictorianViolence.html.

18 Niall Whelehan, *The Dynamiters: Irish Nationalism and Political Violence in the Wider World, 1867–1900* (Cambridge: Cambridge University Press, 2012). See also HIST 230: Violence in Victorian Britain, accessed July 8, 2018, http://cdmyers .info/VictorianViolence2017.html.

19 Rosalind Crone, *Violent Victorians: Popular Entertainment in Nineteenth-Century London* (Manchester: Manchester University Press, 2012). See also HIST 230: Violence in Victorian Britain, accessed July 8, 2018, http://cdmyers.info /VictorianViolence2018.html.

20 Ann K. McClellan, *Sherlock's World: Fan Fiction and the Reimagining of BBC's Sherlock* (Iowa City: University of Iowa Press, 2018).

21 Oxford Brookes University, School of History, Philosophy and Culture, "History of Crime: Professor Anne-Marie Kilday," accessed July 8, 2018, https://www .brookes.ac.uk/hpc/research/history-of-crime/?wid=&op=full&uid=7797.

10

Creating a "Space of Appearance" through the Rollins Foundations in the Liberal Arts Program

•••••••••••••••••••••

HILARY COOPERMAN

In her treatise on the human capacity for action and society's need for plural-ity, political theorist Hannah Arendt argues that the Greek *polis* was created in order to allow a place and forum for ordinary people to distinguish themselves and to be remembered not only for what they produced but for the intangible qualities that move, influence, and persuade: those qualities that distinguish us and define what makes each individual uniquely human. She writes, "[The *polis*] assures the mortal actor that his passing existence and fleeting greatness will never lack the reality that comes from being seen, being heard, and, gener-ally, appearing before an audience of fellow men."[1] The *polis* allowed for the emergence of what Arendt calls "the space of appearance," where the "sharing of words and deeds" constitutes the political sphere and contributes to a sense of a collective and interdependent reality.[2] This idyllic notion is perhaps one of the greatest potentialities of liberal education. However, discursively, its gran-deur is often reduced to conversations about creating campus community or a shared culture. While these activities are important endeavors, they do not capture or reflect the totality of the "space of appearance." In this chapter, I hope to show ways in which the Rollins Foundations in the Liberal Arts (rFLA) program at Rollins College cultivates a "space of appearance" for both faculty and students. Though still in its relative infancy, the greatest potential of the program, beyond its innovative courses and content, lies in its embodied engagement and the creation of a campus-wide endeavor that affords an opportunity to see and hear one another and to act boldly with recognition and accountability.

The following discussion sets out to describe the rFLA program in its inception, development, and current reality. The focus will be on the embodied practice of interdisciplinary education: the way in which bodies come together to create, implement, and assess it, and the pedagogical ramifications of these practices. It will focus on the way the rFLA program creates a "space of appearance" for both faculty and students, and finally will discuss the ways in which a college-wide event, the Foundations Summit, provokes and demands coursework that asks students to speak and act among their peers and to engage with them in discourse around contemporary global issues. This chapter will also gesture toward structural realities within a small liberal arts college setting that are more conducive to the practice of interdisciplinarity when compared to larger research-based institutions. Further, it alludes to the ways in which interdisciplinary education is well served by principles and values small liberal arts colleges wish to foster.

Origins of the Rollins Foundations in the Liberal Arts Program

Rollins College is a small, private liberal arts college with nearly 2,600 undergraduate students. About 550 graduate students, earning degrees from either the Rollins Crummer School of Business or the Hamilton Holt School, are also enrolled.[3] The college is located in central Florida. Over the years, Rollins's faculty struggled with leadership that clearly saw the pendulum swinging toward professional degrees, MOOCs (massive open online courses), and other distance learning offerings, and away from liberal education. This leadership, headed by former Rollins president Lewis Duncan (2004–2014), capitalized on the market's direction, investing its financial and human resources in its business offerings and unilaterally creating the College of Professional Studies.[4] However, in 2015 the college hired a new president, Dr. Grant Cornwell, a philosopher and strong advocate of liberal education. Under his direction, the college refocused and renewed its commitment to a broad-based, civically engaged mission. President Cornwell's hiring occurred the same year as the rollout of a new interdisciplinary and innovative general education program, requiring the input and participation of all departments housed in the College of Liberal Arts. The newly designed rFLA program received widespread support, and in an Arts and Sciences faculty meeting in March 2012, those present voted 59 to 23 to endorse it.[5] Adding to its appeal was the generous support the program received through a three-year Mellon Foundation grant that in part provided training, resources, and course releases in the first year of the program and stipends in the two years following the first year.[6]

The rFLA curriculum replaced what Rollins faculty not-so-lovingly referred to as "the alphabet soup" model, whereby each subject area was associated with a letter, such as "L" for Literature, "S" for Contemporary American Society, "V" for Values, and so on. Students worked their way through the alphabet to eventually complete a sufficient number of courses to satisfy the program's requirements. Whereas the prior curriculum was geared toward broad exposure to many subject areas across the arts and sciences, the new program focuses on skills-based competency through mastery of learning goals rooted in the Association of American Colleges and Universities' LEAP learning outcomes.[7] Skills such as critical thinking, integrative learning, information literacy, and written communication are tied to course levels, ensuring that students achieve proficiency in these areas by the completion of their 300-level capstone course.

For the most part, faculty were optimistic and enthusiastic about developing an interdisciplinary program. In part, this was because many of the faculty were already well-versed in interdisciplinary methods and practices and believed in their value. As Dr. Peggy Maki, an external evaluator for the rFLA pilot program noted in 2011, "If ever there were faculty who are prepared to develop an interdisciplinary GE core, those faculty exist at Rollins. Vita after vita I read reinforced how interdisciplinary faculty are in their research and publications and ways of thinking that led to the design of the RP.[8] It is unusual for me to see these kinds of vitae as the 'typical' background of faculty who become involved in developing an interdisciplinary curriculum."[9] Yet, even for faculty with the experience, ability, and desire to do so, the process of creating an interdisciplinary program was not without difficulties.

One of the early dilemmas was how to organize courses into themed neighborhoods that would eventually cultivate communities of learners.[10] The difficulty lay in finding broad enough categories to comprise a range of courses while providing enough cohesiveness and distinction to be meaningful to students as a grouping.[11] Eventually, the faculty settled on four themes: (1) Mysteries and Marvels; (2) Where Cultures Collide; (3) Identities, Mirrors, and Windows; and (4) Innovate, Create, Elevate.[12]

The way these themes work in practice is that during fall semester of freshman year, students select a "neighborhood" and begin to take courses in their neighborhood in the spring semester of their freshman year. In addition to groupings by themed neighborhoods, courses are developmental, beginning with a 100-level course and ending with the 300-level capstone. rFLA courses also align with divisional goals. For example, students need to take at least one course from each of the Southern Association of Colleges and Schools divisional requirements; humanities, social sciences, physical sciences, and expressive arts.[13] Students take courses in one division twice, for a total of five rFLA seminars. Though the classes have a divisional focus, they must stay true to the interdisciplinary aims of the program and demonstrate through curriculum and pedagogy the interrelationship between disciplines.

How rFLA Creates a "Space of Appearance" for Faculty

According to Rollins faculty, one of the greatest benefits of rFLA is the opportunity to meet one another and gather regularly to share knowledge and pedagogical practices. This type of college-wide, cross-disciplinary knowledge sharing and exchange did not occur formally prior to the rFLA program. From colloquia to intimate neighborhood meetings where we discuss teaching strategies and examples of successful assignments, these forums have greatly enriched our feeling of cohesiveness and community and improved the quality of our teaching and offerings to students. In these forums, individual personalities, research methodologies, shared interests, and ways of approaching problems create strong affinities and alliances among faculty from disparate disciplines. In some cases, these alliances forge the beginning of cotaught rFLA courses, as in the case of What Is Reality?, a 300-level course created by Robert Miller, a theater professor, and Dr. Christopher Fuse, a physics professor. In other cases, gathering together allows us to better understand our colleagues and their fields of expertise in order to create other opportunities and programming unrelated to rFLA.

Another important feature of faculty forums is the opportunity for everyone to participate and express opinions. Particularly for adjuncts and new professors, rFLA provides a collaborative environment to present ideas and become recognized for one's individuality, knowledge, and expertise. Chances to lead subcommittees dealing with specialized areas of rFLA are plentiful, such as planning neighborhood events and conceiving of the 300-level capstone project, and therefore junior faculty are typically selected to fill those important roles. Lastly, part of what contributes to equitable and democratic participation is the acknowledgement on the part of senior faculty that junior faculty hold fresh perspectives that are critical to forming a new, sustainable vision for the program.

How rFLA Creates a "Space of Appearance" for Students

At Rollins, students select their rFLA courses from a broad range of topics. Faculty compete for students and enrollments the way they would for courses in their own discipline. Faculty must think about what appeals to students and what will pique their curiosity and fulfill expectations about what they hope to gain from their college education. Keeping this in mind, faculty create exciting, vibrant, contemporary titles for courses that perhaps speak more to student interest than formal and general ones. For example, a course I teach in the rFLA program is called Rap and Revolution in the Middle East, but on students' transcripts the course title is Performance and Culture of the Middle East. Other student-oriented course titles include The Science of Superheroes; Dog Is Love: The Science of Human–Animal Interactions; Sing Your Heart Out; The Future, What Does It Hold for Us?; Fake News and Critical Thinking; Art Gone Bad; and Shakespeare's A.R.S.E. (Ageism, Racism, Sexism Explored).

The need to interest students has influenced both pedagogical and epistemological choices in terms of not only what students learn but how they learn it. Because courses are created incorporating a contemporary consciousness, a multitude of opportunities affording practical engagement are opened up to faculty and students. Students are able to draw from a broad spectrum of embodied and material pedagogical methods. For example, a class called Conceptual Documentary Practice, taught by art professor Dawn Roe, incorporates a photo documentary project in Hannibal Square to study the impacts of gentrification on a historically African-American neighborhood. In my course Refugees of the Middle East Performance Lab, students create a performance about Syrian refugee experiences. They perform for an audience of their peers and professors and then engage the audience in a discussion about the work. Thus, they deepen their abilities to communicate and reflect with others, and to extend and build on their knowledge.

The Synergy between rFLA and a Small Liberal Arts College

While rFLA has always been an important college-wide endeavor, I don't think anyone expected it to become a pivotal catalyst for change, a tangible platform for shaping, envisioning, and fostering the direction of liberal education at Rollins. I believe our ability to craft a compelling and impactful program has much to do with both the structural realities of our small college setting and culture but also its philosophy: a belief in a centralized, core Rollins experience in which all faculty and students should be able to partake and benefit. It is important to consider that in many ways, a shared collegiate, interdisciplinary experience is almost antithetical to the goals and aims of large research institutions. The teaching goals and learning outcomes of a centralized model lie in opposition to the decentralized model of education based on departmental autonomy. While larger institutions provide both interdisciplinary offerings and general education programs, typically they exist while maintaining separation and isolation from other disciplines and departments. Ironically, interdisciplinary departments such as Middle East Studies, Gender Studies, and American Studies function similarly in practice to other disciplines, in that they are typically housed in their own building and hire their own faculty. It is the content which is interdisciplinary, rather than the practice of intermingling, coming together and sharing in a collaborative experience.

Additionally, interdisciplinary education, while making inroads in university settings, in some ways goes against deeply ingrained hierarchies, tenure structures, claims of authority over bodies of knowledge, and autonomous research and teaching practices, all of which make these institutions attractive to students who wish to specialize in and conduct research in a particular field. It becomes problematic then, within these environments, to introduce a more egalitarian, communal form of education where professors act to facilitate students' production of knowledge in the classroom, rather than predominantly espousing their own. Lastly, with its already small class sizes and discussion-based courses, Rollins offers the appropriate structural requirements and framework for a more intimate, hands-on curriculum.

The Foundations Summit: Creating a Space for the "Space of Appearance"

The importance of a public forum and shared space where people appear to one another in order to be acknowledged and recognized becomes ever more important in today's society, where social media and virtual presence oftentimes outweigh opportunities to be present. It is as performance theorist D. Soyini Madison describes when she writes, "Entering a public sphere enlivens scrutiny, enlarges responsibility, and cracks open into plain sight hidden wrongs. It is said that a dimension of our humanity emerges only when we engage in public discourse."[14] In combining disciplines, much more than content comes together. Through Rollins's interdisciplinary offering, the "inter" of interdisciplinary becomes a call to action, a radical call to praxis. Students and faculty alike are asked to put their bodies on the line, more than just their words, activating a sense of vulnerability and shared responsibility to one another. By engaging in knowledge creation and expression alongside our students and faculty from other departments and disciplines, we must stretch outside areas of comfort to become better and stronger collaborators and public citizens.

The cornerstone of the rFLA program is a consciously and intentionally designed public forum, the Foundations Summit, where the presentation of the 300-level capstone project takes place in the final week of classes each semester. It is this final capstone project and public presentation that drives much of the content and pedagogy of a 300-level course, and, to a large degree, that establishes the outward-facing orientation and practice-based learning of the program in totality. This is due to three important components of the capstone project. First, it usually deals with a global issue or problem that is political in nature. Second, it typically requires what Paul Carter calls "material thinking," the use of found objects and artistic processes to express and create knowledge.[15] Lastly, the projects are presented publicly for the campus, requiring students to face their peers and speak and perform with knowledge and integrity about their topics. Faculty, staff, and students are asked to move among displays and engage presenters in discussions about their work. In the section that follows, I will provide an example using one of my courses to demonstrate the way in which the goal of public presentation and discourse drives the praxis of interdisciplinarity and why this matters.

The Practice of Interdisciplinarity in the Classroom

The campus-wide Foundations Summit requires the production of an object or "artifact," which oftentimes necessitates the use of material objects to fashion, create, or produce a visible sign of what was learned and accomplished. In the past, projects have ranged from poster sessions to performances, photography and art exhibits, and student-created comic books.

For my Refugees of the Middle East Performance Lab course, our capstone project has always been a public performance. Therefore, throughout the course, students are asked to think about the Syrian refugee crisis, using performance as a form of embodied research as well as social critique and activism.

The course content is drawn from migration studies, Middle East studies, visual studies, history, cultural theory, critical race theory, and ethnography. From day one, I ask students to dig deep and to think about epistemology, opening up course material for analysis and critique. We read and discuss a host of textual and visual material and perform monologues from books, create imagistic and gestural performance pieces, and video collages responding in and through our bodies to what we are absorbing through the objects of our study. In this phase of the course, we are actively engaged in what playwright Tina Landau calls *Source Work*, "a series of activities done at the beginning of the rehearsal process to get in touch—both intellectually and emotionally, both individually and collectively—with 'the source' from which you are working."[16] Once students complete this work, they better understand the factual basis of the Syrian refugee crisis, but, perhaps more importantly, they develop an embodied, affective understanding of the refugee as human being.

Though I have taught the course six times, each final performance for the Summit has been vastly different, reflecting the diverse interests and experiences of each class. One cohort created a performance piece about the journey refugees make from Syria to refugee camps, primarily using found objects, such as fabric, cardboard, and plastics. They used the objects to visually depict how quickly one's home (made of cardboard and fabric in our representation) could vanish and how quickly the notion of home is forced to adapt to new places and people in order to survive. Another group chose to play a series of games with the audience—games that were metaphors for how refugees are treated. The games were played in a refugee camp, created by fabric hanging from clotheslines on ropes, on which were written quotations by refugees about their hardships that brought out the meaning of the metaphorical games. Hot Potato signified the refugee passed from one country to another, as the potato passed from person to person, too hot, unwanted, untouchable. In another game, Musical Chairs, the audience marched around the chairs, but each time the music stopped, someone was excluded from the game. This of course signified refugees who were not allowed into countries or afforded opportunities and, in many cases, even died.

Another example of a performance was the adaptation of books dealing with the Syrian civil war and the plight of refugees. One group read an ethnography by Wendy Pearlman, *We Crossed a Bridge and It Trembled*.[17] They chose to reenact a young girl's story from the book in which she gradually begins to starve. They portrayed the young girl asking her mother to get some food at the store. The girl desires peanut butter for her sandwich, but her mother tells her peanut butter is no longer available. Over time, the family runs out of food, and they are forced to eat grass before they ultimately flee the country. One member of the performing group filmed a montage of skillfully rendered pencil drawings of her own lips and eyes interspersed between images of photographs of her family. She incorporated her video in the performance, using it as a backdrop to a dance she choreographed to the ebb and flow of the narrator's emotional state.

The story was painful yet poignant, but what caught my attention was the integration of the student performers' personal experiences: photos of family members, personal sketches of facial features, and peanut butter. These things were not in the factual accounts we read. As they rehearsed and embodied the story, the students brought their own particularities and distinctive experiences to the material. Typically, students studying the Syrian civil war might feel empathy and even identify on some level with the tragedy of those suffering in its wake. However, to begin to suture one's own memories and experiences with those of others requires a profound level of identification with, and immersion into, the experiences and thoughts of someone else.

This attests to the important role the body plays in processing disparate experiences and knowledge. Learning in and with the body and other bodies engaged in shared experience is very different than sitting at a desk listening to lectures and reading texts. When students are allowed to bring disparate objects, experiences, and methodologies together, knowledge is no longer opaque or a finite body of work. Students become part of the knowledge creation process, and it no longer stands apart and away from them. Their bodies become involved in a performative process of arranging, applying, rearranging, collaborating, and engaging. Education becomes active rather than passive, and students continuously work toward the making of meaning for themselves and others. Ultimately, the practice of interdisciplinarity offers students a place to appear and to be recognized in the classroom as a producer of knowledge as well as its receiver. It allows them to be visible among others and to learn to enact and speak that which is deeply meaningful to them.

Conclusion

The practice of interdisciplinarity affords the opportunity to engage in an open and inclusive educational process, inviting many bodies, not only specialists, into the process of knowledge creation. Whether planning a community event, thinking about how to create an interdisciplinary course together, or collaborating on a new interdisciplinary curriculum, these actions cannot be performed in isolation. Interdisciplinary education in practice requires undoing and unbinding the carefully codified organization of territorial assumptions of mastery. "Inter" disciplinarity requires that bodies come together and think, rethink, take apart, put back together, and move knowledge, in the intervals of disciplines, in the interstices of knowledge, at the margins and limits of imagination.

The interdisciplinary classroom, "neighborhoods," and the Foundations Summit offer spaces of connection on campus, for those who care to connect and engage in meaningful conversations about contemporary and global issues and how they relate to our everyday lives. It allows a space where liberal education may be practiced through public discourse, through gathering together to speak, to be heard, and also to listen in and among others. rFLA refutes the idea that general education should be just that, general, not particular, but broad and unrelatable, hidden in the private exchange of term papers and bound in impenetrable canonical texts, written decades ago.

To be sure, what began as an experiment in a different and more impactful general education program is quickly becoming, one could argue, the heart and muscle of the college itself. In part, this was due to logistical needs. But more so, rFLA provided a forum and opportunity for Rollins faculty, a new college president, and new hires to begin to reenvision what pedagogy and practice should look like in the twenty-first-century. It would be an exaggeration to say that the rFLA program allowed us to redefine education at Rollins or even that most faculty are entirely happy with the rFLA program. But what it did do, perhaps unintentionally, is bring people with shared goals and pedagogical desires into a room to speak together about what liberal education is, why interdisciplinary education is vital today, and what interdisciplinary education can achieve in a small college setting. rFLA continues to allow us a voice, a vote, creativity, a community, but most of all, a "space of appearance" to practice plurality, public participation, and engagement, and to play a role in the time in which we live.

Notes

1 Hannah Arendt, *The Human Condition*, 2nd ed. (Chicago: University of Chicago Press, 1958; repr. 1998), 198.
2 Arendt, 198–199, 198.
3 Rollins College Facts and Figures, 2018–19 enrollment, https://www.rollins.edu /about-rollins/at-a-glance/facts figures.html.
4 Jack Stripling, "Behind Rollins College Chief's Battle, a Broader Liberal-Arts Debate," *The Chronicle of Higher Education*, March 28, 2013, https://www.chronicle .com/article/Behind-Rollins-College-Chiefs/138173.
5 Arts and Sciences Faculty, "Minutes, Arts and Sciences Faculty Meeting, Thursday, March 22, 2012," http://scholarship.rollins.edu/as_fac/12.
6 Interview with Emily Russell, associate dean of curriculum, Rollins College, August 9, 2018.
7 This acronym stands for Liberal Education and America's Promise. The full list of LEAP learning outcomes may be found at https://www.aacu.org/leap/essential -learning-outcomes.
8 The acronym RP stands for the Rollins Plan, which was the rFLA pilot program attempted in fall 2009. It lasted until late 2010, when it was overhauled and reenvisioned as the rFLA program. Emily Kelly, "Welcome to the 'Neighbor-hood,'" *The Sandspur*, Sept. 27, 2012, https://stars.library.ucf.edu/cfm-sandspur /1956/.
9 Peggy Maki, "External Evaluation of the Rollins Plan Pilot Curriculum," internal document, November 30, 2011, 6.
10 Maki, 4. Maki's report mentions ten criteria for high-impact learning drawn from George Kuh, *High Impact Educational Practices: What They Are, Who has Access to Them and Why They Matter* (Washington, D.C.: AAC&U, 2008). One of those criteria is the creation of a learning community.
11 Interview with Emily Russell, associate dean of curriculum, Rollins College, August 9, 2018.
12 At the end of 2018, Rollins faculty voted to do away with the neighborhood system altogether and move to an "open borders" policy, giving students the ability to choose from all interdisciplinary courses offered as long as they completed one course from each of the four divisions. Within the open border policy, courses are still "tagged" with a thematic area. The newly created themes are Innovation, Environments, Enduring Questions, Identities, and Cultural Collision.
13 The Southern Association of Colleges and Schools has only three divisional requirements that must be encompassed in a general education program: humani-ties/fine arts, social/behavioral sciences, and natural science/mathematics, as stated in "The Principles of Accreditation: Foundations for Quality Enhance-ment," 6th ed., December 2017, 22, https://sacscoc.org/app/uploads/2019/08 /2018PrinciplesOfAcreditation.pdf. Rollins has separated humanities from expressive arts, the latter of which includes fine and performing arts. In addition, Rollins also requires competencies in foreign language, mathematical thinking,

ethical reasoning, and health and wellness. These competencies must be completed before taking the 300-level capstone course in the junior or senior year.

14   D. Soyini Madison, *Acts of Activism: Human Rights and Radical Performance* (Cambridge: Cambridge University Press, 2010), 6.

15   Paul Carter, *Material Thinking: The Theory and Practice of Creative Research* (Melbourne, Australia: Melbourne University Press, 2004).

16   Tina Landau, "Theories in Practice," in *Anne Bogart: Viewpoints*, ed. Joel A. Smith and Michael Bigelow Dixon (Hanover, NH: Smith and Kraus, 1995), 17.

17   Wendy Pearlman, *We Crossed a Bridge and It Trembled: Voices from Syria* (New York: Custom House–HarperCollins, 2017).

11

Flipping the Humanities Back into Mathematics

● ●

WINSTON OU

The Core

Scripps College's signature program, the Core Curriculum in Interdisciplinary Humanities, is a three-semester sequence taken by all first-year students.[1] In the first semester (Core I), the first-year class is exposed in multiple disciplines to the process by which one becomes aware of contradictions and inconsistencies inherent in one's own framework of values. The course is taught by a team of twelve to fourteen professors in fields ranging from history to biology to dance: in the course of the term, each professor gives one or two lectures to the entire first-year class on a subject linking to a general theme (decided by the participants; recent themes have included structural violence and community) under the Foucaultian rubric Histories of the Present and leads discussions on the lectures and readings for a group of students.[2] Core II courses each have unique topics developed by pairs of faculty members; they were envisioned as opportunities for students to observe the process through which professors from different disciplines engage in civil discourse to explore a single subject in depth. In the third-semester (Core III) classes, students under the guidance of a single faculty member examine a single topic in an interdisciplinary manner, attempt to find some unobserved inconsistency or contradiction in that subject themselves, and then execute a self-designed project that addresses or redresses one or more of those inconsistencies. That is, we heighten the students' awareness, we show them how to engage in civilized revolution, and then we let them act.

Core I: Culture, Knowledge, and Representation

I participated in Core I in 2007 and 2008; at the time, the broad theme was Culture, Knowledge, and Representation, and our goals were partially to make students sensitive to presuppositions in their systems of values as well as caution them against oversimplification (i.e., to attune them to the finer shades of nuance). Tony Crowley's lecture, "Human Rights/the Right to Be Human," had, as its assigned readings, the brutal juxtaposition of the United Nations *Universal Declaration of Human Rights* against selections from Mike Davis's *Planet of Slums*. Newton Copp's lecture, "The Legacy of Galileo's Heresy," was based on Galileo's carefully measured reconciliation of his scientific and religious beliefs in his *Letter to the Grand Duchess Christina*. Roswitha Burwick's lecture, "I Love Man as My Fellow; but His Scepter, Real or Usurped, Extends Not to Me," addressed Mary Wollstonecraft's *A Vindication of the Rights of Women*. My own lecture, "Beyond the Borders of Mathmagic Land: A Lecture with A High Probability of Containing Some Little Truth," was on the sometimes-misleading relationship between beauty and truth and how developments in probability and astronomy during the seventeenth and eighteenth centuries came to alter the very notion of truth itself; the accompanying text was the introduction to Laplace's *Philosophical Essay on Probabilities*. Bridging the distance between my own field of mathematics and other areas with effort, I facilitated discussions on the Enlightenment, philosophy (J. S. Mill's *On Liberty* and others), slavery, communism, racism, evolution, human rights, literature, oppression, feminism, and revolution.

Core III: Women, Girls, and Mathematical Superstitions

In 2008 Scripps received a grant from the Mellon Foundation to implement recommendations made during the last septennial external review of the Core program; in particular, funds were provided to encourage faculty to develop new Core II and III courses. In 2010 I began designing a Core III course in five parts to examine the debate regarding women's innate abilities in mathematics, prompted in part by Larry Summers's provocative 2005 summary of the arguments of the time.[3]

To properly evaluate the argument about women's mathematical abilities, one must first answer some simpler questions. First, what is mathematics? As a mathematician, I am aware of the distinction between Mathematics, the activity engaged in by pure mathematicians, and mathematics, the use of by-products of the first activity to accomplish goals outside the realm of Mathematics, analogous to the distinction between smartphone engineering and smartphone use, or the painting of Picasso and that of fences.[4] Most people confuse the latter for the former, or do not even recognize the former's existence. Before together examining the possible existence of a gender gap in Mathematics, I needed to introduce the general Scripps student to the actual, creative field. I thus started the course with multiple presentations of the foundations of numbers and basic arithmetic, ranging from Fields Medalist Timothy Gowers's *Mathematics: A Very Short Introduction*, in which he argues that a mathematician need not be concerned with what numbers are or if they exist, but only with what properties they satisfy—to Henri Poincaré's "On the Nature of Mathematical Reasoning," in which he, in contrast, proves the basic properties of arithmetic via mathematical induction. That is, the first section of the course introduced students to the most fundamental question of mathematics—How do we know that is true?—by showing how differing esteemed mathematicians justify the most basic phenomena.

The second section introduced students to (for most of them) an incomprehensible or even unimaginable topic: how one creates or discovers new mathematics. The primary materials were the NOVA documentary *The Proof*, on Andrew Wiles's 1993 proof of the 350-year-old conjecture known as "Fermat's Last Theorem"; two of Poincaré's essays: first "Intuition and Logic in Mathematics," on his distinction between "geometers" and "analysts," that is, between those mathematicians who think intuitively in a manner that supersedes language and those who possess an intuition for the logically rigorous constructions themselves, and second, his famous "Mathematical Discovery" on the role of the unconscious in delivering, from an infinity of possibilities, the most beautiful and relevant conjectures to the conscious mind; and finally, Field Medalist William Thurston's essay "On Proof and Progress in Mathematics" on the creation, purpose, motivation, underlying mental processes, and communication of mathematics. Through these general presentations, even students with limited mathematical background could get a sense of the mathematical creative process.

The third part of the course examined the difference between mathematical and general knowledge, using J. S. Mill's *On Liberty* as (as it was partially intended) a model for how one defends a position against an entrenched majority opinion, and Kant's "The Discipline of Pure Reason in Its Dogmatic Employment" (from *The Critique of Pure Reason*), on the distinctions between, and ultimately the mutual inapplicability of, mathematical and philosophical methods. Now that the students had some understanding of what mathematics was and how it was created, we examined the distinguishing characteristics of the field itself.

In the fourth section we read sociological and psychological papers regarding the debate on gender-based differences in mathematical ability and positing explanations for the gender gap in mathematical career success: for example, Levy and Kimura's "Women, Men, and the Sciences," on the correlation of prenatal and postnatal hormonal differences with differences in cognitive abilities between the genders; Aronson's "Stereotypes and the Underrepresentation of Women in Math and Science" on "stereotype effect," the measurable reduction in performance that certain minorities seem to experience on being reminded of their membership in a lower-performing group;[5] and Ceci et al.'s massive literature review, which concluded significantly that "much of the explanation for women's underrepresentation in math-intensive fields can be found in the career–family trade off and in a greater preference for . . . 'home-centered' lifestyle (as well in sex differences in career preferences . . .)."[6]

The fifth part of the course examined the teaching of elementary school mathematics in the United States using Liping Ma's seminal *Knowing and Teaching Elementary Mathematics*, on differences in the nature of the understanding of arithmetic between primary school teachers in the United States and China. Ma distinguishes primarily between the procedural understanding of American elementary school teachers and the "profound fundamental understanding" of their Chinese counterparts, the former geared toward accomplishing certain tasks (long division, multidigit multiplication, arithmetic with fractions) by following the appropriate procedures, and the latter demanding that children be able to, like mathematicians, understand and discuss all mathematical concepts in terms of more fundamental concepts.[7] The students, in light of their new understanding of what mathematics really was and the debate regarding gender differences, examined mathematical pedagogy as a possible cause of both the general ignorance regarding mathematics and the comparatively low number of women who enter the field.

As already mentioned, the course culminated in projects in which students attempted to rectify inconsistencies or contradictions that had struck them during the term. One year the class created, based on the theory in Ma's text, a web of interlinked videos on fundamental topics in elementary school mathematics for adults who wanted to understand what they had learned in only a procedural manner in childhood. Another year the class created a massive examination of the system of support for the STEM (science, technology, engineering, and math) fields at our own women's college, taking paper surveys, online polls, and carefully anonymized video interviews of science, engineering, and mathematics students and alumnae, as well as faculty from all fields, to form a complete picture of that system. Ultimately the students held a public forum to present their findings and recommendations to students, alumnae, faculty, and administrators; I also later gave a condensed presentation to the dean of the Keck Science Department (serving Claremont McKenna, Pitzer, and Scripps Colleges) at his request.

In these ways I attempted to incorporate mathematics into the humanities-centric world of Scripps's Core program: by stretching my own boundaries well beyond the field of pure mathematics in which I was trained, to approach the humanists' world, speaking their language as best as I could (more than one student commented on the "long and awkward moments of silence" endemic to mathematicians); it was a challenge for a mathematician unused to discussion, and a significant use of time and energy. I spent over one hundred hours preparing my fifty-minute 2007 Core I lecture; actual participation in the course took at least triple the preparation time of an upper-division mathematics course. Preparation for Core III was equally daunting: outside of Poincaré's writing, which my high school Senior Humanities teacher Jayne Karsten (who, not incidentally, had received a Department of Education grant to unify calculus and poetry) had introduced to me twenty years before, none of the material was familiar ground; Kant's central essay distinguishing philosophical and mathematical knowledge, in particular, was replete with technical terms. Participation also placed logistical strain on our department of three; at the time, each of us taught only one upper-division course per year, on top of four service courses. Yet I enjoyed the intellectual stimulation and community so much that I volunteered to participate in Core I again the following year, and in Core III even when our department was not scheduled to participate. Perhaps in consequence of my passion, in 2018 I was elected the Core director for the 2019–2021 cycle: the tentative theme, Truth.

Resulting Changes in My Teaching

Creating a course that examined gender issues in mathematics involved explaining the field to laypeople from its very foundations, answering questions about its distinct nature in contrast with that of general philosophical knowledge, the psychological processes involved in its creation and communication, the various methods of its teaching, and sociological influences and concerns. Ineluctably, the process of clarifying the answers to these multiangular questions improved my own work as a teacher within my own discipline. Gaining knowledge of sociological trends had straightforward results, for example, becoming aware of female students' greater propensity to deprecate their mathematical abilities (and the related tendency of women to stop taking mathematics courses despite having the same grades as men who continue) prompted me to make female students aware of this trend and to encourage them about their talents. Knowledge of a measured difference in average spatial ability between the genders allowed me to inform female students that though that gap has been scientifically verified, so has its surmountability. Awareness of the degree of the entrenchment of procedure-based mathematical pedagogy in the United States inspired me to bring all my students face to face with their misunderstandings about mathematical knowledge on the first day of class, with the aid of a central text in the Core at the time, J. S. Mill's *On Liberty*.

What Is Knowledge?

Mill, in distinguishing between "dead dogma" and "living truth" (in describing the pursuit of the latter as one of the great benefits of liberty), makes the following fundamental distinction between truth and superstition: "There is a class of persons . . . who think it enough if a person assents undoubtingly to what they think true, though he has no knowledge whatever of the grounds of the opinion, and could not make a tenable defence of it against the most superficial objections. . . . This is not knowing the truth. Truth, thus held, is but one superstition the more, accidentally clinging to the words which enunciate a truth."[8]

That is, knowledge of the truth comprises at a minimum the ability to defend it against objections; without that, one has merely parroted a statement that fortuitously happens to be true. On the first day of each lower level math class (precalculus, calculus, linear algebra), I always begin the material by discussing Mill's quote. I then ask the class if they can state the Pythagorean theorem; the class, tellingly, invariably recites it like a mantra. I then ask if there is anyone who could defend the theorem against a skeptical child who asks, "Why should I believe that?" Typically, not one student is capable of engaging in the basic mathematical action of explaining this fact in terms of more elementary facts. They have taken its truth—and the truth of much of their fundamental knowledge (e.g., the quadratic formula, long division, multidigit multiplication, division of fractions, etc.)—on faith; one student later confessed that she had had a "panic attack" on realizing how much of her knowledge was in fact not knowledge at all. I typically end the first class by charging the students to, henceforth (not only in this class but in all subsequent classes) not accept any knowledge unless they understand its grounds. With that distinction in place, I can start teaching mathematics.

What Should We Teach?

Mill's general distinction between superstition and knowledge, though potent and fundamental, is not related specifically to mathematics. It was selections from the nonmathematical writings of Kant, Poincaré, and Thurston, the first on the distinction between philosophical and mathematical thought, the latter two on the psychological process of mathematical discovery, that most powerfully clarified for me the mental actions involved in the processes of understanding and creating mathematics and fundamentally altered my view of what we as mathematics professors should be teaching.

In "The Discipline of Pure Reason in Its Dogmatic Employment," Kant examines "whether the [mathematical] method of attaining apodeictic certainty . . . is identical with the [dogmatic] method by which we endeavor to obtain the same certainty in philosophy";[9] he concludes that it is not, in part because of irreconcilable differences in the fundamental objects of study. Mathematics, according to Kant, is founded on "apodeictically certain" definitions, whereas philosophy rather abstracts, from "a multiplicity of suitable examples," *probable* definitions. In other words, "mathematical definitions *make* their concepts, in philosophical definitions concepts are only *explained*." He continues to explain that mathematical knowledge is "the knowledge gained by reason from the construction of concepts," where "[t]o *construct* a concept means to exhibit *a priori* the intuition which corresponds to the concept" by mentally associating with the definition a "single object . . . [that expresses] universal validity for all possible intuitions which fall under the same concept."

The points Kant stresses—that mathematics takes its origin from the study of constructs created via the association of intuition with formal definition, and that that association is both critical and delicate: a universally valid intuition cannot include assumptions beyond the scope of the definition or be so general as to dilute meaning—are clear but easily overlooked. Reading Kant made me far more conscious of both the importance of definitions and the need for delicacy in their construction.

On the next-higher level, Poincaré emphasizes the absolute necessity of intuition not just for constructing definitions but also for understanding proofs. In his "Intuition and Logic in Mathematics," Poincaré divides all mathematicians into two groups: "analysts" and "geometers."[10] The former are "above all preoccupied with logic; to read their works, one is tempted to believe they have advanced only step by step. . . . The other sort are guided by intuition and at the first stroke make quick but sometimes precarious conquests." Though he admits that both logic and intuition are "equally necessary for the progress of science," he values more highly the latter: "Without [intuition] young minds could not make a beginning in the understanding of mathematics. . . . If it is useful to the student, it is still more so to the creative scientist."

Poincaré, significantly, excoriates the analytical teacher who

cuts up, so to speak, each demonstration into a very great number of elementary operations; when we have examined these operations one after the other and ascertained that each is correct, are we to think we have grasped the real meaning of the demonstration? Shall we have understood it even when, by an effort of memory, we have become able to repeat this proof by reproducing all these elementary operations in just the order in which the inventor had arranged them? Evidently not. . . . That I know not what, which makes the unity of the demonstration, will completely elude us.

In other words, what constitutes actual mathematical understanding is not merely the ability to remember the steps of a formal argument, but rather to have grasped the intuition that allows one to reconstruct it in its entirety. Since incorporating this psychological insight about understanding mathematics into my teaching, I have found that even students in first-year calculus (with typically limited comprehension of rigorous mathematics) can grasp various essential intuitions successfully and with pride.

On the other side of the coin, the mathematical creative process is for Poincaré also guided by a holistic intuition: one that critically relies on a sense of beauty, and transcends logic and language. He famously describes some his own experiences of mathematical creativity in which after long, seemingly "absolutely fruitless" periods of conscious effort, he obtained answers in moments of "sudden illumination."[11] Poincaré hypothesizes the existence of an unconscious ego that, on the basis of an aesthetic sensibility, selects from the infinitude of possible logical combinations of syllogisms those which have the greatest potential. Tellingly, he describes the constructions that satisfy that sensibility as "those whose elements are harmoniously arranged so that the mind can, without effort, take in the whole without neglecting the details." Further, this aesthetic sensibility transcends language: "The rules which must guide this choice are extremely subtle and delicate, and it is practically impossible to state them in precise language; they must be felt rather than formulated."

This transcendental quality of the mathematical sensibility is described in greater detail much later by Thurston, who describes his experience of entirely distinct "mental facilities"—the linguistic/symbolic, holographic (visual/spatial/kinesthetic), temporal, logical, stimulus-response (pattern recognition), and intuitive, all communicating together to create mathematics.[12] Reminiscent of Poincaré, he remarks that over-specificity of thought obstructs the creation of precise connections: "I put a lot of effort in 'listening' to my intuitions and associations, and building them into metaphors and connections. This involves a kind of simultaneous quieting and focusing of my mind. Words, logic, and detailed pictures rattling around can inhibit intuitions and associations."

What should we teach, as mathematics professors? Thurston bluntly describes a farce: "We go through the motions of saying for the record what we think the students 'ought' to learn, while the students are trying to grapple with the more fundamental issues of learning our language and guessing at our mental models. . . . Professors compensate by giving homework and tests that are much easier than the material 'covered' in the course." What *should* we teach? At the very least, knowledge and not superstition; but to even discuss mathematics at all we must help the students to construct definitions and see their logical implications and relations. Ultimately, we must also pass on the mental models that we have constructed and, ideally, nurture—through exposure to the arts or the underlying patterns in nature and poetry—the sense of beauty that entices the intuition transcending the cautious tread of logic.

Flipping Precalculus into the Humanities

Teaching in the Core enabled me to more deeply understand various aspects of my own field by providing potent metaphors for the processes of mathematical learning and discovery that facilitated transmission of mental models to the students; it also made me aware of our students' capacity for work, thought, and discourse. The extent of those capacities, and the increasing interest at that time in "flipped courses" (in which the students watched lectures at home and came to class for problem sessions and discussion) prompted me to wonder if it might be possible to create a math course that was run like a humanities course, that is, requiring significant preparatory work, and then actively reasoned complex thought and engaged communication in class. Was it possible for students to learn mathematics in the humanities way? I hoped to create an "augmented flipped" course that would be more effective than any traditional lecture-based math class, a discussion-based experience that could not be duplicated by watching any number of videos.

In the 2012–2013 year I was scheduled to teach precalculus in both the fall and spring semesters. I decided to record all thirty-eight lectures in the fall and teach the spring section in the flipped manner. It seemed to me that doing so would not only provide a richer course but would also address the misperception that mathematics was somehow beyond discussion or did not require it. I hoped to open mathematics, for *all* students (at Scripps, precalculus is the most elementary course satisfying the mathematics general education requirement; the students come from all fields), to active investigation through dialogue. What is knowledge, after all, if not the ability to re-create and further develop a topic via discussion? At this point I had not fully formulated my understanding of Kant, Poincaré, and Thurston but was mainly inspired by Ma's convictions that all human beings have a capacity for mathematics and that any concept in mathematics can be reduced to simpler concepts. According to Ma, the average Chinese elementary school student could engage in mathematical discussion; I believed that the average Scripps student could as well.

The course structure was as follows: before each class, students were required to read the material, watch a relevant video lecture, and do the homework; during class, they asked questions about the lecture or assignment, worked through additional problem sets, and, most importantly, explored concepts through discussion.

Problem sets were relatively straightforward: they simply had to cover techniques that illuminated the concepts while also sufficiently ranging in difficulty. The discussions were more challenging. Of course, they had to clarify basic concepts; but I also wanted them to convey that all concepts arose naturally, from ordinary human concerns. For example, the definition of absolute value, as stated, might seem remote from reality, but it is unavoidable if one begins to consider the notion of distance between two numbers: the distance between numbers A and B is $A-B$ if A is larger, but $B-A$ if B is larger. Thus one recurrent question was to ask why the day's concept was natural. Other basic—but surprisingly beneficial—activities were to ask students to state their understanding or intuition of formal definitions.

In addition, for each class I prepared a list of discussion questions. In hindsight, all questions clarified fundamental logical relations between concepts: they either showed how the day's concepts were related to previous ones (e.g., that the notion of distance in the plane is an extension of absolute value on the line); or forced students to differentiate between concepts (How do you know that an exponential function cannot be a polynomial function? What is the difference in behavior between a rational and a polynomial function?); or illuminated logical implications (If a function has a positive average rate of change over a time interval, can we conclude that it must be increasing? If a function has a constant velocity, must it be linear?); or questioned their compatibility (Could a rational function have horizontal asymptotes but no vertical ones?). That is, they examined whether or not pairs of concepts were logical extensions, identical, consequences, or contradictory. I also hoped they were provocative and stimulated student-driven exploration.

The best discussions consisted of seemingly simple questions that, when more carefully examined, revealed subtleties that could be resolved only by recalling prior concepts. Looking back through my daily record, I think one of the best classes was the following.

Day 22

I began by asking students what the difference was between polynomials and rational functions. Students came up with answers: "Rational functions are not continuous," and questions: "Are they always not continuous?" Someone gave one possible answer to the original question: rational functions can head toward infinity at a finite point (i.e., have a vertical asymptote); polynomials cannot.

Student A then asked an interesting question: "Is it possible for a rational function to have horizontal, but no vertical, asymptotes?" I said, "Okay, let's see if we can *make* one." We broke A's question into two smaller questions: When does a rational function have vertical asymptotes? and When does a rational function have horizontal asymptotes?

The students knew vertical asymptotes occurred where the polynomial denominator had roots. Student B pointed out that a rational function could avoid vertical asymptotes if its denominator had complex roots. So we constructed a simple rational function with no vertical asymptotes: $r(x) = 1 / (x^2 + 1)$. Now, what did we need to ensure horizontal asymptotes? Student C came up with the answer: the top and bottom of the rational function must have the same degree; so we let $r(x) = x^2 / (x^2 + 1)$.

The next subject was the precise graphing of rational functions, so I asked each student to make one observation about this function. One student observed: its graph passes through (0,0); another that the output is always positive; another that it approaches the line $y = 1$, as x goes to positive or negative infinity. Student C observed that the quotient was always less than or equal to 1.

I asked two questions: "Can we say anything about the maximum/minimum? And can we say anything more precise about the behavior near x = 0?" Student C commented (incorrectly) that we needed to find the vertex; I pointed out that this wasn't a quadratic function. Eventually I introduced the technique of more precise graphing and related it to translations. Then I altered the problem slightly: "What about something like $x^2/(x^2 - 1)$, which has vertical asymptotes? How does the function behave near those points? Notice that we can use the symmetry. . . ."

In that class, students both questioned and verified their knowledge through conversation, engaged cooperatively and actively in the extended examination of a question they had generated themselves, and invoked prior knowledge. In other words, like Ma's young subjects, they engaged to some degree with their elementary problems as mathematicians.

Results and Reactions

The difference in exam scores between terms was considerable: on average, students in the discussion-based course scored about one standard deviation higher on every exam, excluding the final (on which they were about half a standard deviation higher). Although one might suspect the higher grades were due to extra time spent in preparation, the average reported time commitment per week was virtually identical.

Despite the higher scores, the discussion-based format was not popular. At two points in the term, I solicited anonymous feedback; the second time, a majority of the students commented that they did not like the video lecture format. One said, "It brings a lot of extra work to my weekly schedule and it makes the overall homework extremely daunting," another that "The [structure] just doesn't fit my learning style. I would suggest going back to the original method." Because the majority disliked the flipped structure, we switched back to the standard in-class lecture format for the final fourth of the term; the slightly lower, if still superior, performance on the final exam might be a consequence.

Interestingly, after switching back to the regular format, I noticed that some students still committed certain basic errors that, in previous semesters, had for the most part been caught by that point. Normally, during the deliberate construction of basic facts in lecture, students have opportunities to trouble-shoot their prior knowledge; perhaps the focused, one-on-one nature of dia-logue provides more leeway for uncertain students to conceal their ignorance and prevents one from noticing the usual cues of confusion.

Conclusion

By some measures, the course had significant success: students exercised their curiosity, explored questions using their own observations, and were able to dis-cuss concepts; further, their numerical performance was markedly higher. Yet the students themselves did not value that success despite having been informed of it; they had become, perhaps, so used to the comfort of procedural problem-solving that they had no desire to enter the prickly door to actual mathe-matics. If I were to run such a course again, I would include significant clarification regarding the connection between mathematics and other fields of thought, as well as more of what I learned through more recent iterations of examining mathematics from the view of other disciplines: that we must help the students construct definitions via association with intuition, acquire and listen for the insights that inspire the logic, create mental metaphors for phe-nomena via faculties that supersede the linguistic, and cultivate a delicate sense of beauty. Interplay between teaching, reflections from other fields, and my own experience of mathematics creates a recursion that tends, inevitably, toward more powerful teaching.

Notes

1 The program was designed in 1994 in reaction to the traditional liberal arts core curriculum, after "two decades of lively experimentation and debate." Nathalie Rachlin, David Lloyd, Jane O'Donnell, Amy Marcus-Newhall, and Steve Naftilan, "The Core Curriculum in Interdisciplinary Humanities" (internal Scripps self-study, September 2000), 2.

2 Faculty are required to participate in the program regularly as part of their five-course teaching load.

3 https://www.pbs.org/newshour/science/science-jan-june05-summersremarks_2-22.

4 Edward Frenkel, *Love and Math: The Heart of Hidden Reality* (New York: Basic Books, 2013), 1.

5 Jerre Levy and Doreen Kimura, "Women, Men, and the Sciences," in *The Science on Women in Science*, ed. Christina H. Sommers (Washington, D.C.: AEI Press, 2009); Joshua Aronson, "Stereotypes and the Underrepresentation of Women in Math and Science," in Sommers, ed., *The Science on Women in Science*.

6 Stephen Ceci, Wendy Williams, and Susan Barnett, "Women's

Underrepresentation in Science: Sociocultural and Biological Considerations," *Psychological Bulletin* 135, no. 2 (2009): 232.

7   Liping Ma, *Knowing and Teaching Elementary Mathematics* (London: Routledge, 2010), 120ff.

8   J. S. Mill, *On Liberty* (Indianapolis: Hackett Publishing, 1978), 34.

9   William Ewald, ed., *From Kant to Hilbert* (Oxford: Oxford Press, 1996), 137ff.

10 Ewald, 1012ff.

11 Henri Poincaré, *Science and Method*, trans. Francis Maitland (New York: Cosimo Classics, 2007), 47ff.

12 William Thurston, "On Proof and Progress in Mathematics," *Bulletin of the American Mathematical Society* 30, no. 2 (April 1994): 164ff.

12

Arts in the Laboratory

• •

A Multidisciplinary Approach
to Honors Education in a
Small College Setting

LANA A. WHITED AND

SHARON E. STEIN

A Ferrum College student observing Titian's painting *Venus with a Mirror* (ca. 1555) at the National Gallery of Art is likely working on a class assignment. If the student is in the Boone Honors Program (BHP), he or she will be quite familiar with the artist's work, having learned about the Venetian Renaissance master in class—from a chemistry professor. The course, Honors 215, Science and Art, exemplifies the synergistic nature of Ferrum's honors seminars. Students explore connections between the physical sciences and the visual arts in a course combining the perspectives of art, chemistry, economics, history, religion, and Italian Renaissance geography. Guided by faculty in both the sciences and humanities, students learn how pigments are detected and change over time, using techniques such as x-radiography and infrared reflectography. They apply these techniques to analyze works by Renaissance masters, including Titian, Giorgione, and Bellini. Through such assignments, students are challenged to exhibit superior analytical ability and sophisticated aesthetic appreciation. The class also includes a field trip that brings students, some of whom have never visited the nation's capital (about five hours from campus), face to face with art by world masters. Students' experiences in multidisciplinary seminars, such as Science and Art, are typical of honors education at Ferrum, although our research and observation reveal that honors students and honors faculty view and value these multidisciplinary experiences differently.

Background: The Boone Honors Program

Ferrum's honors program was launched in 2001 at a school founded in 1913 as a Methodist training (or "mission") school for students in the Blue Ridge Mountains without access to public education.[1] The college granted only associate's degrees until 1976; these degrees were relatively uniform versions of today's general education program, except that some opportunity for electives allowed customization. An associate's in applied sciences, for example, prepared students to transfer to the University of Virginia to study engineering. When the baccalaureate programs debuted, the curriculum followed a model that some called "two plus two": students earned a two-year degree before entering one of several programs in the two-year Senior Division, all of which were tied to the concept of service and led to baccalaureate degrees. One such program was in public administration. Ferrum's environmental science program, the second oldest in the nation (after that at Stanford), also evolved then. Beyond their work in such specific programs, every student in the Senior Division completed eighteen credit hours in a Humanities Core. This comprised interdisciplinary courses, many with titles that included the word "man": a course grounded in mathematics, for example, was called Quantitative Man, and a course combining anthropology, geography, and history was called Non-Western Man. This two-plus-two model constituted the baccalaureate experience until the inauguration of a new presidential administration. Partially in response to faculty concern that students lacked sufficient preparation in disciplines, the curriculum was revised to require more specialization at the upper level.[2]

Named after the college's then outgoing president and his wife, the Boone Honors Program thus emerged at a moment of institutional and curricular transition. The demands of some faculty for greater curricular specialization notwithstanding, the honors program maintained an interdisciplinary focus that reflected the commitment of its founding faculty, who had taught under the two-plus-two system and remained committed to the college's tradition of humanistic education. Faculty in the arts and humanities still lead the way in developing interdisciplinary curriculum; more honors course proposals (eleven of fifteen since 2001) have been written by arts and humanities faculty than by those in the natural and social sciences combined.

From the program's inception to the end of the 2017–18 academic year, approximately 265 students entered Ferrum as program members or (rarely) joined after matriculation by making the Dean's List and petitioning the BHP Steering Committee for membership. In most years, total membership falls between 50 and 60 students at a school with an enrollment of about 1,050 in fall 2019. While arts and humanities faculty have guided the program's development, recruitment data indicate that programs in the natural sciences attract the most new honors program members, with environmental science and pre–professional health sciences consistently the most popular. While these facts suggest at least some interdisciplinary interests among the students, it is worth noting that students pursuing degrees in English have the highest ratio of honors completion (one hundred percent) among the college's majors. In the meantime, non-honors students are permitted to enroll in honors seminars after review by course faculty and the program director. Approximately 150 have done so, usually because the subject matter complements their own major or because the course meets a Liberal Arts Core requirement. Beyond the substantive contributions that these students can make in the classroom, their presence offers a welcome enrollment boost for honors seminars whose size seldom exceeds fifteen.

Although Ferrum has joined the trend toward standardized-testing-optional admissions requirements, eligibility criteria for honors continue to include SAT or ACT scores because high school GPA alone is an inadequate predictor of success in honors.[3] Ferrum's honors program requires a cumulative high school GPA of 3.5 or higher and a math/verbal SAT score of 1200 or higher (or the ACT equivalent). Admission officers place applicants meeting these criteria automatically into the program, unless they opt out (which is rare). Before fall 2012, students were notified of honors eligibility and invited to opt in; the current practice of automatic placement, however, has increased the size of each incoming cohort from an average of twelve or thirteen to an average of eighteen or nineteen. Members take five multidisciplinary seminars, all of which, except the capstone, fulfill Liberal Arts Core requirements. For example, Honors 100, a leadership seminar, replaces the gateway course required of first-year students. Honors seminars bear titles such as Science and Art, Political Satire, Reason and the Individual, and Expressionism in Art, Literature, and Film. The program also requires twelve hours of independent enrichment projects, language study through the intermediate level, and a study abroad experience (for which a travel scholarship of up to three thousand dollars is provided).

The interdisciplinary nature of honors education at Ferrum distinguishes honors students' experiences of the Liberal Arts Core requirements from those of non-honors students. Although Ferrum briefly required all students to take two courses designated as Integrated Learning (IL), even then the IL-designated course need not cross disciplines; it could involve assignments integrating other material within the major. For example, the psychology capstone course includes a project requiring students to discuss their "psychology philosophy" and apply it to future career goals, such as school psychology or substance abuse counseling. These seniors must integrate previous psychology courses and experiences into their paper; some may choose to integrate minor coursework in social work or criminal justice, but this is not required. Thus most non-honors students can miss the interdisciplinary component found in honors seminars, except those who enroll in experiences such as the Appalachian Cluster (discussed in chapter 15) or the Holocaust course. Honors students also tend to embrace the multidisciplinary philosophy in their major/minor combinations, which include, for recent graduates, chemistry and music, horticulture and Spanish, preprofessional science and philosophy, and international relations and Russian.

Honors seminars also have a team-teaching component following one of two models. In the first model (about a third of the seminars), two faculty members participate fully; for example, Honors 213, Media and Violence, is taught by a developmental psychologist and a mass media specialist. The remaining two-thirds follow the second model, which have a primary teacher and guest faculty for limited lectures or experiential activities; for example, Science and Art is taught primarily by a chemistry professor but includes lectures in Renaissance art and Italian sociopolitical history by faculty guests. The main obstacle to having all honors seminars fully team taught is workload demands of faculty home departments; on a small campus, preparing a program's class schedule is like cooking without a recipe.

The Student Perspective

For honors program members, the goals of the seminar design are numerous, and our recent research affirms that students perceive and appreciate the benefits that the courses are designed to foster.[4] Two questionnaires were created to gather student and faculty perspectives. The first was for students and alumni who have taken at least one honors class. It contained questions concerning demographic information, including the respondent's major, whether the respondent was an honors member, and whether the respondent had graduated. The student questionnaire contained ten statements inviting students to compare their honors seminars to non-honors courses with regard to such aspects as being more challenging, fostering different perspectives, offering multidisciplinary content, exposure to new concepts, and developing critical thinking skills. The questionnaire also included two open-ended questions asking about problems and benefits students experienced exclusively in honor seminars.

Forty-eight students completed the questionnaire, a participation rate of 12.3 percent. Twenty-seven of forty-eight respondents had graduated, and twenty-one had not. Forty respondents were honors program members, while five were not (three did not specify). Respondents' majors represented all academic schools existing at the time of the research, with nine from Arts and

Table 12.1

Student responses to statements comparing honors to non-honors classes

The honors course(s) was more challenging than other courses.	3.87
The honors course(s) was more interdisciplinary than other courses.	4.18
The honors course(s) was more enjoyable than other courses.	3.9
The honors course(s) taught material that exposed me to new concepts more than other courses.	4.0
The honors course(s) integrated technology more than other courses.	2.73
The honors course(s) helped me develop critical thinking skills more than other courses.	3.93
The honors course(s) helped me see connections between different courses and/ or disciplines more than other courses.	4.11
The honors course(s) reduced my fear of taking courses outside my major or minor area more than other courses.	3.36
The honors course(s) introduced me to more or different perspectives than other courses.	4.05
The honors course(s) has (or will) help(ed) me obtain my future career goals more than other courses.	3.23

Humanities, twenty-one from Natural Sciences/Mathematics, and fifteen from Social Sciences/Professional Studies. Three students completed majors from two or more schools. Table 12.1 depicts students' mean responses on a Likert scale, with 5 indicating the highest rate of agreement.

Results clearly show that respondents recognize the value of seeing connections across disciplines. Mean responses exceed 4.0 for statements affirming that honors courses are more interdisciplinary than other courses, likelier to help students connect disciplines, and likelier to encourage multiple-perspective thinking. Respondents also believe honors seminars provide greater enhancement to critical-thinking skills. The challenge in honors seminars may arise from students' being asked to contemplate two subjects that they do not customarily study *together*, such as politics and psychology (Honors 222) or religion and the visual arts (Honors 206). Respondents called the multidisciplinary design "fun" and "amazing." Of thirty-two responses to the open-ended question concerning benefits of honors courses, almost all singled out interdisciplinarity and examination of multiple perspectives as seminal features of the honors curriculum.

The Media and Violence course taught by the authors illustrates how students are encouraged to see interdisciplinary connections and hone their critical thinking skills. Students learn from a developmental psychologist about risk factors such as family dynamics and psychopathologies that predispose young men to be violent or tolerant of violence. Another risk factor, exposure to violent media, is discussed by a mass media expert. Correlations connecting media violence and social violence are complex, so explaining why individuals with different risk factors are affected differently by the same media requires higher-order critical thinking skills and advanced formal reasoning. Faculty model precise vocabulary; for example, explaining the difference between "causation" and "correlation" helps students to think deeply in other contexts. Because professional work is less compartmentalized than academic preparation reflects, interdisciplinary coursework helps prepare students for the complexity of this work. A student comment that discussion in seminars was "more advanced" than discussion in classes in the student's major affirms this effect. Another said, "One of the things I loved about the honors courses I took was the consistent challenging and intellectual conversation. It was harder to find on a consistent basis, but it was always present in honors courses."

Multidisciplinary honors courses also offer more challenges for talented students, who may achieve good grades but experience boredom in other courses, particularly those meeting general education requirements and enrolling students of diverse abilities. Respondents agreed at a mean of 3.87 that honors courses are more challenging than other courses. For one thing, students taking honors seminars are presented with concepts from areas they might not study otherwise, and strong students can cover more material more quickly. Survey respondents agreed about being exposed to new concepts, at a mean of 4.0. Students also agreed (3.36) that taking honors courses diminished their fear of taking courses in disciplines outside their major or minor area. As one respondent put it, "The course opened up my comfort zone in subjects outside my area of interest." Religion is a subject outside some students' comfort zones, for even those with significant exposure to faith communities are unlikely to have been asked to examine scriptures with a critical eye, as scholars approach other literatures. In Honors 206, The Bible and the Arts, students examine biblical texts and analyze their interpretation in films and works of visual art; these assignments challenge some students to move out of their comfort zones. One student noted that, prior to the course, she would not have read works such as the Talmudic story of Lilith, which she had particularly enjoyed, with the same critical eye that she might use for reading a narrative in English class. This student said the course "pushed me to read more and to write more." Other students, particularly those who have grown up in nonreligious families, find that the intellectual, analytic approach to religious texts is a comfortable means of meeting the college's general education requirement for religion or philosophy.

Of course, the material is only one source of challenge. Another is talented classmates who are curious, work hard, and see each other and their faculty frequently on a small campus. In the Media and Violence course, students undertake some assignments in pairs, a factor that tends to increase motivation. A famous story in our honors program concerns the English major in an ordinary freshman composition course (there is no honors-designated section) who went directly to her adviser's office after the first class, announcing that she had listened to classmates' complaints about the amount of writing to be done and decided on the spot, "I cannot make it through a whole semester in a class with these people." By contrast, another respondent described the learning environment in honors seminars as cooperative. Echoing this sentiment, another wrote, "The benefit of taking these classes was being able to collaborate with other students to discuss sincerely different perspectives. Inside of a single major, people usually have a similar mindset, but in honors classes, we all had something different to bring to the table, and those shared experiences were noteworthy." Add to the interplay of more difficult or less familiar content and highly motivated classmates the encouragement of two faculty members (in team-taught courses), and the increased level of challenge is readily apparent.

Because the honors program is small, team projects and regular contact also help members build strong relationships with both peers and faculty. The requirement of five honors seminars means that the same cohort of students will find themselves in classes together repeatedly, a phenomenon generally common only to students who share a major. In their first year on campus, honors students live together in a centrally located residence hall near the library. This insular initial experience of residence life helps to assure that program members develop a sense of community early on. Research such as that of Nichols, Ailts, and Chang confirms that communal living boosts honors retention.[5] Program members support each other in their various activities around campus, whereas non-honors students attend performances, lectures, and the like primarily as required or for extra credit. Even honors students' social media habits reflect developing networks of friendships that often extend past graduation; it is not unusual to find honors alumni serving as attendants in the weddings of their former program mates. In light of the multiple benefits students perceive in honors seminars, it is not surprising that they agreed at a mean of 3.9 that these courses are "more enjoyable than other courses."

Students' perceptions of the multidisciplinary experience is more uniformly positive than that that of their faculty. When students were invited (in our survey) to identify problems in taking honors courses, the only issue to elicit a substantive response was negotiating scheduling conflicts. Of thirty-three responses to this question, seven specifically mentioned scheduling, while thirteen said they experienced no problems. It should also be noted that one of the seven students who mentioned scheduling was completing *three* majors. Tensions that arise in scheduling usually result from Ferrum's small size. In any semester, two or three seminars are offered; because all except Honors 100 rotate on a two-year cycle, a student enrolled for four years has only two chances to take any particular course. This problem is compounded by the trend of talented students pushing themselves to earn baccalaureate degrees in fewer than eight semesters by pursuing dual enrollment or advanced placement credit while still in high school. This phenomenon is more common at small, nonselective, enrollment-driven institutions, as first-tier schools may refuse to accept dual-enrollment credits. The truncation of the undergraduate experience increases the likelihood that an honors seminar may conflict with a required major course and makes delivering the honors curriculum more challenging.

After scheduling, the problem of "fit" for students who were not honors program members drew the most discussion. This concern was cited by only two students, one of whom noted that non-honors students "were not as invested in the learning as honors students and affected the learning environment." The second student said the course was "intimidating" at the outset with unfamiliar classmates, noting that it was hard for nonmembers to interact. However, on balance, this student offered more praise than criticism, observing that honors students "were very welcoming" and that her experience in the course was ultimately one of growth: "I don't think I heeded my friends' warnings when they told me how difficult the course load would be for a single class. I was definitely challenged by that, but in the end it taught me how to better manage my time."

We also anticipated discussion of some problems that were barely mentioned. Primarily, we were surprised by lack of attention to the challenge of navigating the teaching and assessment methods of two faculty members rather than one (in team-taught seminars). Only two students commented on consistency in multiple faculty members' approach to the course, although this seems—at least to faculty—an obvious tension in team-taught courses. One student noted that "there didn't seem to be an equal distribution of content—one professor seemed to really take control and run with it," a comment that suggests an imbalance but not a difference in grading standards. A second student addressed the issue of students' expectations more directly: "Typically with one teacher, as a student you can figure out exactly what that teacher expects of you, but when you have two[,] both teachers['] expectations change throughout the course to adapt to each other's teaching styles." The difference in faculty and student perceptions on this point suggest that students attribute variations in the faculty approach to the oversimplified concept "expectations," whereas faculty recognize differences in methodology arising from their disciplinary backgrounds. In Media and Violence, for example, students writing papers in American Psychological Association format are expected to make more frequent references to research dates in the text, whereas those using Modern Language Association format do so only in bibliographic contexts. Students may view this as a difference in what faculty members "want," but it is a distinction arising from disciplinary practices.

One additional issue virtually ignored by students is the heavy humanities emphasis in Ferrum's honors curriculum, an aspect magnified by the language requirement. The recent addition of two courses involving political science has mitigated the dominance of the humanities overall, yet only three courses besides Science and Art have emerged from natural science–related disciplines. The inclusion of more honors seminars involving science could ease the scheduling burden for science majors with hefty lab commitments, especially if such courses also met non-honors requirements. Nevertheless, only one student mentioned the honors curriculum's disciplinary balance. This peculiarity merits further investigation, especially if it represents an attitude that might serve as counterpoint to currently increasing hostility against the liberal arts. Such hostility is often attributed to perceptions concerning what work is most valuable; a prime recent example is the Trump administration's emphasis on STEM (science, technology, engineering, and math) degrees in making immigration and citizenship decisions.[6] Budget cuts involving the arts and humanities also suggest diminished value, and young women are choosing nonhumanities fields more than in previous generations. All of this suggests that for our honors students, the interdisciplinary honors curriculum plays a role in connecting the humanistic tradition with their work in majors that are increasingly focused on technologies.

The Faculty Perspective

While students appear to focus more on the novelty of taking interdisciplinary seminars, faculty clearly perceive more challenges in leaving our home disciplines or merging them with those of colleagues. Eleven of thirteen current honors faculty were sent the second questionnaire, containing four open-ended questions designed to clarify how faculty and student perceptions of the multidisciplinary course experience differ. Eight faculty members participated, a 73 percent response rate. (This essay's authors did not complete the survey.)

Faculty are very aware that workload dynamics pose major complications at a small institution with a fixed rotation of courses within majors and a constant eye on the instructional budget. Workload tensions and faculty compensation "in an environment of budget cuts" were mentioned by two faculty respondents as problems. Most Ferrum faculty teach eight courses in an academic year (for those teaching lab science and arts performance courses, workload is calculated differently). The impact of workload on staffing honors courses in the current financial environment illustrates a domino effect. In many majors, faculty have a set rotation of courses which they may be the ideal (or only) person to teach. In the courses with a primary professor, guest faculty are compensated with a per diem stipend. While the survey indicates that faculty are focused more on other problems, workload issues nevertheless add to the costs of a program benefiting a relatively small population of students—a general concern for the honors director.

Most of the challenges faculty experience in teaching honors seminars may be benefits in disguise. The issue of preparation is a notable example. The initial design of honors seminars is quite time consuming; when we designed the Media and Violence class, we met for about two hours a week for an entire semester. Course design and even preparation for an honors seminar taught regularly is more strenuous than for many other courses and undertaken without additional compensation (though sometimes during sabbatical). In all honors courses and particularly in team-taught ones, ongoing preparation involves some reading outside the faculty member's primary discipline and staying current on a broader range of content. One respondent said, "Sometimes my class does nontraditional things[,] which possibly means more work from me to keep on top of the new stuff." However, most faculty, being lifelong learners, tend to see this work as a benefit of honors involvement—an enhancement, not a burden.

The ability to foster creative student responses hinted at in the comment about "nontraditional" assignments was a benefit mentioned on multiple surveys. One faculty member said, "I generally allow [students] more free reign to complete assignments in a way that fits their learning styles, aesthetic preferences or even their sense of humor. For instance, the final project in one BHP class featured a skit, a video, a Minecraft world, a student-created game, a diorama, and others." This faculty member, who is known for his creative assignments, noted that it is sometimes challenging to develop a rubric for evaluating such projects. The program director strongly encourages creativity in the work students undertake for their independent enrichment credits, and while some students still extend the length of a paper or prepare an extra presentation, others venture farther from the typical: A chemistry student developed an app for mastering the periodic table. Psychology students designed and produced a board game used for test review. A Spanish student made a Bingo game featuring vocabulary words. An international relations major minoring in Russian wrote and designed a Russian–English dictionary of diplomatic terms. An English and journalism student wrote and designed a newspaper that might have been published in Shakespeare's lifetime. Working with students who think not only analytically and deeply but also creatively can alleviate the tedium of a faculty member who might also be teaching a survey course for the seventeenth time.

Praise for the team-teaching experience was common in faculty responses, although some recognized that the experience might be different with a partner "who is rigid or possessive about the course." The team-teaching aspect of some honors courses allows faculty "to build off each other's expertise," one respondent said. Another stressed the advantage of students' exposure to "integrated learning from multiple disciplines": "We would often be teaching and I would share the term used for a phenomenon in my discipline[,] and my co-instructor would share a different term in [his or her] discipline that meant nearly the same thing. These connections are helpful to students."

Faculty were more likely than students to point out the potential for tension in the team-teaching paradigm. One confessed to being sometimes "out of my comfort zone," noting that veteran teachers (often the most likely to be recruited for honors assignments) have well-established "rules and methods and styles" and that "compromising those [is] sometimes uncomfortable." A common source of tension in team-taught courses is student perception of different grading standards. One faculty member observed, "Dual grading is difficult in terms of communication and perspective on expectations. Communication needed to be continual and clear between co-instructors. Some students took feedback really hard and were borderline disrespectful regarding constructive feedback." According to multiple faculty members, because honors students are accustomed to academic success at high levels, they may have a harder time accepting constructive criticism than other students.

Continual discussion between team-teaching faculty about expectations is indeed critical in preventing or diffusing student complaints about differing grading standards and other expectations. Rubrics are very useful toward this end, including feedback forms for evaluating essays. Team teachers should also remember that both need not grade all assignments. In the Media and Violence course, both faculty read all assignments, but a psychological abstract early in the course is assessed by the psychology professor, while the media theory test later in the semester is evaluated by the professor teaching that portion of the course. Finding enough time for the faculty dialogue essential to the team-teaching model was cited by one faculty member as a problem. The most common way our faculty have solved this problem is meeting during the workday for meals.

Many faculty members who responded to the survey said they felt a synergy in the team-teaching experience that carried over to non-honors courses. One wrote, "Team teaching proved to be a great experience. Being able to step outside of tried (and regularly employed) approaches to teaching and evaluating student progress by consulting with and observing the other professor not only encouraged me to be more creative in the honors class; it also encouraged revision in non-honors courses." If the honors program serves to reinvigorate the teaching of its faculty in non-honors classes, then it truly serves a larger population than its comparatively small membership.

Perhaps the faculty response that we least anticipated concerned multiple levels of student ability in the same classroom. Because all honors seminars except the first and last are offered at the 200 level, a teacher might have freshmen and seniors in the same class. Obviously, some of these students will have much more academic experience than others. While faculty clearly enjoy having a range of students from many disciplines, teaching students with vastly different preparation is difficult for everyone, although the more experienced students may serve as role models for the less experienced. Students newer to college expectations "seemed to be a bit overwhelmed" being in a classroom with juniors and seniors, one faculty member found, adding, "The range of experience and abilities occasionally made it difficult to teach both the best and least prepared students." At least one faculty member who discussed this problem advised that the honors director investigate the possibility of further differentiating seminars by academic level, a change the program's steering committee has begun discussing. With an increasing number of talented students entering college with numerous credit hours already earned, the Ferrum model of honors seminars meeting Liberal Arts Core requirements is no longer as attractive as it was in the program's early years. While most four-year colleges and universities are grappling with increasing student interest in less expensive transfer credits, smaller institutions, in particular, are worried about the declining, or shortened, enrollment that such a trend entails. At Ferrum, at least, this reality may drive a program revision that would see fewer lower-division and more upper-level honors seminars.

These potential challenges notwithstanding, the best benefit for faculty teaching honors courses almost goes without saying: the opportunity to work with some of the institution's most talented and ambitious students, young people who show up in the classroom prepared and willing to engage sometimes difficult material with relative confidence. Because honors class size is generally capped at fifteen, seminars are significantly smaller than most survey courses, which range from twenty to thirty unless they are writing intensive. Students "take responsibility for their learning," one faculty member said, and behavioral problems are almost nonexistent. Even cell phones are seldom visible in an honors class. One faculty member's description of the benefits of teaching honors sounds exactly like an affirmation of synergistic education: "I had a wide range of students . . . with a great variety of majors from all three colleges. The differences . . . allowed for much more engaging and fruitful class discussions, where nearly every class a student was able to use her [or his] knowledge almost as a quasi-expert on a topic that developed out of class conversation, and the students were able to learn much more collaboratively than in other classes I have taught." One faculty member noted that by the time honors students graduate, some feel more like colleagues. Any integral feature of an honors class—multidisciplinarity or team teaching or exceptional students—would be enough to "synergize" a typical classroom. But when these features are combined in an honors classroom, the impact is exponential, almost magical.

In July 2018, a new honors program graduate, chemistry major Joshua Sanders, published his first book, with Dr. Jason Powell, professor of chemistry and physics. The book, *Harry Potter Potions for Muggles*, is a collection of chemistry demonstrations inspired by potions classes in the Harry Potter series. It evolved from "lessons" conducted by Ferrum's chemistry faculty for local high school students and participants in Ferrum's Summer Enrichment Camp. The project was supported by a professional development grant, rehearsed in a required departmental lyceum, and presented at the 25th Biennial Conference on Chemical Education at Notre Dame. Powell and Sanders's work represents the very best qualities of honors education at Ferrum: the opportunity for a well-prepared student to work collegially with a faculty member, merging ideas from vastly difference academic disciplines (chemistry and literature) and developed in collaboration with peers, to achieve a result that is academically sound, creative, and inspiring to faculty colleagues and classmates alike. At a time when small schools such as Ferrum struggle to distinguish ourselves from larger institutions, the project by Powell and Sanders shows that a small college can deliver the individualized growth and achievement that talented students and faculty alike still seek.

Notes

1   Ferrum's honors program was named in recognition of our ninth president, Dr. Jerry Boone, and his wife, Mrs. Shirley Boone, upon Dr. Boone's 2002 retirement.

2   The authors are grateful to Dr. Peter Crow, Dr. Jody D. Brown, Dr. Richard L. Smith, and Mrs. Kathleen Holt Smith for this information.

3   Timothy Nichols, Jacob Ailts, and Kuo-Liang Chang, "Why Not Honors? Understanding Students' Decisions Not to Enroll and Persist in Honors Programs," *Honors in Practice*, 12 (2018): 33–58, https://eric.ed.gov/?q=why+not+honors&id=EJ1104368.

4   Surveys described herein were conducted for the purpose of writing this article. For more about this research, email lwhited@ferrum.edu or sstein@ferrum.edu.

5   Nichols et al., "Why Not Honors?"

6   Joey Ye, "STEM Students to Benefit from Visa Extension," *Yale Daily News*, April 25, 2016, https://yaledailynews.com/blog/2016/04/25/stem-students-to-benefit-from-visa-extension/.

Part III

**Exploring across
the Disciplines**

●●●●●●●●●●●●●●●●●●●●●●

13

Science and Cultural Competence

• •

Incorporating Hispanic
Migrants' Knowledge
and Experience in the
Spanish Curriculum

MARTHA BÁRCENAS-MOORADIAN

Speaking with immigrant women from
CLEAR about their healthcare experiences, both in the U.S. and in their
countries of origin, was enormously
informative. Hearing them speak with
such passion about family traditions and
personal sacrifices was important in
putting the course into perspective. It
took the lectures from theoretical to
tangible, from the page to a thinking,
feeling people.
—Ellery Koelker-Wolfe (CMC student)

Our participation in this class was an
opportunity to develop ourselves as
women. We never went to school.
However, we were able to speak, to teach
our cultural traditions. We also learned
from the students as we shared our
stories. Students made us feel very
important for they expressed interest in
our conversations and explanations.
—Leticia Martínez and Julia Barrios
(CLEAR members)

Introduction

This chapter presents the case of an advanced, interdisciplinary Spanish course
(Science and Cultural Competence) that I redesigned, restructured, and taught
for the first time in the spring of 2018 at Scripps College. The course integrates
community-engaged pedagogies and experiential learning methodologies following an interdisciplinary content approach. It remains part of the curriculum of the Department of Spanish, Latin American and Caribbean Literatures
and Cultures and will continue to be offered on an annual basis in its new form.
The pages that follow provide contextual and background information about
the course as well as a discussion of the steps and strategies that proved helpful
for the successful development and delivery of a class that combines interdisciplinarity with experiential learning activities. The chapter also discusses how a
partnership with a local community-based group of Hispanic women (named
CLEAR, the Spanish acronym for women leaders, entrepreneurs, allies, and revolutionaries) was developed and how it contributed to the objectives of the class
while posing challenges that needed to be addressed. A final section on experiential learning and critical pedagogies provides a framework for introducing the
kinds of learning opportunities required for a course like this to succeed.

Contextual and Background Information about the Course

Medical Spanish courses were incorporated within the American college curriculum in the last decades of the twentieth century to provide physicians and
health care providers with linguistic tools to better communicate with their
patients of Hispanic descent. Since then, most medical Spanish courses at the
college level have focused primarily on linguistic and communicative approaches
to improve the language skills of future health professionals. In contrast, my
redesigned course emphasizes and promotes not only linguistic skills but

cultural competence to better prepare future health providers to understand their patients in relation to cultural aspects that may affect diagnosis, treatment, and instructions for preventive medicine.

There is a lack of literature regarding the incorporation of cultural competence in medical Spanish courses, including guidelines, methodologies, and evaluation systems consistent with second language acquisition recommendations for curricula created for medical Spanish courses and programs.[1] Therefore the course that I redesigned was created on the basis of my own expertise in second language acquisition, community-based pedagogies, and culture. The course was designed to be interdisciplinary because the cultural competencies targeted can only be realized holistically. For example, linguistic competencies cannot be separated from the practices, institutions, and cultural contexts in which they are situated. I therefore integrated a broad spectrum of topics pertaining to Spain and Latin America that went beyond linguistic and communicative proficiency. These topics included traditional medicine, public health, ethnomedicine, gender and power relations, migration and border medicine, technology and the environment, cultural perspectives about the stages of life, and cultural perspectives about mental health and incapacities. Further, because these competencies require practice and experience, I also integrated an experiential learning aspect by connecting with a Hispanic women's program, part of the local nonprofit Pomona Economic Opportunity Center.

As already mentioned, the course was taught at Scripps College, a women's liberal arts college with approximately a thousand students, and a member of the Claremont Colleges Consortium, located in Southern California. Our students most commonly pursue majors in biology, psychology, media studies, English, economics, and computer science. Scripps College students who enroll in my course are interested in pursuing studies in the health professions and public health, and many of them are enrolled in the Post-Baccalaureate Premedical Program, which provides support, guidance, and multiple resources for students entering medical/health care school.

A core value of Scripps is to provide a well-rounded education that combines humanistic and scientific study and connects both with practice. The inclusion of this course within the Scripps College curriculum fits this paradigm and addresses the demographic changes of the Hispanic population that will condition future professional practice.[2] Scripps College introduced this course with the objective of preparing students interested in pursuing a career in science or the health professions to be culturally competent, as well as linguistically proficient at the advanced level. The course can serve as a prerequisite for the department major in Spanish and has the goal of providing foundational knowledge to promote students' curiosity to explore and advance their research following ethical principles in the health professions and to better communicate with diverse communities in Spanish.

Steps and Strategies: Creating Interdisciplinarity with an Experiential Learning Approach

Upon recommendation of the chair of the Spanish department, I was invited to redesign and teach the Science and Cultural Competence course from a more defined cultural/historical/inter-American perspective that considers topics related to indigenous traditions and ways of thinking in a colonized context, as well as power relations, including gender and border/migration medicine. This new focus was needed, as all of these factors now inform the experience of migrant patients within the medical system and are therefore essential for medical professionals to understand. For this reason, themes having to do with sociopolitical struggles, gender inequality, racism, ethical and regulatory practices, among others, fell within the scope of the course. I also considered topics such as the role of religion within colonial and globalizing societies, the relevance of technology, science and cultural perspectives during various life stages (pregnancy, childcare, adolescence, adulthood, terminal illness, and the end of life), nutrition, and cultural myths, especially those that may affect one's health or promote disadvantages for individuals that suffer certain handicaps or belong to alternative communities.

The range of themes presented in the course allowed me to draw on an interdisciplinary background that included graduate studies in higher education, and Spanish and Latin American literature, as well as research and publication on indigenous knowledge and languages, traditional healing practices, migration studies, and second language acquisition. My own background as a Mexican migrant woman gave me a unique and deep perspective into the conditions and needs of minority communities. Nevertheless, preparing for the course took considerable work that included two semesters of research into topics, with which I was not initially familiar, identified as relevant to the class.

Designing a course that prepares health professionals and scientists to understand and communicate culturally with minority communities presents challenges and opportunities that lead the instructor to consider alternative pedagogies. These pedagogies are more conducive to motivating students to engage the subject matter and immerse themselves in the community because they encourage a more collaborative approach to learning in which the instructor is a guide, as opposed to the expert. The student and teacher co-create the curriculum, and the community participants function as additional instructors rather than mere subjects.

Inclusion of alternative pedagogies led to reconsidering the format of the course. An important design change was the structuring of immersive experiences in which students could engage in authentic dialogue with community partners in an egalitarian setting. With this in mind, I planned field trips to local traditional pharmacies (*farmacias* or *botánicas*) and organic community gardens where students could interact and learn from Hispanic community members with knowledge of alternative medicines and traditional practices pervasive in their cultures.

The incorporation of a robust experiential learning component raised the problem of how to fund field trips, honoraria for community partners, and other activities. Because the experiential component was not part of the course as taught by previous instructors, funding sources had not been previously identified. I therefore had to investigate grant opportunities within Scripps College and the Claremont Colleges Consortium. After a period of inquiry and submitting applications, I received two grants. One was provided by a center associated with Pomona College (part of the Claremont Colleges Consortium), the Sontag Center. This center promotes and supports interdisciplinary and experiential learning initiatives. The other grant that I received came directly from the dean of faculty's office at Scripps. This grant, from the Oshita Fund, was received for curriculum development purposes. With the support of these two grants, the course could be redesigned and delivered as an interdisciplinary endeavor with enhanced experiential learning.

The interdisciplinarity of the course was manifested in the content and through the participation of guest speakers, invited with the support of honoraria from the Oshita Fund, with expertise in various areas. Among these were Tongva elders, traditional healers, and other professionals who offered talks about cultural issues having to do with health, nutrition, emotional health, gender issues, socioeconomic disparities, and race. Speakers were chosen because of their first-person knowledge of practices, institutional contexts, and roles, or for their academic and professional knowledge of particular topics, such as the health care system in Spain or hospice care in the United States.

Adding to the interdisciplinarity provided by the guest speakers, the Sontag Center award facilitated the integration of interdisciplinary experiential learning. Workshops, meetings, and field trips were organized for students and local active migrant women to connect, reflect, and exchange thoughts about topics included in the course. All these engagement activities were planned to motivate participants to expand and reflect on course topics through alternative mechanisms and to explore knowledge that has not been included in traditional academic coursework. To be sure, these and other initiatives were only possible with the support of the various grants received, thus revealing a broader institutional need for continued support for courses with strong experiential and interdisciplinary components. The following section presents how academic-community engagement in an experiential learning mode was realized in this course.

Identifying and Creating Sustainable Partnerships with the Local Community

Creating partnerships with the local community is both time consuming and challenging for faculty members. Many colleges and universities have an office in charge of identifying and connecting the curriculum with various organizations to create sustainable partnerships that result in internship and service learning opportunities for students. These offices, centers, or programs are increasingly desirable in view of the need to create opportunities to develop practical knowledge and skill sets that complement their academic learning. They have been important in recruiting students, who see experiential learning and internship opportunities as critical to their professional and personal development and something a college should offer.

Among members of the Claremont Colleges Consortium, most have an office that serves these purposes. The Sontag Center at Pomona College is an example of this. In addition to material support, it offers guidance for faculty members seeking to develop experiential learning courses. Unfortunately, my institution does not have such a center. While I was grateful to receive funding from the neighboring Sontag Center, I had to draw on my own previous experience working with the local community to establish the relationships necessary for my course. Indeed this served me well when I tried to connect my course with the local Pomona Economic Opportunity Center (PEOC) women's program, and I received a positive response from the organization and the CLEAR leadership.[3] I have worked as a volunteer, researcher, and member of the PEOC's board of directors for approximately fifteen years. PEOC staff and clients view me as both a professional and a trusted ally and friend. For faculty seeking to make connections with the community to support their pedagogy, college centers may provide initial inroads into relevant organizations. Nevertheless, the initiative and commitment to this pedagogic approach have to spring from the faculty member's own conviction. Faculty members must be ready to invest time, energy, and resources into cultivating relationships, exploring a broader spectrum of community-based groups and material resources beyond what is already available through the campus. This is perhaps truer at smaller institutions, where resources are limited.

CLEAR (Compañeras, Líderes, Emprendedoras, Aliadas y Revolucionarias) is a women's program created in 2016 under the auspices of PEOC. The Spanish acronym defines this group as women leaders, entrepreneurs, allies, and revolutionaries, a group that is currently active in the city of Pomona. The group promotes mental health and health in general, and is active in local politics in relation to immigrant issues and workers' rights. Most of its members are migrant women from Mexico and Central America. Despite their differences in educational levels, age, ethnic backgrounds, and places of origin, they all share a similar story as migrant women of Hispanic cultural traditions. They sustain themselves and the group by offering services in the cleaning and catering industries.

When connecting academia with another community, it is important to establish a mutually beneficial relationship based on respect, while recognizing the needs and talents of each group. CLEAR was very enthusiastic about their participation in the class, contributing their knowledge of traditional medicine and sharing their experience facing the American health care system. They were also eager to help coordinate field trips to *botánicas* (traditional pharmacies) and help students find engaging opportunities to immerse themselves in the culture of the Hispanic persons residing in Southern California.

To engage CLEAR members with the subject matter and with the group of students they were to encounter, I provided each member with a copy of my syllabus that included a course description, learning objectives, learning goals, attendance and decorum policies, a list of experiential learning activities and workshops, and the schedule for specific themes to be covered, including the readings, videos, and assignments for each segment of the course. Assessment and evaluation criteria as well as information about other assignments (formal presentations and research papers) were not discussed in detail, but CLEAR members understood the academic demands that students would face in the semester. There was also discussion about the Spanish linguistic abilities of students enrolled (at the advanced level), as well as their professional/academic interests and preferences. Finally, basic information about Scripps College was shared in order to familiarize CLEAR members with the campus and its resources.

Experiential Learning/Critical Pedagogies

Liberal arts colleges provide an environment conducive to introducing alternative pedagogies and experiential learning activities because of their character and historical ability to connect with neighboring communities. Small class sizes allow a level of intimacy and flexibility that facilitates such connections. At the same time, the small college is usually committed to immersing their student body in unique experiences that are fulfilling and engaging through study abroad programs and internships. In my experience, these programs helped make available a variety of mechanisms and material support for alternative experiential pedagogy.

Taking critical pedagogies and experiential learning approaches as foundational for this course, an intentional experience was created to engage students in critical reflection on selected topics with members of a minority local community in order to promote positive social change and enhance critical thinking.[4] Furthermore, a student-centered learning approach was used as much as possible, taking into consideration students' knowledge and background as well as their academic and professional interests. The use of experiential learning methodologies and critical pedagogies (e.g., students' engagement with CLEAR members) enhanced the academic curriculum, while empowering participating members of CLEAR. Through these interactions, CLEAR participants revalorized their knowledge, experience, and culture. In fact, exchange of knowledge among students and participating women allowed for "traditional knowledge" to be valued and viewed as worthy of consideration in understanding deep cultural concepts that are collectively shared (*within* Hispanic culture) and that may interfere with medical treatment offered in typical American health care settings.

According to this alternative pedagogy, the teacher–student relationship is established in a nonhierarchical relationship, in which both develop themselves as agents of social change. This different approach provides an important opportunity, discussed in greater depth in this volume's opening chapter, for both the student and the teacher to reflect on background experiences, socioeconomic and historical factors, ethnicity, gender, and classroom dynamics.[5] I will share some instances that illustrate how this pedagogic approach proved successful in creating a more democratic classroom.

Interdisciplinary work (pursued through scholarly readings, oral presentations, written assignments, and research papers) prepared students to more fully engage with community members by introducing them to the value of diverse perspectives. At the same time, exposure to community-based activities reinforced interdisciplinary interests on the part of the students and motivated students to research additional topics beyond their narrow interests and from multiple angles. For example, for their weekly essays, students were excited to reflect on assigned readings because they were given the option of choosing two to three texts of interest to them. Furthermore, because students were so engaged with the readings and the concepts introduced through the dialogical exchange with CLEAR members, they often submitted papers much longer than the assigned length to further develop their thinking on these topics. When guest speakers introduced certain subjects, students were always prepared and motivated to engage in serious discussions; when CLEAR members led the conversations, students carefully listened and respectfully asked well-informed questions.

Students were encouraged to apply theory learned in class during meetings and other sessions outside of the classroom. For example, workshops and field trips allowed students and community members to reflect together on the subject matter explored in class and to do so in a friendly and safe environment that was conducive to learning. This produced a variety of collaborative exchanges on issues having to do with gender, marginalization, economic disparity, leadership, cultural traditions, religion, and misconceptions, as they relate to the medical system and the health professions in general. For example, students of Hispanic descent were able to express their feelings about belonging to marginalized migrant communities, who see themselves as second-class citizens. These students openly shared information that they had never shared before in a class setting. They also showed their pride in their cultural traditions and were appreciative of how this class validated their knowledge.

In my reimagined, nonhierarchical role as instructor, I tried to respect CLEAR members' decisions and suggestions in relation to their participation in the class. Prior to the start of the semester, it was decided that CLEAR would facilitate three presentations on topics included in the syllabus and would participate in two field trips. With respect to the former, CLEAR members helped to select course topics that were related to their knowledge, experience, and interests. They also contributed to the design of their visits to class. They thought, for example, that it was important for them to attend the first week of the semester to meet the students; they also considered that their participation would contribute to topics such as cultural perspectives on traditional medicine, ethnomedicine, the doctor–patient relationship, sexuality, adulthood, and care of the elderly. When participating, CLEAR members brought stories that captured the attention of the students and allowed for an engaged and respectful dialogue. Laughter, and occasional tears, were inevitable when some CLEAR members remembered past stories about their youth in relation to sex education, pregnancy, motherhood, and being the main care providers of their own families, including their elders.

As for arranging field trips, the process was not easy since the members' work and meeting schedules conflicted with the schedule already set for the course. Fortunately, CLEAR responded with flexibility. In a similar vein, I remained open to suggestions from CLEAR leadership. A field trip that I planned to visit an organic local farm, for example, was reworked upon invitation from a CLEAR member to visit her own private garden. She organized all the activities to be held that day, including a cooking presentation of a traditional Salvadorian meal and multiple presentations by various CLEAR members on healing herbs and foods used in Mexico and Central America. The reworked field trip exposed students to an intergenerational family setting and to a recyclable-sustainable home garden that bore a resemblance to a rural Mexican backyard. This provided an opportunity for the students to reflect on the value of family and the importance of the elderly in Hispanic cultures. Students learned about rural ethnic food and its properties for healing while they cooked *pupusas* (a Salvadorian dish). Eating *chapulines* (crickets) as well as tasting diverse medicinal beverages prepared by CLEAR members added amusement and an opportunity to connect more personally. CLEAR board president, Julia Barrios, and events coordinator, Leticia Martínez, took full responsibility for the coordination of the group in relation to their participation in the class.

CLEAR members helped facilitate additional excursions as well, including a visit to a traditional medicine pharmacy (*botánica*) that took place during class time. Although the instructor had original plans for this field trip, CLEAR members used their networks to locate a pharmacy where a healing demonstration could take place. Unfortunately, due to a family emergency, the family-run pharmacy had to close on the day of our visit. Immediate and alternative plans were made to visit two nearby pharmacies where students were immersed in the Hispanic culture while driving and walking the streets of a neighboring city that is very different from the city where the campus is located. The students were informed about preventive alternative/traditional medicine during this trip while touring the pharmacies and hearing an improvised but well-structured lecture by one pharmacy manager.

Learning Opportunities and Recommendations

The fusion of various teaching approaches during the semester enhanced the educational experience of students. The combination of experiential learning activities, small and large group discussions, seminar-style lectures, weekly research/reflection essays, and student presentations on topics of choice, motivated students in their intellectual inquiry and desire to competently communicate (linguistically and culturally) with their future patients. For example, writing weekly two-page reflection papers about the readings and incorporating their reflections about their conversations with CLEAR members and other guest speakers provided an opportunity to critically analyze health systems while recognizing and respecting each participant's perspective, as well as discussing the relevant theory. Moreover, some minority students in the class felt comfortable sharing their families' experiences while navigating the American medical system, using traditional medicine healers (*hueseros* and *curanderos*), because their experiences were reinforced by the comments made by CLEAR members. Minority students felt that their knowledge and experiences (as well as those of their own community) had been valued through these interactions. Additionally, the positive effects of valuing the voice and knowledge of students with their contribution to the curriculum through sharing knowledge, experience, readings, and videos enhanced the motivation of each student. This marked a first step to co-creating curriculum with students.

One key to facilitating this creative process was to establish a learning environment in which all members had the flexibility needed to pursue their curiosity. Not unlike interdisciplinarity, in general, this environment marks an important departure from conventional academic practice, in which a syllabus distributed at the start of the term prescribes the actions of both the instructor and the students for the entire semester. In order to provide such an environment, plans to deliver and discuss the material had to be readjusted and modified often. For this reason, in-class sessions (twice weekly) were organized into four sections. The first part was an introduction of the topic by the instructor followed by students' presentations of the topic of their choice (approved by the instructor) and related to the theme. The third section of the class consisted of discussion in small groups (four to six students) focusing on specific readings and topics that students found more interesting and connected with their future careers. Small group discussions were summarized by one or two members of the group toward the last part of the class and followed by questions and comments made by members of the larger group. To accommodate such dialogue, the traditional classroom setting had to be physically reconfigured in order to form a large circle. Smaller groups were also formed to have more intimate discussions that took place inside the classroom and outside of it (in a terrace under the shade of trees). This physical readjustment of the classroom provided a comfortable and relaxed environment conducive to teaching/learning where the role of the teacher followed more closely the definition of a teacher as a guide and motivator for the student to engage in the learning process. Most students appreciated the versatility that the class dynamics allowed in relation to the learning process, as the comment of one student (Sammy Little) demonstrates: "But most importantly, the small group discussions created a space where the students could share their own stories with the CLEAR members as well. The exchange of lived experiences was very valuable because it fostered a feeling of collaboration and understanding that was missing during the whole group meetings."

Connecting CLEAR members with Scripps College students through this class allowed various generations of women with various backgrounds to discuss issues that are of concern to all. Through engaging activities (meetings, field trips, and workshops), students were challenged to reflect on their own experiences and were responsible for their own learning and development during the semester. Exposure to unfamiliar settings (e.g., field trips in the city of Pomona) where Hispanic representation is above 80 percent, and knowledge of migrant stories, presented the students with ambiguity. This exposure and immersion in a different culture offered an opportunity for students to enhance not only their linguistic but also their cultural expertise. One of the students (Grant Steele) made a comment that is representative of those made by others regarding this experience: "By getting off campus and learning from individuals who do not attend the Claremont Colleges, I feel that I learned more than I ever imagined while also becoming part of a larger community. Although classroom readings and discussions are very informative, nothing can compare to learning from community members themselves.... The field-trips and guest speakers.... enhanced what I learned in the classroom and readings and helped me put a face to the theory."

Integrating cultural competence through experiential learning activities requires resources and commitment from all stakeholders. It requires more physical resources (e.g., space and honoraria for guest speakers and community members) and more investment of time and energy to plan activities and to realize such activities with success. Furthermore, the creation of policies for field trips and the adaptation of guidelines in relation to interactions with members of the local community are necessary, while making sure that protocols are followed and paperwork is arranged in advance so that all members involved are able to fully participate in all activities planned.

It is important to be aware that when using alternative pedagogies, all stakeholders need to have the capacity for improvisation and adaptation in order to face unexpected situations. There are many anecdotes about how stakeholders had to use alternative plans to complete their objectives. On one occasion (in spite of making van reservations) transportation became an issue; however, students with cars volunteered to drive other classmates without receiving any monetary compensation. On another occasion an emeritus professor of psychology auditing the course volunteered to serve as a guest speaker on the topic of the end of life in relation to cultural Hispanic practices. CLEAR members were also expert improvisers and flexible when their initial plans had to be changed. In those situations they demonstrated that they had a very strong support network that immediately responded to their needs. The two field trips were examples of this.

Creating bridges between academic and underserved local communities is an important pedagogical endeavor that promises benefits for all involved. My course empowered local migrant communities, revalidating their cultural knowledge and recognizing their dignity and contribution, while immersing students in the reality that migrant women face on a daily basis throughout the diaspora and in their roles as leaders in their own community. At the same time, the integration of experiential learning methods with an interdisciplinary approach allowed students to thoroughly engage with the subject matter and their interactions with members of the community and thus avoid the limitations of a traditional disciplinary focus. This motivated students to engage on a deeper level in order to identify solutions to specific problems raised by CLEAR members. Through this reflection, students were a step closer to becoming agents of social change in their current work or internships and future careers.

Based on students' excellent evaluations and informal comments made to the Spanish department leadership about this course, the Department of Spanish, Latin American and Caribbean Literatures and Cultures at Scripps College has plans to allocate funds for this course to continue to be taught and to further integrate the experiential learning and interdisciplinary approaches. Plans for the next course to be taught in the following spring are already under way, with community partners fully engaged and collaborating. Moreover, students who took this course have volunteered to be contacted to serve as mentors for future students enrolled in this class or to be guest speakers for future classes. With more persons interested in this kind of approach to teaching/learning in the Claremont Colleges Consortium, volunteering with their time, knowledge, and resources, I feel confident that this kind of work can be replicated in other fields throughout the nation's small colleges and universities.

Notes

The author asked students and CLEAR members (CLEAR is the Spanish acronym for women leaders, entrepreneurs, allies, and revolutionaries) to provide comments about a Spanish 100 course (Science and Cultural Competence) and their interaction and engagement with each other to assess methods, content, and assignments. A questionnaire was created for this purpose and sent to students after they had received their final grade. Students and community members gave permission to include their comments and names in this chapter.

1   Karol Hardin, "An Overview of Medical Spanish Curricula in the United States," *Hispania* 98, no. 4 (December 2015): 640–661; Karol J. Hardin and Mike Hardin, "Medical Spanish Programs in the United States: A Critical Review of Published Studies and a Proposal of Best Practices," *Teaching and Learning in Medicine: An International Journal* 25, no. 4 (2013): 306–311.

2   For information on demographic statistics and projections, please see Pew Research Center, August 3, 2017, http://www.pewresearch.org/fact-tank/2017/08/03/u-s-hispanic-population-growth-has-leveled-off/.

3   Information about PEOC can be found at http://pomonadaylabor.org/.

4   Paulo Freire, *Pedagogy of the Oppressed* (New York: Bloomsbury, 2000); Paulo Freire, *Pedagogy of Freedom: Ethics, Democracy, and Civic Courage* (Lanham, MD: Rowman & Littlefield, 2001); bell hooks, *Teaching to Transgress: Education as the Practice of Freedom* (Philadelphia, PA: Routledge, 1994).

5   Freire, *Pedagogy of the Oppressed*; Freire *Pedagogy of Freedom*.

14

Authenticity and Empathy in Education

• •

Team-Teaching "The Voices
Project: Mental Health"

AMANDA M. CALEB AND
ALICIA H. NORDSTROM

Rita Charon and other scholars of narrative medicine have emphasized the need
for doctors to develop close listening skills that translate to meaningful engagement, attentive interpretation, and better patient care.[1] These skills that
emphasize both empathy and authenticity are fundamental to education more
broadly, particularly at Misericordia University, a small Catholic University
that enrolls approximately 1,900 undergraduates and espouses a mission of "all
are welcome." Founded and sponsored by the Sisters of Mercy, Misericordia
deeply infuses the charisms of mercy, service, justice, and hospitality within a
broader identity of advocating social justice for marginalized and stigmatized
populations. The need to listen to and bear witness to stories of experiences that
differ from our own is at the heart of developing world citizenry.

Such was the framework for our approach to team-teaching two general education courses—PSY 123: Introduction to Psychology and ENG 151: University Writing Seminar: Literature of Health and Illness—to a total of fifty
students. In combining our classes for a unit on mental health, we sought to

challenge stigmas about mental health conditions through two uses of narrative: reading a graphic narrative and writing a personal memoir of mental health. In this endeavor, we blended the teaching of symptoms with stories and causes with personal chronicles.

Both PSY 123 and ENG 151 share goals of cultivating ethically and socially responsible behavior and developing written and oral communication skills that address the goals of our general education curriculum and utilize the habits of mind associated with a liberal arts education. These goals can be achieved in a number of ways, but we were motivated to combine the courses to pose essential educational questions. How does the act of reading contribute to our ethical worldview? What are the ethical responsibilities of writing another's story? How can writing cultivate social responsibility? Broadening this approach, we also sought to find ways to create an authentic experience of empathy through oral and written communication that could effectively engage our students to think about their social responsibility not only to empathize with those living with a mental health condition but also to educate others in order to reduce stigma. By combining our classes for a third of the semester, we demonstrated to our students the interconnectivity of educational experiences that could—and did—shape their understanding of mental health.

Our approach was twofold: to dissolve disciplinary boundaries through our team teaching about mental health and to have our students practice empathetic reasoning and imagination by interviewing individuals with mental health conditions and developing a first-person memoir. We chose to focus on mental health because of the prevalence of stigma about it, which owes to problematic narratives in the media, in society, and even in education. We integrated this approach throughout the semester, both during team-taught sessions and in individually taught classes: approximately a third of the semester was team taught, which the students were notified about on the first day of class (by arranging to teach at the same time, we avoided the need to structure student schedules). By combining classroom teaching with experiential learning that culminated in a theatrical performance of student interviews of people with mental health conditions, we emphasized to the students the need to understand individual experiences of mental health and our responsibility to reduce stigma through education.

Conditions and Constraints for Interdisciplinary Teaching

Our position at a smaller institution makes interdisciplinary pursuits relatively simple: we were easily able to coordinate our class times and request neighboring classrooms with the help of the registrar; we also had support from our online learning manager to create the necessary space on Blackboard for the two classes. Given the flexibility of our departments' curricula, which allows for selection of textbooks and, to a degree, themes, we were able to examine mental health as a unit without straying from the disciplinary expectations of these core classes.

One potential challenge of such interdisciplinary work, however, is loading: given that our university loads fully team-taught courses (meaning team taught for an entire semester) as only two credits for the faculty member, there are challenges to achieving our required twelve-credit load while engaging in creative and effective teaching methodology. While our university is supportive of innovative and interdisciplinary teaching, the administration is currently wrestling with how to balance the need for appropriate faculty compensation that accounts for the workload of team teaching (which is considerably more than teaching a class as an individual) with the concern of loading equity. Fortunately, our compromise of only team teaching for a third of the semester avoided this issue, limited the additional work we would have if we team taught for longer, and allowed us to address the disciplinary conventions of each course while still exposing students to the importance and value of interdisciplinary inquiry. It did, however, require additional, uncompensated time to develop the team-taught and specific skill–focused sessions as well as recruit the interviewees and supervise the student interviews. Preparation of the theatrical program also required additional work to facilitate the script creation, recruit actors, and execute a fully memorized and technical production. Thankfully, one of us received a three-credit course release each semester through an internal research grant, which provided some respite to buffer these time pressures. We ultimately persisted in our decision to team teach our courses because we believe in the value of such an approach—an opinion our students shared—and we were willing to work around institutional constraints.

Experiencing Stigma

We began the semester by doing the opposite of what good teaching suggests: we purposefully alienated our students. Assigning them numbers on the first day of class, we refused to acknowledge them by name, and we criticized their answers to complicated questions based on their majors, athletic status, and the like. The exercise created the experience of stigma and of dehumanization that we wanted the students to dissolve over the course of the semester; in other words, we created what we wanted them to destroy. Having then explained that the exercise was not real, we asked the students to write responses to the following: How did this experience of only being identified by a number make you feel? and Write about an experience when you were treated as insignificant or your voice did not count. We used the students' responses to develop a verbatim theater script, which grouped similar responses together but maintained the original syntax; we also added our responses to the exercise.

Verbatim theater is an established genre of documentary theater in which the playwright interviews individuals about a topic and then uses their exact words to create a coherent script. Verbatim theater can be used to achieve a number of goals, including establishing each individual as valued by allowing everyone's voice to be heard; encouraging individuals to listen to others' stories, creating a sense of community and connectivity; and "challeng[ing] normative and oppressive ideals, broadening our consciousness and transforming our understanding."[2] By using verbatim theater at the beginning of the semester, we could model expectations for our later writing project and demonstrate to students the power of narrative and their own words.

The results were heartbreaking but revealing: nearly all fifty students described the experience as dehumanizing, likening it to being a prisoner or being in a concentration camp; they also noted that they felt silenced regarding their own education. In our follow-up discussion, we asked the students to reflect upon how it felt to hear their own words aloud, to hear their classmates' words, and if the sharing experience created a sense of empathy or connectivity. They all agreed, both in person and through reflective writing, that they felt more connected with their classmates. Although they shared individual past experiences of being treated as just a number, they also revealed a sense of anxiety, insignificance, and the desire never to treat others in the same manner.

Reading about Stigma

This first class set the tone for subsequent meetings and helped establish a deep-felt need to reduce stigma about mental health conditions. In four subsequent class periods during the semester, we discussed Daryl Cunningham's *Psychiatric Tales*, a graphic novel depicting the author's experience as a psychiatric nurse working with individuals with varying mental health conditions and struggling with his own. Using this text presented several challenges: students were exposed to mental health conditions through subjective experience before being provided textbook definitions, diagnoses, and so forth, which could lead to confusion; and not all students were familiar with graphic narratives and how to interpret them. The first challenge we embraced as a way of reimagining how we teach about mental health, whereby the individual's experience and perceptions about mental health drive the conversations about depression, bipolar disorder, and other conditions, rather than viewing mental health only within the limited, distant scientific view. Engaging with the verbal and pictorial narrative offered students the means to understand mental health conditions outside the top-down medical structure and in cases when words fail to describe the condition and the experience of it.

We addressed the second challenge, that of the unfamiliarity of graphic narratives, through traditional guided readings and by using Visual Thinking

Strategies (VTS)—a means of encouraging student engagement with images through careful observation of details to cultivate deep understanding.[3] Given the small size of our university, we were easily able to use Misericordia's Pauly Friedman Art Gallery to preempt our discussion of *Psychiatric Tales* with a VTS session, asking the students three simple questions: What's going on in this picture? What do you see that makes you say that? What else can you find?[4] This art gallery experience helped develop the students' critical observation and thinking skills, requiring them to slow down their observations to comprehend more of the image. This training translated to their careful and detailed examination of *Psychiatric Tales* that went beyond the obvious to consider the page layout, use and repetition of images and symbols, use of contrast, and so forth. It also helped developed students' critical thinking skills, whereby a claim for meaning was always and clearly supported by specific details from the image. This attention to detail and critical meaning making was essential in cultivating their understanding of mental health conditions.

For our first discussion on *Psychiatric Tales*, we asked the students if they ever used words like "spaz," "psycho," "crazy," "freak." Unsurprisingly, all the students acknowledged their own usage, almost shamefully. We then asked them to interrogate why these words are problematic, which introduced students to how stigma is embedded in our word choice and our culture: our willingness to use such language demonstrates the challenge of breaking down stigmas about mental health conditions. Cunningham points out that "we don't tolerate sexism and racism these days, but people with mental health problems are still fair game. . . . Mockery, discrimination, and stigma persist despite research showing mental illness to be as real as any other illness."[5] The challenge is to educate about mental health, not only the biological component, but also as an individual condition: while those with depression share symptoms, their experience is as individualized as anyone's experience of any health condition or situation. Encouraging the students to see a person with a mental health condition as an individual helps break down the stigma about what a certain condition looks like and how a person with that condition should act, and it ultimately creates an empathetic understanding of mental health.

Subsequent classes followed the structure of the book, which defied easy groupings: purposefully, Cunningham moves from dementia to self-harm to schizophrenia to depression to antisocial personality disorder to famous people with mental health conditions, and on, ending with suicide and his own experience with anxiety and depression. While the structure might seem disorganized, the students noted that it is anything but: Cunningham prevents us from the very human tendencies to group like things together. We cannot claim a shared experience with dementia and self-harm; what we can do is observe individual experiences of each condition. The structure denies the possibility of progressive blame—that conditions somehow worsened from an individual's actions or inactions; it also denies the reader a traditional narrative structure (rising action, climax, resolution) because mental health conditions are neither so simple nor so predictable. In reflecting upon the authorial decision to structure the work in this way, students were able to see mental conditions in their own right and the individuals in their singularity.

Class discussions included close readings of the text and images paired with clinical presentations of each condition through various articles and websites. The purpose was to expose students to how mental illness is diagnosed—which is not always evident in *Psychiatric Tales*—and to offer multiple perspectives as to what a specific mental health condition would look like to an individual. The result was a rich engagement of psychology with narrative presence; several students reflected how symbols—which require interpretation to understand their meaning—are similar to symptoms, noting that viewing both requires seeing/listening carefully, looking for evidence to support an interpretation (and not just preconceived notions), and asking more questions.

This clinical, close-reading approach culminated in the students' discussion of the final chapter, in which Cunningham discusses his depression. With guidance from us, students noted his repetition of images from early chapters, making connections with the chapters on antisocial personality disorder and suicide. When asked why the author would make these visual connections, students offered a range of answers: to suggest the relationship between the different mental health conditions; to connect the author with the patients he treated; to connect the reader to all the stories. It is this last explanation that students found the most functional and valuable: the students recalled an early chapter entitled "It Could Be You," suggesting the reader's connection to the text because mental health conditions do not discriminate and are not something that can be anticipated or prevented. This realization at the end of our discussions demonstrated the students' development in thinking critically and empathetically about mental health conditions.

Writing about Stigma

Midway through the semester, our students shifted from consumers of storytelling to producers through their next assignment, called The Voices Project: Mental Health. The Voices Project (TVP) is a narrative-based assignment using contact theory as a means to reduce college students' stereotypes and prejudice toward stigmatized groups. In psychological literature, contact theory states that bringing individuals from conflictual groups into direct contact with each other reduces stereotypes and prejudice. This principle has been empirically supported with over fifty years of research evidence, even in countries with strongly entrenched attitudes.[6] However, the parameters of contact matter; this stigma-reducing effect works best when the interpersonal contact promotes equal status among group members, shared goals, and cooperation, and it provides opportunity for friendship and positive emotional and cognitive outcomes.[7] TVP framework was first developed in 2009 and has been empirically shown to reduce racism in college students.[8] A TVP assignment involves several components that apply contact theory in a college-based general education course. The goal of TVP is for students to capture the "voices" of individuals from stigmatized, ignored, and misunderstood social groups and disseminate them publicly to promote education, social justice, and advocacy. TVP achieves these goals through student interviews with individuals from stigmatized groups and subsequent memoirs reflecting life themes of the interviewee from the first-person perspective.

We applied TVP framework in a version of the project focused on persons with mental health conditions (PMHCs) and their family members to examine if direct contact would reduce mental health stigma. First, students completed surveys assessing their attitudes toward the target group as a baseline measure of stigma. As part of the survey, students also ranked the mental health conditions that they (1) were most familiar with, (2) were least familiar with, (3) found most interesting, (4) found least interesting, and (5) had experienced themselves or through a family member or friend. The mental health conditions evaluated included anxiety/obsessive-compulsive disorder/post-traumatic stress disorder, depression/bipolar disorder/suicide, schizophrenia, autism spectrum disorder, eating disorders, Tourette syndrome, drug abuse/alcoholism, dyslexia/learning disabilities, Alzheimer's disease/dementia, and intellectual disabilities (attention-deficit/hyperactivity disorder, or ADHD, was included later). Based on their rankings, we assigned students to interview a PMHC or family member of a PMHC who related to a condition that they ranked as being (1) least familiar and/or (2) did not experience themselves or through a family member or friend. This matching process was to ensure that students were unfamiliar with the mental health condition that they would experience to enable the most academic and emotional growth over the course of the project.

Interviews

To accommodate the participation in TVP for the fifty students enrolled in our two classes, we recruited fifty PMHCs or family members of PMHCs for interviews. Interviewees were recruited through personal contacts and community outreach to local and regional mental health support, education, and advocacy groups, including National Alliance on Mental Illness, the Pennsylvania Tourette Syndrome Alliance, and the Alzheimer's Association. Interviewees signed consent forms acknowledging that their stories would be shared publicly and confidentially, unless they requested otherwise. Interviewees spanned a range of ages from nine to ninety years old and included PMHCs as well as mothers, fathers, siblings, and children of PMHCs.

Once students were matched with the appropriate interviewee, they arranged a one- to two-hour interview to learn about how the mental health condition affected the life of their interviewee. To alleviate scheduling and logistical concerns, students independently contacted their interviewees and scheduled an individual interview on campus at a time convenient for themselves and their interviewee. We provided students with training in safety procedures, and we encouraged them to record the interview on a device so they could focus on asking questions and building rapport during the interview. We also briefed the students on the importance of confidentiality and protecting the identity of their interviewee on the recordings and in their memoirs.

We provided students with guidelines of suggested interview topics, including childhood experiences of mental health (e.g., first time realizing condition, school experiences); family experience of mental health (e.g., reactions of parents, nuclear and extended family); experiences of mental health with the outside community (e.g., assumptions and stereotypes encountered, decisions about disclosure, perceptions of media portrayal); experiences with others who have a mental health condition (e.g., feelings of connection or disconnection with those having similar conditions); cultural and economic issues (e.g., effect of condition on finances and work); and personal experiences with mental health (e.g., definitions of "mental illness," lessons learned, three wishes). To prepare students for their interviews, we dedicated two class periods to interview training during which we reviewed skills, such as how to build rapport, asking effective questions, how to acknowledge and respond to emotions, anticipating challenges, and observing verbal and nonverbal details. Students role-played skills in class with instructor support and debriefed their concerns and questions, such as what to do if their interviewee talked too much, talked too little, or cried during the interview. Students reported feeling nervous that they might offend their interviewees or might not know what to say in the moment. We gave students an opportunity to voice their concerns and helped problem-solve their anticipated anxieties.

Memoirs

The final component for the students' involvement in TVP is to create a memoir from their interviews, using a first-person perspective to transform expression from participant to student that "fictionalizes" the story and gives students their own venue to express the ideas and meaning of their interviewee's story while still maintaining the accuracy and authenticity of the interviews. Adopting an autobiographical (as opposed to third-person biographical) writing style enables empathetic perspective taking, which we consider to be a key feature in stigma reduction.

To support the writing process, we offered a memoir-writing workshop in which we provided students with examples of different types of memoirs, including Alison Piepmeier's blog about living with (and eventually succumbing to) brain cancer, two excerpts from *Reading Lips and Other Ways to Overcome a Disability*, and memoirs written by students who participated in previous incarnations of TVP.[9] These workshops were developed from existing writing workshops from English classes and a previous First Year Experience class focused on memoirs of individuals with disabilities. In discussing the sample memoirs, we instructed the students to consider what was engaging about each one, how they conveyed a central and lasting message, and what narrative techniques they employed; we also asked students to consider the ethics of how someone tells another person's story. These samples, along with *Psychiatric Tales*, exposed students to various ways of telling stories and conveying meaning, including the use of traditional linear or topical narratives, letters, blogs, poems, graphic novels, and diaries.

Students then analyzed the content of their interviews to extract and identify main ideas and themes from the life of their interviewee. We encouraged them to distill these main ideas and themes as creatively as possible using the VTS skills they had cultivated at the beginning of the semester. Students brought their laptops and interview notes to class, and each instructor floated from student to student to provide feedback as they began writing. Students asked for help with organization of their memoir, how to select a point of view or format (e.g., first-person account versus a letter), and how to pare down and find a focus from the wealth of information they gathered from the interview. We required each student to meet with their respective instructor for a conference during which the instructor reviewed a draft of the memoir and provided feedback. Students also conducted peer reviews and provided feedback to other students writing on similar topics. This scaffolded approach—from reading to analyzing to creating—not only helped students with their written communication skills but also helped them to understand their ethical responsibility when writing another person's story.

Theatrical Production

Given that the goal of TVP is to educate and share the voices of stigmatized groups, the project aims to disseminate the stories written by students as widely as possible beyond the classroom; in this process, students become storytellers to the larger public arena. For the mental health version, a team of seven faculty from the disciplines of English, history, psychology, and mass communications and design—who are committed to interdisciplinary collaboration and who had helped with previous iterations of TVP—worked together to excerpt the stories and thematically arrange the excerpts into scenes to create a play script. These faculty were selected based on their expertise on stigma of mental health as well as their pedagogical strength in analyzing themes of discrimination and identity through narrative texts. The scenes ranged from topics such as specific disorders (e.g., Tourette syndrome, substance abuse, the spectrum) to broader themes (e.g., fix it, gratitude) and included stories from all interviewees. Scenes varied in format with monologues, interspersed dyads, trios, and more, with a finale that involved the full cast of twenty-one actors. The theatrical production was performed as a memorized play in the campus auditorium across four days with a total audience of over six hundred people in attendance.

In addition, we had the opportunity to share the students' stories in a larger theatrical context as well as a documentary format. A research grant enabled the filming of six of the live interviews (with permission of the students and interviewees), which were edited into a thirty-minute documentary. One of the filmmakers had a colleague who was organizing the Broadway Bound Theatre Festival (BBTF) in New York City and was looking for a socially conscious piece that highlighted mental health issues. Through this pipeline, the script for TVP was submitted and accepted for the festival and revised with the help of a professional dramaturge to focus on only fourteen stories in order to give each story more depth. The stories were also arranged to create a holistic arc across the show from the most to least familiar conditions. This BBTF version was performed in New York on two days with professional TV, film, and theater actors and a professional director. Audience members provided feedback during a talkback session after the show, which reinforced the authenticity of the stories and made personal connections with the mental health conditions portrayed in the show. Both shows were filmed for future educational use.

Impact Assessment

The overarching goal of our team-teaching union was to apply two narrative methods of pedagogy—the reading of a graphic novel and writing a first-person memoir—to increase empathy and reduce students' stigmas about mental health. Students completed survey packets during the first and last week of the semester asking them to report on their attitudes toward PMHCs. We used the California Assessment of Stigma Change, a psychometrically reliable and valid measure that evaluates four dimensions of attitudes toward mental illness.[10] The attribution subscale involves a brief vignette describing "Harry," a thirty-year-old man with schizophrenia, and asks respondents to rate Harry across different domains (e.g., pity, blame, danger). The recovery subscale asks about "people with serious mental illness in general" in regard to their level of hopefulness, future goals, and coping. The empowerment subscale explores respondents' perceptions of the capability, worthiness, and competence of PMHCs. The care-seeking subscale inquires about respondents' care-seeking choices if they were in the position of having mental illness. Each item is evaluated on a nine-point scale.

We statistically compared the survey data from the first week of the semester to the last week of the semester for all students who completed the project. Although fifty students were enrolled in both sections, one student did not complete the project. Results showed that students significantly decreased in their attribution stigma toward mental health from the beginning to the end of the semester. Students reported significantly reduced perceptions that PMHCs were at fault for their disorders, were dangerous and should be avoided, and should be pitied after completing TVP compared to before the project. These stigmas reflect the most common manifestations of public stereotypes about mental illness and often result in discrimination toward PMHCs.[11] However, no significant changes emerged for the recovery, empowerment, or care-seeking subscales. Given that the interviewees were speaking from a detached vantage point—as opposed to being in the throes of their mental health condition—students may not have had the opportunity to witness the severity of mental illness, and therefore may not have changed these specific facets of mental health stigma.

Conclusions and Lessons Learned

In our experience, the value of interdisciplinary teaching, particularly at the core level, cannot be overstated: the act of team teaching across disciplines allows faculty to model effective learning through the act of learning from each other. Nearly all students in our two classes indicated in their final course reflections that they found great value in the team-taught component of the courses, citing the benefit of looking at literature and mental health conditions from a variety of disciplinary perspectives and the positive impact of learning from each other. Several students noted how the combined courses brought together the core curriculum in ways that made sense to them and built upon skills that were developed in the individual course sessions that were not team taught; these same students reflected upon how they imagined this experience modeled what their careers would entail: working across boundaries and disciplinary backgrounds.

The blended course assignments helped develop students' empathetic and imaginative reasoning, and had significant impact on their worldviews. While this transformation could occur with the input or drive of only one discipline (psychology), the addition of another (English) cultivated the students' understanding of narrative and authenticity and ethical responsibility in writing. The addition of psychology to English provided students with a broader understanding of the nature, symptoms, and life experience of mental health conditions. The survey data we collected demonstrated the impact of both textual and direct contact narrative techniques on reducing common public stigmas of mental health. During our team-taught portions, our courses integrated seamlessly such that we essentially "adopted" each other's students and treated all students as our own. By examining and catalyzing empathy through verbatim theater, *Psychiatric Tales*, and TVP, our disciplines overlapped so obviously that students could not feel the boundaries between subjects. Students developed personal relationships with their interviewees, which enabled them to replace their preconceived stigmas with real-world experiences with individuals with mental health conditions. The theatrical production raised empathy and social connectedness to an even higher level. Interviewees and audience members expressed feelings of validation, understanding, and inclusion after watching the program. Several interviewees introduced themselves to the actors portraying their stories and thanked them for representing them on stage. Many interviewees also introduced themselves to us and thanked us (often with hugs and tears) for sharing their stories. We believe that our united courses created a lasting understanding of how seemingly different disciplines work together, enabled students to produce original works for social advocacy and stigma reduction, and ultimately broadened and enriched how students see others in the world as well as themselves.

Notes

1 Rita Charon, "Narrative Medicine: A Model for Empathy, Reflection, Profession, and Trust." *JAMA* 286 (2001): 1897–1902.
2 Sara Peters, "The Impact of Participating in a Verbatim Theatre Process," *Social Alternatives* 36, no. 2 (2017): 33.
3 Abigail C. Housen, "Aesthetic Thought, Critical Thinking, and Transfer," *Arts and Learning Research Journal* 18, no. 1 (2001–2002): 99–131; Craig M. Klugman, Jennifer Peel, and Diana Beckmann-Mendez, "Art Rounds: Teaching Interprofessional Students Visual Thinking Strategies at One School," *Academic Medicine* 86, no. 10 (October 2011): 1266–1271.
4 Abigail C. Housen and Philip Yenawine, "VTS: Visual Thinking Strategies," California State University, Northridge, 2013, http://wrocc.csun.edu/~sch_educ/assets/take-away-tools/2013/hoel-moca.pdf.
5 Darryl Cunningham, *Psychiatric Tales* (London: Bloomsbury, 2011), 25.
6 Gordon W. Allport, *The Nature of Prejudice* (Cambridge, MA: Addison-Wesley, 1954), 487–491; Jens Binder et al., "Does Contact Reduce Prejudice or Does Prejudice Reduce Contact? A Longitudinal Test of the Contact Hypothesis among Majority and Minority Groups in Three European Countries," *Journal of Personality and Social Psychology* 96, no. 4 (2009): 843–856; John F. Dovidio, Samuel L. Gaertner, and Kerry Kawakami, "Intergroup Contact: The Past, Present, and the Future," *Group Processes & Intergroup Relations* 6, no. 1 (2003): 5–21; Miles Hewstone and Hermann Swart, "Fifty-Odd Years of Inter-Group

Contact: From Hypothesis to Integrated Theory," *British Journal of Social Psychology* 50, no. 3 (2011): 374–386; Thomas F. Pettigrew and Linda R. Tropp, *When Groups Meet: The Dynamics of Intergroup Contact* (New York: Psychology Press, 2011), 1–27.

7   Allport, *The Nature*, 487–491.
8   Alicia H. Nordstrom, "The Voices Project: Reducing White Students' Racism in Introduction to Psychology," *Teaching of Psychology* 42, no. 2 (January 2015): 43–50.
9   Alison Piepmeier, *Every Little Thing* (blog), accessed March 20, 2020, http://alisonpiepmeier.blogspot.com/.
10   Patrick W. Corrigan et al., "The California Assessment of Stigma Change: A Short Battery to Measure Improvements in the Public Stigma of Mental Illness," *Community Mental Health Journal* 51, no. 6 (2015): 635–640.
11   Corrigan et al.

15

Experiential Learning in the Rural, Small College Setting

•••••••••••••••••••••

Creating an "Appalachian Cluster"

TINA L. HANLON, PETER CROW,
SUSAN V. MEAD, CAROLYN L.
THOMAS, AND DELIA R. HECK

Designed primarily for first-year students, Ferrum College's Appalachian Cluster is a group of liberal arts classes that examines modernization in Appalachia from several points of view, through the study of English, sociology, and environmental science. One cohort of students takes all three classes together during the fall semester, with faculty and students forming a unique learning community. While students fulfill their usual core requirements and faculty members include one cluster class in their normal workload, students also benefit from a variety of high-impact learning activities, planned collaboratively by the faculty, while experiencing and bolstering the strong relationship between the college and our region's mountain communities.

The Appalachian Cluster has four main aspects that, taken together, constitute an especially meaningful entrance into college life and learning:

1 It encourages learning as a communal activity.
2 It embodies both disciplinary and interdisciplinary perspectives.
3 It utilizes place-based, experiential learning.
4 It provides unique insight into modernization issues critical to the future.

The cluster is a learning community in that the students are together in three introductory courses. Thus they spend ten hours a week in class together, often collaborating on projects outside of class as well. Though they are not housed together on campus, by the end of the semester they have spent significant blocks of time participating in off-campus field experiences, including a three-day trip. Research from the past several decades on academic success and retention documents the benefits of such a learning community, especially for first-year students.[1] When recent students wrote about their experiences in class, a few said they would have liked to get acquainted with a wider variety of classmates in each course, but most were extremely enthusiastic about having a built-in, close-knit group of friends in their first semester and working closely with professors who cooperatively arranged extracurricular activities and deadlines in ways that would help them succeed.

The Appalachian Cluster comprises three classes that are part of Ferrum's core curriculum and meet the objectives required of all sections of those courses. As such, they are discipline focused, with grades determined separately by the professor for each course. Being introductory classes, they lay out the very parameters and methodology of their respective disciplines, one based in the humanities, one in the social sciences, and one in the natural sciences. An interdisciplinary perspective emerges from the integrated treatment of the theme of modernization in Appalachia. Coal from Appalachia, for example, powered much of the modernization in the United States. So sociologists examine economic benefits and liabilities of the industry, medical and safety issues, cultural and religious resources of communities, power dynamics, and other systemic human issues. At the same time, environmental scientists focus on systems in nature and effects of coal mining, coal burning, and coal waste on ecosystems. The students thus begin to wrestle holistically, rather than piecemeal, with hidden costs of modernization, of which most had been only vaguely aware. The English professor helps them apply critical thinking skills, organize essays, and edit in a drafting process that leads to writing clearly about what they read and observe for all three courses. Cluster students also get literary perspectives on coal country from writers such as Lee Smith, Denise Giardina, and George Ella Lyon.[2] By semester's end, the students have witnessed how different academic disciplines approach and evaluate knowledge and how knowledge is often enhanced by synthesizing those disciplines.

As our college evolved over the past century from Ferrum Training School to a junior college and then a four-year liberal arts college, the faculty has developed a variety of synergistic, interdisciplinary projects and courses, often supported by consortiums such as the Appalachian College Association. The college's small size (under 1,500 students) and tradition of housing many faculty and staff on campus have facilitated collegiality and necessitated cross-disciplinary cooperation. The Appalachian Cluster has contributed to recent revisions in Ferrum's general education program, which addressed trends in higher education and modernization in society—the need for global citizens who can synthesize as well as specialize, by requiring every student to take two Integrated Learning courses, designated IL.

Ferrum's location in the foothills of Virginia's Blue Ridge Mountains provides a remarkable setting for place-based educational experiences, with diverse opportunities for hands-on activities. In addition to coal country in Southwest Virginia and adjoining states, iron was once mined to the north, timber covered the whole area, and a railroad industry emerged in Appalachia to transport these resources. Appalachian Cluster classes have had extended field experiences around the region, extracting not natural resources, but stories of communities that grew up because of these industries; some of them have nearly died, and some carry on a gallant effort to survive. Our favorite location for place-based learning is along the biologically diverse Clinch River, where the town of St. Paul is at once the home of loyal workers and a large coal-fired electric plant built in the twenty-first century, a center of resistance to coal domination, and an area standard bearer for community resilience and resourcefulness. Between Ferrum and St. Paul is Whitetop Mountain, where a popular music festival in the 1930s promoted traditional music and dancing. Today the railroad bed once used for transporting timber off the mountain (and presumably festival participants) is transformed into a paved trail where biking is mostly coasting eighteen miles through verdant forests (testimony that they can grow back), to Damascus, Virginia, and the Appalachian Trail.

It is hard to imagine issues more critical in education, indeed in essential decision making everywhere, than those related to the ubiquitous reach of modernization as led by the Western world. Once seen by many as the superhighway to a better future for all the earth, modernization now finds itself the center of sharply divided views, including the belief that economic progress in some areas requires economic plundering of others. In Central Appalachia strong opinions on these matters have a long, contentious history. These issues encompass "power and powerlessness," shifting understandings of history, even the hidden risks of establishing folk museums such as Ferrum's Blue Ridge Institute and Farm Museum.[3] Issues of race, gender, migration, and white privilege are embedded throughout.[4] Running through the center of it all are ecological imperatives at or near flood stage.[5] The Appalachian Cluster has proven over time to be a compelling vehicle for examining these matters, given proximity to clear demonstrations of why modernization needs questioning, rigorous scholarship readily available, and learning tools the cluster makes available.

Peter Crow and a group of colleagues created the Appalachian Cluster in 1999, after an American Council of Learned Societies grant provided preparatory release time for four professors and one campus folklorist, as well as travel funds to begin field research and plan service learning. The cluster began as a four-course learning community, but the difficulties of enrolling enough students in the same four classes at once led to the decision to phase out the American history course. They are freshmen, and occasionally sophomores, at a small college with limited options for fitting in other courses they need without encountering schedule conflicts. Honors students can count any cluster course as one of their required interdisciplinary honors seminars. In 2013 the cluster was moved from spring to fall semester for several reasons related to the college's changing calendar, the need for warm weather not too late in the semester for the field trip, and the desire to attract students interested in environmental science who would take their introductory course in their first semester.

Susan Mead, current coordinator of the program, has taught the sociology course since the cluster began, Tina Hanlon took the English course after Peter Crow retired in 2008, and four different professors have taught science in the cluster due to faculty turnover and sabbaticals. Recently Delia Heck took over as Carolyn Thomas phased into retirement after many years of teaching environmental science. The cluster design allows for flexibility in individual teaching methods and course content as the faculty and the world around us change. Moreover, in addition to linking our teaching in the cluster with a wide variety of our own research and community service projects across the region and world, the faculty benefit from sharing resources and experiences with colleagues from other institutions. We have discussed the cluster at professional conferences and, from 2002 to 2008, four National Endowment for the Humanities grants enabled Appalachian Cluster professors to sponsor month-long summer institutes for college and university teachers on regional study and interdisciplinary learning in the liberal arts. Ferrum College was one of only a few small colleges to receive these grants, presumably because the National Endowment for the Humanities recognized the value of replicating our methods of place-based interdisciplinary study in other regions.

After external grants were no longer available to support multiple field trips in the same semester, the college provided a modest budget that covered about one quarter of the field trip expenses. Donations to the college from those keenly interested in Appalachian Studies have filled the gaps so that students have never been charged for field trips, aside from buying themselves extra snacks and one restaurant meal. To stabilize the funding, some years ago one administrator expressed her belief that this unique opportunity for students should not have to start depending on their ability to pay, and arranged for an annual supplemental amount from Academic Affairs to cover the field trip. In a typical year, fifteen students and three faculty can spend a long weekend exploring Appalachia for under three thousand dollars, nearly all of which goes to community organizations that host our visits and, in two locations, prepare meals for us. As time and local needs allow, the cluster also contributes to these communities by helping with a gardening or renovation project, or sharing poems in a classroom. We pack a busy schedule of activities into three full days of travel, but we can't manage a visit to every place of interest every year, so examples mentioned in this chapter represent different places the cluster has visited over the years.

The cluster's science course includes a lab one afternoon a week and class meetings on days that the other cluster courses don't meet. The English and sociology classes meet on the same days during consecutive morning hours, so the professors can blend their hours together and trade times if needed. Although faculty aren't paid extra for team teaching or administering this program, these two professors usually attend both hours, most often sitting in as observer and participant while the other is teaching. The blended class time makes it possible to watch a full-length film during the first week and later study a novel in depth to explore sociological examples, literary traditions, and essay topics. Within the first two weeks, cluster students and faculty have dinner together, at a rural faculty home or the Phoebe Needles Center, a former mission school up the mountain from the campus. We review some local history and participate in get-acquainted activities, with informal discussion that relates to integrating our thinking about environmental science (favorite places outdoors), social sciences (most significant social justice issues), and the arts (favorite fictional characters).

In their introductory sociology course, cluster students study standard sociological concepts through an Appalachian lens. They take quizzes and a final exam on terminology related to sociological theory and methods, culture, socialization, family, social stratification, religion, education, politics, economy, race and ethnicity, sex and gender, deviance, social groups, and social movements. Simultaneously, students must apply this terminology to examples from poetry, novels, film, music lyrics, essays, visual art, collected interviews, role plays exploring environmental issues, scientific field experiences, and lab experiments. Their culminating project is "ABCs of Appalachia," an illustrated collection of slides applying randomly assigned terms to examples they have studied for each topic area throughout the semester, drawing from field trips, assigned texts, and activities from all three classes. For example, a student assigned "language" as a sociological term about culture designed a slide for the letter "L" with photographs taken at the Mountain Heritage Museum in St. Paul. The student's text and pictures of periodical pages show that the *United Mine Workers Journal* has been published in multiple languages, including Italian and Slovak, "for all of the different immigrant miners who spoke different languages and worked in the mines."

The key to the Appalachian Cluster is weaving course content and experiences with regional community partnerships, developed for over twenty years, into a holistic semester of critical thinking. On the first day of class students begin watching John Sayles's acclaimed film *Matewan*, about the 1920 "mine war" in southern West Virginia. The first frames of that film put students into the atmosphere of darkness within a deep mine, where miners struggle to make a living and stay alive; weeks later students experience that same literal darkness when they visit an exhibition coal mine in West Virginia, Kentucky, or Virginia. They delve deeper into power struggles between unions and workers when they visit the town of Matewan itself, and stand on ground where union and company men killed one another, just behind the West Virginia Mine Wars Museum.

One focus of the Appalachian Cluster is to explore economic, ethnic, environmental, and experiential diversity within the region. Stereotypes of a monochromatic Appalachia are first dispelled through *Matewan*'s cinematic depictions of Italian, African American, and white miners first clashing, then working together, as symbolized through the film's integration of music and food traditions. Ethnic diversity in the coalfields is reinforced on the field trip when students see communities with formerly segregated hollows and steep hills of tombstones carved with difficult-to-pronounce names of eastern European miners. To further explore the region's racial-ethnic diversity, we read poetry by NAACP Image Award recipient Frank X Walker, who coined the word "Affrilachia,"[6] as well as the work of Monacan Indian Nation member Karenne Wood.[7] In some years students even meet these authors on campus, giving greater meaning to the sociological connections made with textbooks then signed by the authors. When they travel to the Museum of the Middle Appalachians, a site in Saltville, Virginia, recommended by Karenne Wood, they see artifacts left behind by Monacans and others of the Woodland Indian period. At Southwest Virginia Community College, students see brick sculptures representing regional folktales, wildlife, and Native American petroglyphs on nearby Paint Mountain that are now inaccessible on privately owned land. Within this context, students can reflect further upon how to apply sociological theory to the Appalachians' loss of land; the loss experienced by indigenous inhabitants centuries ago and the more recent loss of mountain land to modern development are the subject matter of another cluster text, Sharyn McCrumb's novel *The Rosewood Casket*.[8]

In addition to exploring human diversity within Appalachia, we consider diverse ways people interact with the land itself, by, for example, studying effects of underground mines versus mountaintop removal mining, with that learning occurring in the classroom, the lab, and the field trip. On the road, students can see three different ways communities have implemented flood control: building a flood wall embellished by relief sculptures of Matewan's history; moving an entire commerce district from a low river bank to a higher flat surface blasted from a mountainside in Grundy, Virginia; and rerouting a biologically diverse river so that residences wouldn't flood and recreation, retail, and manufacturing sites could flourish in St. Paul. While visiting these sites, students meet and learn from people who have been partners with Ferrum College for decades; they see communities that are barely holding on and ones that are rising up. And they learn more about sociology through every interaction.

The Appalachian Cluster's original design as a spring semester experience included English 102, the second half of freshman composition. With that course's emphasis on research, students explored a variety of primary and secondary sources over the years. Their interviews with community members during field trips are archived in the college library. Students who already have advanced placement or transfer credit for freshman composition can enroll in the cluster English class for sophomore literature credit. Although they do some extra reading and give an oral report on a literature project, they generally study literary works with more depth and less breadth than they would get in a literature survey course. Since typically no more than one to three students enroll for literature credit, the professors are willing to work with individual students if they have special interest in a particular Appalachian author or type of literature. Susan Mead's use of detailed examples from literature to teach sociology augments the English course assignments, helping all the students get a broad introduction to the study of fiction, poetry, film, nonfiction, folktales, and traditional ballads. We usually look at one or more picture books as well, and added a regional book of photographic essays in 2017.

Since the cluster was moved to fall semester, having most of the students enrolled in English 101 provides more flexibility in writing assignments without having to fit topics into the English 102 requirements for longer critiques and research papers. Students write response papers about readings and other cluster activities, practicing basic skills in stating and supporting a precise thesis. We tried requiring integration of a sociological concept into the thesis statement of some English papers, but that can put awkward limitations on students inexperienced at analyzing literature, so we changed that requirement to a recommendation. When they write about cultural diversity, family and community relationships, living off the land, or labor struggles depicted in a poem or novel, students are discussing sociological concepts even if they don't use a sociology definition that restricts the examples they might choose to support their main ideas.

Students also practice writing summaries by reporting on different chapters of Peter Crow's book *Do, Die, or Get Along: A Tale of Two Appalachian Towns*.[9] Since this 2007 book of oral history grew out of interviews by Peter Crow and early cluster students with residents in St. Paul and Dante, Virginia, it now introduces students to regional history and some of the places and people they will encounter on the field trip. All the composition students also write about the field trip, with the requirement added in 2017 to integrate one or more photographs into their essay.

For a folktale project in the English course, students analyze variants of the same Appalachian folktale in small groups that report to the class on their tale type, such as "Jack and the Robbers," "Whitebear Whittington," or "John Henry." After the class discusses one tale together, such as Tina Hanlon's favorite folktale "Mutsmag,"[10] the groups use packets she provides with folktale texts, links to online resources, guidelines for analyzing motifs and enduring values in folktales, and outlines for planning essays. Each student then practices analyzing, comparing, and documenting stories by writing an essay about two tales they choose. Since the Blue Ridge Institute on our campus hosts the Blue Ridge Folklife Festival every October, teaching the cluster in the fall enhances an in-class introduction to different types of folklore that links the festival, the folktale project, the study of culture within sociology, and literary depictions of folkways.

Sometimes an invitation to watch The Jack Tale Storytellers perform for schoolchildren on campus is a bonus that fits into the cluster students' schedules. Whenever possible, we take the class to meet authors they are studying or related lectures or performances on or off campus. In 2017, for example, Sharyn McCrumb, who had lectured on campus years before, gave a library talk ten miles from campus that was a required activity for the cluster.

The final exam in English is an open-book essay using examples from course readings and cluster activities, with a choice of topics focusing on education, folklore, the land, gender, or modernization in Appalachia. The biggest challenge of the English class, as with other composition classes that include compelling thematic content, is balancing time devoted to learning about the region and time spent on writing skills. Since Susan Mead has such a strong interest in teaching sociology with examples from the arts, much of the content of literature assignments is discussed during her hour. Many English class periods are divided between discussing content and working on different types of writing and editing skills. We constantly seek ways to motivate students to edit their work more carefully, so, for example, they may be required to have the English professor check their editing of slides they prepare for their "ABCs of

Appalachia" project in sociology, with text applying sociological concepts to images they select.

The science offering in the Appalachian Cluster was initially based on two half-semester team-taught lab science classes (called Humans within Ecosystems and Our Home/Our Habitat), developed as general education courses at Ferrum in the 1990s as part of a Council of Independent Colleges national project on integrating environmental science and the arts. Introduction to Environmental Science eventually replaced the two short science courses in the cluster. Like English and sociology, this course fulfills a liberal arts core requirement for all students as well as providing an introduction for anyone interested in a major or minor in that discipline. Since natural sciences both gave rise to modernization and reveal its limits, the cluster's focus on modernization in our region provides exemplars for studying basic concepts of environmental science as a global subject in relation to natural resources and environmental degradation in the Appalachian Mountains.

The emphasis in this freshman-level class is to study the necessities of life—food, shelter, and water—by observing organic community agricultural farms, visiting energy-efficient homes and schools, and evaluating water quality in mountain streams and other bodies of water. The primary learning outcome is to demonstrate understanding of the history and effects of practices with high environmental impacts and to observe that some practices can minimize these impacts. Southwest Virginia and adjacent states provide many opportunities for students to experience the natural ecological environment, while the prominence of fossil fuel industries presents different examples of environmental issues associated with the mining and use of coal and natural gas. In addition to ecological degradation, human health implications overlap in many ways with sociological impacts and the aesthetic paradox of the beautiful mountains being destroyed. The intersection of ecology, sociology, and artistic expression through literature provides the natural collaboration among the three courses in the Appalachian Cluster program. The science class typically reads poems with environmental themes by Cherokee poet Marilou Awiakta and supplements scientific study with other readings and films.[11]

One experiential requirement includes the planning, completion, and reflection associated with an environmental outreach program for each student or team of two students. A few examples of the many projects designed by students are organizing a white paper recycling program for campus, building and installing bluebird and bat boxes, planning Earth Day activities, and conducting stream sampling for the Save Our Streams program.

After the field trip into the coal fields, an in-class role-playing exercise simulates a public hearing about a coal company proposing to open a new mine in the immediate area. Students play roles including coal miners, miners' spouses, mine executives, school teachers, local and state environmental officials, health department doctors, high school students, and other stakeholders in the community. Thus, in addition to traditional tests, papers, and lab reports, the science course engages students in actively debating complex issues and tackling environmental problems.

Some students who completed the Appalachian Cluster in previous years like to become lab assistants, enjoying their repeat experiences with cluster activities while serving as role models for new students. Other students have shared their cluster work at intercultural festivals, academic talent shows, and public schools, as well as co-presenting at professional conferences.

One remarkable story represents the sustained power of experiential learning through the Appalachian Cluster. In the early years, students watched the popular film *October Sky*,[12] about young men from McDowell County, West Virginia, who defied all Appalachian stereotypes and became national science fair winners. Through a variety of channels, Ferrum faculty got to visit McDowell County, establishing an ongoing partnership with Big Creek People in Action and its director, Franki Patton Rutherford, the granddaughter of a fierce union organizer and graduate of the same high school as the *October Sky* "Rocket Boys." As a passionate community organizer, Franki worked with colleges across and beyond the Appalachian region, hosting college students for a week at a time to work on local house repair, community-based research, and other projects filling community needs. When Franki decided to complete her undergraduate degree, she chose Ferrum College and enrolled in the Appalachian Cluster to integrate her first-year intellectual pursuits. Franki embraced every aspect of the cluster as the centerpiece of her return to college, and in turn, she mentored other cluster students. Excelling in all her academic work, she chose a sociology minor to supplement her political science degree. The world lost a great social justice champion when Franki died just eighteen months after graduating. From her memorial service at the Ferrum College chapel to international travel that has kept Susan Mead connected with Franki's family since that time, her meaningful longtime association with Ferrum's faculty and students lives on and is the sort of relationship that the Appalachian Cluster fosters.

Franki's connection was unique but not unusual. Team Estonoa in St. Paul, Virginia, has been a partner with the Appalachian Cluster since the very beginning. St. Paul community members, especially high school students, have restored and protected Wetlands Estonoa, an environmental treasure that helps filter water draining into the most biologically diverse river in the continental United States, the Clinch River. Under the direction of their Appalachian ecology teacher and mentor, Terry Vencil, St. Paul High School students wrote hundreds of thousands of dollars' worth of grants to establish an internationally acclaimed environmental learning center that the cluster visits each year. After reading about Estonoa in *Do, Die, or Get Along*, and visiting with people she had read about, Ferrum student Lindsey Shelton later reflected,

One of my very first college papers was about Terry Vencil and her husband Dean and what they worked to accomplish. My trip to Estonoa my freshman year became one of the most inspiring events in my college career and one of the main reasons I majored in Environmental Planning and Development with an emphasis in Sociology. . . . Their hard work and determination lit a type of fire in us that made us want to achieve more for ourselves and the Ferrum community. . . . I have remained in contact and have built friendships with some of the students from Estonoa that have remained till this day. . . . Their determination and passion for the environment pushed me and my fellow Appalachian Cluster students to achieve more by working together and with the community to create a more promising future.

Lindsey's entire 2010 Appalachian Cluster cohort illustrated the interdisciplinary synergy of their experience when, after an afternoon in that community, they joined with Team Estonoa students to write sentences about "Where We've Been Today" (fashioned after the "Where I'm From" poetry tradition created by Kentucky author George Ella Lyon).[13] These lines from our collaborative poem show the integration of the disciplines and the strength of the partnership:

"Where I've been today the native tongue tells the name of a place where the water is placid and there is life all around."
"Where I have been students are the teachers."
"Where I've been wonderful greetings have never ended! As we pass by mountainsides, if you listen you can almost hear them cry."
"Where I've been is a place with dedicated students who are inspired to save their community and made a difference in the world."
"Where I've been today, the money is low but the morals are high."
"Where I've been I have seen a human passion meet God's wonder and beauty in every green mile."
"I have been where our students amaze me, and where inspiration resides."
"I've been to a place where the students taught me to eat violets."
"Today I've been into black mulch; luscious fruity cake; tiny green leaves; and tie-died, talented students who work wonders at their wetlands."
"I'm from a place where my best friends play; where I've been is the past yet I get to see the future."

Once again, the partnership forged between the Appalachian Cluster and the community goes far deeper than a visit once a year. Ferrum faculty have attended school functions, community festivals, and regional revitalization seminars in St. Paul and other communities; they have been invited to groundbreaking and dedication ceremonies for the Estonoa Learning Center, and were recognized at the final graduation ceremony when St. Paul High School was closed during consolidation. Appalachian Cluster community partnerships continue far beyond the semester, and now span more than two decades of experiential learning. While the places and people of Appalachia have historically been marginalized and misinterpreted, Ferrum's beautiful rural setting and the college's long tradition of serving the region from a close-knit, collaborative campus community have provided our students and faculty with exceptional opportunities for exploring contemporary social and environmental problems while experiencing rich cultural traditions of the region.

Notes

1   Alexander W. Astin, *Preventing Students from Dropping Out* (San Francisco: Jossey-Bass, 1995); Jodi H. Levine, ed., *Learning Communities: New Structures, New Partnerships for Learning* (Columbia: University of South Carolina, 1999).

2   Lee Smith, *Fair and Tender Ladies* (New York: Putnam, 1988); Denise Giardina, *The Unquiet Earth: A Novel* (New York: Norton, 1992); George Ella Lyon and Christopher Cardinale, *Which Side Are You On?* (El Paso: Cinco Puntos Press, 2011).

3   John Gaventa, *Power and Powerlessness: Quiescence and Rebellion in an Appalachian Valley* (Urbana: University of Illinois Press, 1980); Altina Waller, *Feud: Hatfields, McCoys, and Social Change in Appalachia, 1860–1900* (Chapel Hill: University of North Carolina Press, 1988); David E. Whisnant, *All That Is Native and Fine: The Politics of Culture in an American Region* (1983; repr., Chapel Hill: University of North Carolina Press, 2009).

4   Frank X Walker, *Affrilachia* (Lexington, KY: Old Cove Press, 2000); Mary K. Anglin, *Women, Power, and Dissent in the Hills of North Carolina* (Urbana: University of Illinois Press, 2002); Thomas E. Wagner and Phillip J. Obermiller, *African American Miners and Migrants: The Eastern Kentucky Social Club* (Urbana: University of Illinois Press, 2004); Mychal Denzel Smith, "What White Privilege Looks Like When You Are Poor," *The Nation*, May 22, 2014, http://www.thenation.com/article/what-white-privilege-looks-when-youre-poor.

5   Steve Nash, *Blue Ridge 2020: An Owner's Manual* (Chapel Hill: University of North Carolina Press, 1999).

6   Walker, *Affrilachia*.

7   Karenne Wood, *Markings on Earth* (Tucson: University of Arizona Press, 2001).

8   Sharyn McCrumb, *The Rosewood Casket: A Ballad Novel* (New York: Penguin, 1996).

9   Peter Crow, *Do, Die, or Get Along: A Tale of Two Appalachian Towns* (Athens: University of Georgia Press, 2007).

10 "'Mutsmag' and Other Girls Who Outwit Giants," in *AppLit: Resources for Readers and Teachers of Appalachian Literature for Children and Young Adults*, ed. Tina L. Hanlon, last modified November 24, 2017, http://www2.ferrum.edu /applit/bibs/tales/Mutsmag.htm.

11 Marilou Awiakta, *Selu: Seeking the Corn-Mother's Wisdom* (Golden, CO: Fulcrum, 1993).

12 *October Sky*, directed by Joe Johnston (Universal City, CA: Universal Studios, 1999), DVD.

13 George Ella Lyon, "Where I'm From," in *Where I'm From: Where Poems Come From* (Spring, TX: Absey & Co., 1999; repr., George Ella Lyon, 1999), http://www.george ellalyon.com/where.html.

16

"Hold My Piña Colada"

• •

Operational and Ethical
Considerations for
Interdisciplinary Experiential
Learning Study Abroad

PAOLA PRADO AND

AUTUMN QUEZADA-GRANT

As student enrollment at U.S. colleges and universities lags, many institutions of higher learning have sought to drive student retention through innovative town and gown collaborations in which faculty and students connect theory to practice with the aid of partners outside the ivory towers. As a result, more and more instructors at colleges large and small find themselves in open classroom settings, experimenting across disciplines, and reimagining best practices in contemporary pedagogy. At Roger Williams University, where the authors teach, administrators in search of a competitive edge for a small private liberal arts institution have embraced faculty-led experiential learning programs as an institutional core value and tout them often in fundraising and marketing materials. Although such support is essential for the development of experiential learning and study abroad programs, their success depends on the ability of faculty and their institutions to resolve the kinds of ethical dilemmas that these programs can entail. Existing at the intersection of higher education requirements and local community needs, the growth of these programs invites educators to reflect on how best to place global and national debates—about, for example, social justice, development, and the conduct of democracy—in a local context that serves the interests of faculty, students, and the communities that they visit.

To be sure, all experiential learning and service-learning courses are different. Yet, whether dishing out food at the neighborhood food kitchen or lounging under coconut fronds at a glitzy Caribbean beach resort, most engage socioeconomically underprivileged communities as a learning space for more privileged students and faculty. In environments where precarity abounds, such as the Global South, it is not uncommon for power imbalances to play out in ways that replicate or reproduce the very inequalities that a course or campus–community partnership is meant to alleviate. Having grappled with this reality in our own work, we have found that the best approach to global experiential learning study abroad is one in which institutional agents are invited into a community to carefully listen and plan a collaboration that prioritizes the intentions and objectives of all partners. Versed in the foundational scholarship of pioneers in the field of global service learning (GSL),[1] the authors of this chapter adhere to a Freirean dialogic model[2] whereby faculty and institutional agents approach community collaborations imbued with conscious awareness that each party has knowledge to give and to gain in a "fair-trade" exchange. We understand ethical community engagement as a practice of fair-trade learning that promotes transparency, encourages self-reflectivity, and privileges what we have come to call an "empathy-first" approach.

This chapter is a result of years of interdisciplinary practice based on a shared philosophy that informs how we as faculty interact with the world. Our analysis evolved in part from discussions at our small campus's faculty learning communities—intellectual spaces that afforded us room to question our methods, reflect upon our goals, and consider how those align with best practices. Funded through a Hassenfeld Grant from the Office of the Associate Provost for the Advancement for Teaching and Learning, a group of teacher-scholars at Roger Williams University examined the ethical dimensions of community engagement, questioning how our university interacted locally and globally. This yearlong collaboration, which leveraged learning across a network of scholars, educators, and practitioners, yielded many of the recommendations in these pages. Here, we parse out what we learned from these experiences, as we identify and examine the synergetic origins of these partnerships, and some of the ethical and operational challenges of community-based interdisciplinary global experiential learning.

In this chapter we ask two questions: Which institutional practices at a small college best support community-based experiential study abroad programs? and Which factors impact interdisciplinary collaboration in these programs? In response, we first briefly describe the operation and learning outcomes of one of our interdisciplinary experiential learning study-abroad programs. Next, we pinpoint high-impact practices that guide students across disciplinary boundaries, examine operational challenges and identify ethical dilemmas that arise in the field. In closing, we evaluate successes and failures of the program, reflect upon best practices, and assess the value of interdisciplinary study abroad programs at smaller institutions of higher education.

"Hold My Piña Colada": Interdisciplinary Experiential Learning in the Caribbean

Situated on the waterfront in Rhode Island, our private coeducational liberal arts university remains primarily tuition driven. In a residential, small-college-town setting, 217 full-time faculty and a robust roster of adjuncts teach 4,019 undergraduates and 762 graduates. Over the last decade, efforts to boost enrollment, diversify the student body, and promote retention included a flagship program whereby the university paid passport fees for undergraduates who studied abroad. Yet, even with such institutional support, we have found that short-term interdisciplinary study abroad experiences often evolve organically, spurred by a subset of junior faculty eager to build programmatic curricular innovation on their path to tenure. Within this group, synergistic collaborations have emerged among faculty whose scholarship straddled common interests. In one such program, a historian whose research focuses on indigenous peoples of Mexico joined a biologist with public health expertise to teach social justice on a Caribbean island. With these and other partnerships, shared learning outcomes and a commitment to ethical values and principles that privilege the common good provided a foundation for success.

Take the example of one faculty-led study abroad program in the Dominican Republic; a program that offers an attractive midwinter Caribbean jaunt delivers an immersive sixteen-day in-country experience where students are confronted with evidence of social justice challenges embedded in the operations of luxury beach resorts. The course also takes issue with programmatic practices at our own university, leading students to question matters of privilege and whiteness as they engage in experiential learning facilitated by elites whose wealth is inextricably tied to conditions of precarity in surrounding communities. As the course unfolds, it uncovers global controversies that sour the taste of the piña colada served at the beach resorts. Taught on rotation by two faculty from different disciplines, the program delivers 225 contact hours and awards six credits that may count toward requirements or electives, depending on a student's major. Juxtaposed and intermingled activities and assignments provide firsthand knowledge about the confluence of socioeconomic and historical dynamics in global society. Learning outcomes vary in relation to the disciplines at each iteration but can include the ability to analyze and explain relationships through the lens provided by disciplinary context; identify and apply appropriate research methods in study of local communities; demonstrate competent use of particular skill sets or technologies; examine local issues within a perspective that interrogates a wider global context; and achieve group objectives through effective collaboration with others.

Lectures and workshops provide the scaffolding for the academic coursework in the program. Grounded in fair-trade learning pedagogy, the format requires students to participate in open classroom settings and research social justice issues on site. Faculty leaders and local bilingual aides help students navigate linguistic and cultural barriers as they hear from local experts, visit key cultural and historical landmarks, participate in experiential learning youth engagement projects, and conduct hands-on fieldwork in local communities. Beyond traditional learning through directed readings, in-class discussion, and writing assignments, the program incorporates experiential service learning planned and executed in collaboration with local communities; the latter provides the basis for reflective group discussion and student journaling about community engagement, service learning, and global citizenship.

Guided by tools of ethnographic inquiry, students uncover dilemmas and place the lived experiences of community members within a larger, interdisciplinary context. As an example, in the collaboration between history and journalism, students discover how social factors such as race, nationality, gender, class, and regional histories affect how communities gain access to or control over economic resources (land, water, agricultural properties, culturally significant landscapes, etc.). Next, they practice daily reporting and newswriting assignments. Learning assessments evaluate how accurately the resulting news stories incorporate the viewpoints of local stakeholders and whether the reporting provides a balanced account that demonstrates a newfound understanding of the historical factors that impact resource allocation, migration, and human development.

High-Impact Practices: Community Engagement, Openness, and Empathy-First Approach

The practice of global service learning at our university is the exception to, rather than the standard for, faculty-led study abroad programs, most of which still conform to traditional models where field trips illustrate classroom lectures within disciplinary boundaries. Given that our institution encourages faculty creativity to propose curricular enhancements, faculty members conversant in GSL practices reconsidered how to best deliver student-centered experiential learning that met standards of ethical community engagement. For that reason, we focus intentionally on "global" rather than "international" service learning, emphasizing civic education, democratic action and engagement, geared to shape our students to become global citizens. Clarifying the distinction between the two models further, Bringle and Hatcher cite the America Council of Education's definitions:

- *International Service Learning*—focusing on nations and their relationships
- *Global Service Learning*—denoting systems and phenomenon that transcend national borders
- *Intercultural Service Learning*—focusing on knowledge and skills to understand and navigate cultural differences[3]

One might presume cultural competency a prerequisite for GSL and experiential study abroad programs, yet as noted by other scholars, many programs underemphasize that capability. We have found that where cultural competencies are underscored, students are better equipped to bridge the gap in critical consciousness through reflection. Tracy Rundstrom Williams discusses the importance of self-reflectivity within a broadening of cultural competency: increased knowledge, increased flexibility, open-mindedness, curiosity, and enhanced critical skills.[4] The scaffolding of learning outcomes within the GSL study abroad experience emphasizes intentionality. After all, meaning is not inherent in the learning and can be socially contrived. Constructivist theories in teaching and collective learning consider that experiential education can be critical to connect experience to learning. Intentionality between planned experience, community interaction, individual work, and group reflection embedded within skill-building presents a path that connects experience to learning outcomes.[5]

Our small faculty cohort roughly ranging around six faculty members at Roger Williams University together identified three high-impact practices within the umbrella of GSL experiential education: fair-trade community engagement, openness to experiment with dynamic or challenging situations, and an empathy-first approach.[6] At our school faculty learning communities allowed for the synergy of thinking on high-impact practices to provide a philosophical and pedagogical foundation for those of us active in this teaching. Curricular models for our short-term study abroad course center on these principles, using best practices within each field.

Our first high-impact practice, that of fair-trade community engagement, provides an entry point for ethical collaborative engagement between faculty, students, the institution of higher education, and community members.[7] Girded by the principles of fair-trade experiential learning,[8] participants share and exchange knowledge within a framework that emphasizes collaboration, diversity, and reciprocity,[9] where each group is treated fairly and benefits equally from the interaction. For the relationships to remain on an equal footing with all parties rotating through positions of power requires a conscious effort and presents an immense responsibility. The equitable nature of the exchange must be seeded prior to the establishment of a program, with consideration of potential obstacles and challenges that may arise. Once an agreement is reached about the nature of the community engagement, partners are better equipped to plan, step-by-step, in an inclusive manner, how to best achieve common goals.

A second high-impact practice that contributes to the success of these programs emerges from the ability of faculty leaders to reimagine and adapt lessons to opportunities that result from unforeseen encounters and unexpected situations that present in the field. Equally paramount is the skill and willingness each faculty member deploys to leverage a partner's strengths. The most successful collaborations happen among faculty who display the nimble agility to fold emergent talking points into a lesson plan, or to expand the scope of inquiry beyond disciplinary borders. Indeed, thoughtful interdisciplinary collaboration has the potential to illuminate aspects of one's own discipline; existing knowledge can seed vibrant new paths for scholarship when it is framed against an unexpected context or viewed from a different lens. An openness to explore new ways of understanding and a willingness to engage with the other are essential for interdisciplinary collaborations to thrive.

Our guiding principles for student-centered practices reinforce these values: our lesson plans encourage group problem-based learning exercises, allow for sustained critical analysis and reflection, and focus on development of critical consciousness that is globally minded.[10] Having students think and work together rather than in isolation extends group reflection to include what leaders in the tech field call "liquid networks."[11] Good ideas and solutions for problems arise from working in collaboration and across disciplinary boundaries. The intentionality of group work alongside individual work teaches students how to think on their feet, how to engage in face-to-face communication, and how to reflect thoughtfully about the lived experiences of community members who face the realities of oppression and inequality we examine in academic study.

The third high-impact practice relates to the infusion of an empathy-first approach amid those who partner in pursuit of a common good. An empathy-first approach is one that *shares power* and allows that, for portions of time spent together, community members hold the source of knowledge. In this conception, the role of faculty leaders is to validate that positioning and to facilitate student learning in a space of mutual respect. Experiential learning collaborations grounded in an empathy-first approach establish a path to hold institutional agents accountable and help control expectations. It is a given that power relations frequently tip toward institutional interests, and that communities in the Global South operate within a framework of inequity. Yet faculty and institutional agents who appreciate the bonds that tie community life and can identify shared values are better equipped to interrogate power structures that thwart sustainable program development. Ultimately, we must always remember that we are invited into collaboration by the community, and that is a privilege. The most effective and empathetic educators teach by the following creed: *we shall not leave the community partners worse off than we found them.*

Operational Challenges to Collaborative Experiential Education

Faculty-led study abroad programs can substantially enhance the breadth and scope of the educational opportunities available on a small college campus. The adoption of an open classroom model with ethical and fair-trade community engagement has the potential to expand learning resources through access to offsite facilities and professional experts. As students and faculty engage with outside constituencies, the experiential education environment offers a bridge from theory to practice and, in some settings, can build student comprehension of expressions of diversity and identity. Crossing that bridge, however, at times exacts a heavy toll on faculty: the coordination and oversight of community engagement activities add a layer of supervisory complexity to lesson plans and often pose hurdles in the form of scheduling and transportation. What amounts to trivial concerns at large institutions nevertheless presents time-consuming impediments for faculty at small teaching colleges, where heavy course loads are the norm, administrative assistance may be underresourced, and access to equipment—from vans to instructional materials—remains competitive. Institutions that systematically require advance planning, transparent budgets, and academic oversight of credit-bearing experiential learning courses help manage the demands imposed on faculty and campus resources. However, those demands can contribute to faculty burnout and disengagement with the educational model, specifically at institutions that fail to establish clear incentives and compensation in exchange for the time and effort instructors dedicate to experiential learning initiatives.[12]

The sustainability of global experiential learning programs also depends upon rather practical matters: affordability, scheduling, and other liabilities can impact enrollment. At small colleges where low faculty–student ratios add a mark of distinction, small class sizes can make study abroad programs prohibitively expensive. To counter this obstacle at our school, an administrative official helped establish a special scholarship for global travelers working in the developing world. Elsewhere, expenses associated with foreign travel can discourage financially strapped students. As the cost of higher education reaches dizzying levels, and more students work full time to meet tuition payments, fewer are free to enroll in study that will take them abroad during the summer months. Yet another challenge to enrollment may originate from risk-averse parents who discourage college-age offspring from travel abroad. Last but not least, in an increasingly corporatized model of education, legal counsel often balks at the liabilities posed by travel abroad. All along, one is reminded of the need to establish and adhere to stringent criteria of participant selection. To begin, travel to the Global South is not for everyone. Students are prone to romanticize the study abroad experience, and those flights of fancy do not reflect the harsh realities of fieldwork. A careful review process for all applicants is key to enrollment of a balanced cohort. Programs ought to implement application and interview processes that allow faculty to gauge a student's ability to handle the difficulties of such work, and ideally also verify that the students are medically fit and mentally prepared for the hardships inherent in foreign travel.

At the institutional level, discretionary decisions about community engagement are all too often led by administrators unfamiliar with state-of-the-art practices or scholarship. Yet there are knowledgeable resources and advice available for institutional managers willing to consult with experienced practitioners of ethical community engagement. Interdisciplinary experiential learning succeeds at small colleges that (1) accurately promote and disseminate the goals of community engagement programs throughout the institution, and (2) set tangible measures of faculty support that promote recognition and foster innovation. An executive task force comprising faculty members and administrators provided input as our university took positive steps to ensure institutional change with revised core values, expanded funding opportunities, fellowships, and mentorship aimed at promoting faculty engagement in experiential learning.

Lastly, collaborative work between faculty and administrators in small institutions is critical in developing a shared campus philosophy that actually reflects practice. As is often the case in university settings across the country, the composition of the administration at our institution does not reflect that of the faculty body. At small colleges where the administration remains a preserve dominated by white males, minority and female faculty members can often feel unheard and underappreciated. Faculty collaboration can counter this dynamic through effective team-building strategies that strengthen female and minority faculty voices and combat the marginalization of overlooked constituencies.

Ethical Issues and Dilemmas That Arise in the Field

Small liberal arts colleges that embrace core values of experiential, collaborative, and engaged learning provide a supportive platform from which faculty can innovate upon the idea of what accounts for classroom space, interrogate which approaches to community partnership conform to high ethical standards, and expand access to intellectual spaces beyond the university campus, returning cultural, social, and symbolic capital to the community where it originated through collaborative practices. For the most part, practitioners of global experiential learning consider it a *privilege* to teach and to learn in a community-based setting, but we believe that ethical learning and exchange can only be built upon a fair exchange between all parties.

The temporal nature of the exchange, along with the ability of the guests to depart and leave behind the many challenges of daily life in impoverished communities, has given rise to the label "poverty tourism," to describe affluent visitors who tour poverty zones in the Global South. Ethical, fair-trade community engagement considers the unintended consequences of short-term study abroad and reflects on questions of potential harm, inequity, power relations, and social responsibility. Programmatic learning outcomes and partnership agreements address such pitfalls when faculty prepare students for the course with predeparture workshops, sustained reflection throughout the course while in the field, and conscious assessment and evaluation of the successes and failures of the course upon return to the home campus. Mindfulness among faculty leaders is just as important as it is for students.

Furthermore, where students of color remain underrepresented, it can be a challenge to recruit minority (and commuter) students who, deterred by the high costs of education and limited alternative funding, opt out of study abroad. Among those able to afford program fees, few consider study abroad in the Global South as a first option. The underrepresentation of marginalized and minority student voices in innovative study abroad programs transposes the challenges of majority-white classroom settings to the field, where the opportunities for transformational learning increase exponentially as participants practice cultural competency and learn from lived experience. Absent a diverse student body, and lagging in foreign language skills, the composition of study abroad cohorts from small New England colleges reconstitutes in foreign soil deleterious class and racial inequalities imported from home.

Assess Success, Learn from Failure, and Move Forward

Student assessment in the various programs that adhere to this model of interdisciplinary faculty-led study abroad collaboration at our college have yielded evidence of successful attainment of learning outcomes. In addition to standard assessment measures, course evaluations and postcompletion debriefing responses characterize these programs as "life-changing" and indicate that students emerge emboldened with a sense of possibility, agency, and self-awareness. It is common to find that students who had previously never traveled abroad, upon return to campus position themselves as global citizens who aspire to explore new foreign locales or plan to return to the site of the study abroad. Indeed, we found ample evidence that participation in experiential study abroad coursework provides a gateway for a substantial number of students who, as a result of having participated in one initial program, subsequently enroll in further elective study abroad. Graduates who successfully completed community-based experiential study abroad have reported that they receive positive feedback from potential employers based on their participation in study abroad.

Self-evaluation of the course by participants and stakeholders helps faculty to reassess the next iteration of the course. Pre- and postassessment and evaluations provide valuable guidance to educators who lead study abroad programs in the Global South, where various factors outside the instructors' control can make it nearly impossible to replicate consistent teaching practices from one trip to the next. Careful tracking of the impact of field activities on learning outcomes allows for recalibration, as do follow-up interviews with community leaders to gauge the impact of field visits on community members. Best practices in fair-trade community engagement recommend that program leaders maintain open channels of communication and check back regularly to ensure that the community continues to perceive value in the collaboration and is willing to maintain the partnership.

Yet we know that innovative program development travels in lockstep with failure. Community partnerships can become mired in local power imbalances, or disputes over community goals, or solicitations for charitable donations and dependency, or disruption caused by students who fail to disclose drug dependency or preexisting mental health conditions in advance. In one such instance, participants in a study abroad program where students built a water reservoir for irrigation of community gardens operated by a local nongovernmental organization learned from local villagers concerned that the reservoir was a ploy to control access to water resources. Unbeknownst to the faculty leaders, the program ran headfirst into a local dispute over water rights. These types of issues inevitably do occur; they require facilitators to be cognizant that local realities can engender tense situations that alter the course of the program. It is important to set up and adhere to firm boundaries with the community, which is easier to do in programs where faculty members display cultural competency to help steer difficult conversations. Faculty members who work in regions of the world where they lack either language skills or cultural knowledge court disaster.

Ultimately, our ability to practice interdisciplinary experiential learning in a global setting owes much to institutional commitment to faculty training supported by commensurate compensation, public recognition for the production of scholarship, and practical incentives for those engaged in programmatic and curricular experimentation. Our own institution proved curious about our methods, and encouraged us to share in workshops with fellow faculty members what we have learned. Of course, ethical, effective experiential learning collaborations inevitably demand resources in excess of those required in standard classroom or lab settings; absent tangible rewards, perfunctory acknowledgment and promises of prestige fall short of fair compensation for work that is time consuming and requires continuous reinterpretation and calibration due to its dynamic, constantly evolving nature. In small-college settings, specifically where heavy course loads combine with expectations of service, student advising, and mentoring duties that demand a substantial time commitment, faculty learning communities can build an important gateway to successful development of ethical experiential learning programs.

In our experience, faculty learning communities deliver measurable positive results when members meet regularly in structured sessions for workshop-based discussions based on directed readings of foundational concepts and theories. Provided tangible rewards and incentivized to develop a scholarly interest that links theory to praxis, faculty are empowered to generate awareness among the campus community. As a corollary, these groups can facilitate the compilation of literature about strategies that serve as a roadmap of best practices for other educators. Faculty incentivized to provide feedback on experiential courses, and to identify and support experiential learning constituencies on campus can foster an atmosphere of engagement and renew commitment to shared goals. Where financial pressures prevent adequate monetary incentives or professional development funding, grant awards present a lifeline that enables faculty to attend innovative workshops and to invite experts to campus.

Conclusion

Supported by the scholarship and practice of a network of educators who generously shared their experience in this work, we were motivated to drive the pace of change at our small liberal arts college. We are privileged to have found collaborators and community partners imbued with curiosity, courage, and heart who were eager to actively experiment across disciplines with new modes of teaching and learning. A series of demonstrably successful innovative interdisciplinary study abroad collaborations led administrators to revise global experiential learning guidelines, recognize faculty who act in accordance with best practices, and expand collaboration with local communities and global partners. They also encouraged expert faculty to share their methods and provide practical advice in public presentations, publications, and recordings archived in the library. The innovation spearheaded by faculty emboldened administrators to support tenure-track faculty in pursuit of best practices, and the Hassenfeld Fellows Program was launched to mentor faculty engaged in this endeavor.

Our embrace of fair-trade global experiential learning flows organically from a pedagogy that thrives in dialogic engagement between educators, students, and community partners. This pedagogy succeeds where participants are open to experiment and are able to respond with curiosity and openness, even when unforeseen challenges threaten to alter the course of instruction. Ultimately, the practice of what we have come to call an empathy-first approach to social interaction is at the core of what connects us to the other; whether the other is a colleague, a student, or a community partner, it is through empathy that we can reach across differences and collaborate beyond borders. We have found that faculty who model ethical global engagement in experiential learning help raise awareness of what it means to be a catalyst for social change in a manner that places our humanity front and center.

A final thought: not all study abroad is experiential or interdisciplinary, nor does it have to be. Fair-trade GSL is not easy; more often than not, it can present instructors and institutions with daunting pedagogical and ethical challenges. Yet, for educators who thrive on active experimentation and dynamic learning, interdisciplinary faculty-led study abroad collaborations can place into brilliant context what it means to be ethically engaged in a global world.

Notes

1 Eric Hartman, Richard Kiely, Christopher Boettcher, and Jessica Friedrichs, *Community-Based Global Learning: The Theory and Practice of Ethical Engagement at Home and Abroad* (Sterling, VA: Stylus Publishing, 2018); Eric Hartman, Cody Morris Paris, and Brandon Blanche-Cohen, "Fair Trade Learning: Ethical Standards for Community-Engaged International Volunteer Tourism," *Tourism and Hospitality Research* 14 (2014); Building a Better World: The Pedagogy and Practice of Global Service-Learning Conference, 2013; Robert G. Bringle, Julie A. Hatcher, and Steven G. Jones, eds., *International Service Learning: Conceptual Frameworks and Research* (Sterling, VA: Stylus Publishing, 2012).

2 Paulo Freire, *Education for Critical Consciousness*, (New York: Continuum, 1974).

3 Robert. G. Bringle and Julie. A. Hatcher, "International Service Learning" in *International Service Learning: Conceptual Frameworks and Research*, ed. R. G. Bringle, J. A. Hatcher, and S. G. Jones (Sterling, VA: Stylus Publishing, 2011), 18.

4 Tracy Rundstrom Williams, "The Reflective Model of Intercultural Competency: A Multidimensional, Qualitative Approach to Study Abroad Assessment," *Frontiers: The Interdisciplinary Journal of Study Abroad* 18 (2009): 289–306.

5 Ann Lutterman-Aguilar and Orval Gingerich, "Experiential Pedagogy for Study Abroad: Education for Global Citizenship," *Frontiers: The Interdisciplinary Journal of Study Abroad* 8 (2002): 44.

6 Autumn Quezada de Tavarez and Kerri Staroscik Warren, "Designing the Curriculum for Global Service-Learning Abroad: Power and Health in El Salvador," in *Passport to Change: Designing Academically Sound, Culturally Relevant, Short-Term, Faculty-Led Study Abroad Programs* (Sterling, VA: Stylus Publishing, 2018), 133. Also see Becky Spritz, Paola Prado, Autumn Quezada-Grant, and Kerri S. Warren, "Translating Transformational Learning: Applying ISL Principles to Local Community Engagement" (paper presented at the International Service-Learning Summit, Manhattan, KS, October 23–25, 2016). Also, Paola Prado and Autumn Quezada-Grant, "Best Practices for Digital and

Social Media Integration in Experiential Service Learning: A Case Study of Community Engagement Study Abroad in the Global South" (paper presented at NSEE Conference, St. Petersburg, FL, 2015); Paola Prado, Kerri S. Warren, and Autumn Quezada-Grant, "Global Service Learning Best Practices" (paper presented at NSEE Conference, Baltimore, MD, September 2014).

7 For further reading on best practices within community engagement see D. W. Butin, "Of What Use Is It? Multiple Conceptualizations of Service-Learning within Education" in *Teacher College Record* 105, no. 9 (December 2003): 1674–1692; B. W. Head, "Community Engagement: Participation on Whose Terms?" *Australian Journal of Political Science* 42, no. 3 (2007): 441–454; and J. J. Zuiches, "Attaining Carnegie's Community Engagement Classification," *Change* 40, no. 1 (2008): 42–45.

8 Hartman, Paris, and Blanche-Cohen, "Fair Trade Learning."

9 S. Mintz and G. Hesser, "Principles of Good Practice of Service-Learning," in *Service-Learning in Higher Education*, ed. B. Jacoby and Associates (San Francisco: Jossey-Bass, 1996).

10 Quezada de Tavarez and Warren, "Designing the Curriculum," 139–140. See also Paulo Freire, *Education for Critical Consciousness* (New York: Continuum, 1974).

11 S. Johnson, "Where Good Ideas Come From," 2010, https://www.ted.com/talks /steven_johnson_where_good_ideas_come_from.

12 Elaine Ward, "Navigating Institutional Culture: The Promotion and Tenure Process for Community-Engaged Scholars" (campus talk in Ethical Engagement: Faculty Learning Community, Roger Williams University, Bristol, RI, April 26, 2017); John Saltmarsh and John Wooding, "Rewarding Community Engaged Scholarship: A State University System Approach," *Metropolitan Universities* 27, no. 2 (Summer 2016): 7–18.

Notes on Contributors

AARON ANGELLO is the Sophia M. Libman Professor of Humanities and visiting assistant professor of English at Hood College in Frederick, Maryland.

ALLAN W. AUSTIN is professor of history at Misericordia University in Dallas, Pennsylvania.

MARTHA BÁRCENAS-MOORADIAN is visiting assistant professor in the Department of Spanish, Latin American, and Caribbean Literatures and Cultures and Community Engagement/Mellon Interdisciplinary Humanities Initiative coordinator at Scripps College in Claremont, California.

APRIL M. BOULTON is associate professor of biology and dean of the graduate school at Hood College in Frederick, Maryland.

AMANDA M. CALEB is professor and director of medical and health humanities and professor of English at Misericordia University in Dallas, Pennsylvania.

COREY CAMPION is associate professor of history and global studies and director of the master of arts in humanities program at Hood College in Frederick, Maryland.

MARYANN CONRAD is associate professor of hospitality management and chair of the Hospitality Management program at Nichols College in Dudley, Massachusetts.

HILARY COOPERMAN is assistant professor of theater at Rollins College in Winter Park, Florida.

PETER CROW, founding coordinator of the Appalachian Cluster, is professor emeritus of English at Ferrum College in Ferrum, Virginia.

CHRISTINE DEHNE is dean of the School of Arts and Sciences and professor of communication and media at Manhattanville College in Purchase, New York.

AUDRA L. GOACH is professor of chemistry at Monmouth College in Monmouth, Illinois.

PATRICK L. HAMILTON is associate professor of English at Misericordia University in Dallas, Pennsylvania.

TINA L. HANLON is professor of English at Ferrum College in Ferrum, Virginia.

DELIA R. HECK is professor of environmental science and chair of the Natural Sciences Division at Ferrum College in Ferrum, Virginia.

JULIA F. KLIMEK is professor of interdisciplinary studies and English and the director of the Interdisciplinary Studies program at Coker University in Hartsville, South Carolina.

PATRICIA MARCHESI is assistant professor of English at LaGrange College in LaGrange, Georgia.

SUSAN V. MEAD is assistant professor of sociology and coordinator of the Appalachian Cluster at Ferrum College in Ferrum, Virginia.

JONATHAN MUNSON is professor of computer science at Manhattanville College in Purchase, New York.

CHRISTINE D. MYERS, PHD, is an independent historian based in Monmouth, Illinois.

ALICIA H. NORDSTROM is professor and chair of psychology at Misericordia University in Dallas, Pennsylvania.

WINSTON OU is associate professor of mathematics and the Elizabeth Hubert Malott Endowed Chair for the Core Curriculum in Interdisciplinary Humanities at Scripps College in Claremont, California.

PAOLA PRADO is associate professor, journalism and digital media, and program coordinator for Latin American and Latino studies at Roger Williams University in Bristol, Rhode Island.

AUTUMN QUEZADA-GRANT is associate professor of Latin American history and faculty in Latin American and Latino studies at Roger Williams University in Bristol, Rhode Island.

PAUL D. REICH is associate professor of English at Rollins College in Winter Park, Florida.

ERIKA CORNELIUS SMITH is assistant professor of political science and international business and chair of the Civic Leadership and Politics program at Nichols College in Dudley, Massachusetts.

SHARON E. STEIN is professor of psychology at Ferrum College in Ferrum, Virginia.

CAROLYN L. THOMAS retired in 2019 as professor of biology and environmental science at Ferrum College in Ferrum, Virginia.

LANA A. WHITED teaches English and directs the honors program at Ferrum College in Ferrum, Virginia.

Index